Philosophical Foundations of Quantitative Research Methodology

Chong Ho Yu

University Press of America,® Inc.
Lanham · Boulder · New York · Toronto · Oxford

4501 Forbes Boulevard
Suite 200
Lanham, Maryland 20706
UPA Acquisitions Department (301) 459-3366

PO Box 317
Oxford
OX2 9RU, UK

Printed in the United States of America
British Library Cataloging in Publication Information Available

Library of Congress Control Number: 2006921671
ISBN-13: 978-0-7618-3429-8 (paperback : alk. paper)
ISBN-10: 0-7618-3429-X (paperback : alk. paper)

∞™ The paper used in this publication meets the minimum requirements of American National Standard for Information Sciences—Permanence of Paper for Printed Library Materials, ANSI Z39.48—1984

Contents

Preface

When I was a graduate student, my mentor Professor John Behrens, an expert on Exploratory Data Analysis (EDA), always emphasized the importance of maintaining a detective mentality for a data analyst by stating, "Always know where the numbers come from." I adopted a similar approach as Professor Behrens and thus have always held a skeptical view to all data sets. Later in my career I extended Dr. Behrens' notion of tracing back where the numbers come from to a broader domain. I started asking questions such as: "Where did those statistical procedures originate from? How were the numbers in the t–table and the F–table generate? How could statisticians synthesize the Fisherian and the Pearsonian frameworks while they are substantively different in their philosophies? What does it mean that the parameter is consistent and eventually residuals converge to zero? Are we making an implicit assumption that parameter estimation can discover some sort of objective and invariant truth and thus people regard quantitative methods as being tied to logical positivism? Significance testing is said to be based upon a hypothetico–deductive paradigm and empirical study is said to be inductive in nature. Besides deduction and induction, is there another type of reasoning to facilitate exploratory analysis and to address unstructured research questions? What do those numbers mean in a regression model or a structural equation model? Do these numbers signify some cause and effect relationships or just mere association?" My list of questions can go on and on.

This book is a crystallization of my contemplation of the meanings of quantitative methods in the perspectives of history and philosophy of science throughout the last several years. To be frank, many statistical and philosophical texts are not accessible to most audiences in terms of readability. The former type of texts tends to be excessively loaded with mathematical notations and equations whereas the latter is usually packed with unexplained jargon. Hence, this book is written for readers who have the intermediate level of statistical and philosophical backgrounds. I hope that the preceding meaningful issues can be further pursued by more quantitative researchers who might be motivated by my writing.

Chapter 1 is a discussion that reviews where the Fisherian and Pearsonian methodologies originate from in the perspective of the history of science. By citing the history of these two prominent statistical methodologies, this chapter attempts to debunk the myth that statistics is a subject–free methodology derived from invariant and timeless mathematical axioms. Instead, biological themes and philosophical presumptions, in part, lead Pearson and Fisher to develop their statistical schools. Pearson, in general, is pre–occupied with between–group speciation and thus his statistical methods, such as the Chi–squared test, are categorical in nature. On the other hand, variation within species plays a central role in Fisher's framework and therefore Fisher's approach, such as partitioning variance, is more quantitative than Pearson's in terms of the measurement scale. In addition, Fisher adopted a philosophy of embracing causal inferences and theoretical entities, such as infinite population and gene, while Pearson disregarded unobservable and insisted upon description of the data at hand. These differences lead to the subsequent divergence of two hypothesis testing methods, developed by R. A. Fisher and Neyman/E .S. Pearson, son of Karl Pearson, respectively. Hypothesis testing in the current form is a fusion between the Fishe-rian and Pearsonian Schools, but their core elements reflect two different philosophies that have risen from the context of biological inquiry.

The objective of Chapter 2 is to demystify a popular misconception that quantitative research is based upon logical positivism and to promote ecumenicalism in research methodology. This chapter examines the relationship among quantitative research and eight major notions of logical positivism: (a) verification, (b) pro–observation, (c) anti–cause, (d) downplaying explanation, (e) anti–theoretical entities, (f) anti–metaphysics, (g) logical analysis and (h) frequentist probability. It is argued that the underlying philosophy of modern quantitative research does not subscribe to logical positivism. Associating an outdated philosophy with quantitative research may discourage social science researchers from applying quantitative research approach and leads to misguided disputes between qualitative and quantitative researchers. Researchers and students should be encouraged to keep an open mind to different methodologies because mixed methods have the potential to achieve the goals of convergent validity and completeness.

Chapter 3 is concerned with how various reasoning modes can be synthesized to gain a holistic view in research. The philosophical ideas introduced by Charles Sanders Peirce (1839–1914) are helpful for researchers in understanding the underlying logic of quantitative methods specific to the foundational concepts of deduction, abduction and induction. In the Peircean logical system, the logic of abduction and deduction contribute to our conceptual understanding of a phenomenon, while the logic of induction adds quantitative details to our conceptual knowledge. At the stage of abduction, the goal is to explore data, find a pattern, and suggest a plausible hypothesis; deduction is to refine the hypothesis based upon other plausible premises; and induction is empirical substantiation.

Chapter 4 discusses philosophy of mathematics with an emphasis on the schools of Carnap and Quine, and their implications for quantitative researchers. Both Carnap and Quine made significant contributions to the philosophy of mathematics despite their diverse views. Carnap endorsed the dichotomy between analytic and synthetic knowledge and classified certain mathematical questions as internal questions appealing to logic and convention. On the contrary, Quine was opposed to the analytic–synthetic distinction and promoted a holistic view of scientific inquiry. The purpose of this chapter is to argue that in light of the recent advancement of experimental mathematics such as Monte Carlo simulations, limiting mathematical and statistical inquiry to the domain of logic may be unjustified. Robustness studies implemented in Monte Carlo Studies demonstrate that mathematics and statistics is on a par with other experimental–based sciences.

Chapter 5 pertains to philosophical issues of factor analysis, and to a larger extent, the latent construct model. It is undeniable that factor analysis has been under severe criticism in the arenas of philosophy of science, psychology, and statistics. Nonetheless, it is important to point out that most of these criticisms are applied to Exploratory Factor Analysis (EFA) rather than Confirmatory Factor Analysis (CFA). One of the focal points concerns whether EFA could yield a hypothesis or just a mere description of the data. This question reflects the notion of maintaining a distinction between interpretation and computation. The preceding dichotomy is a variation of the dichotomy between logical and synthetic questions, which is a questionable epistemology. Nonetheless, EFA and CFA can work together in the sense that the former suggests a factor structure and the latter provides support for the proposed factor model. According to the Peircean philosophy that is discussed in Chapter 3, long term scientific inquiry is a self–correcting process; earlier theories will inevitably be revised or rejected by later theories. In this sense, all conclusions, no matter how confirmatory they are, must be exploratory in essence because these confirmed conclusions are subject to further investigations.

Causal inference is an intriguing but controversial topic in philosophy, statistics, as well as social science research. Chapter 6 is a brief overview and evaluation of the current mathematical/statistical causal models, including the SEM, TETRAD, and the graph theory. The efficacy of these approaches will be discussed in the philosophical context of the Duhem–Quine thesis, realism, simplicity, identifiability (testability), empirical adequacy, and probabilistic causality.

Chapter 7 continues to explore issues of causal inferences left off by the previous chapter. The Causal Markov Condition and its sister, the common cause principle, provide the assumptions to structure relationships among variables in the path model and to load different variables into common latent constructs in the factor model. In addition, the Faithfulness Assumption rules out those models in which statistical independence relations follow as a result of special coincidences among the parameter values. The arguments against these assumptions by Nancy Cartwright as well as those for these assumptions by James Woodward will be evaluated in this paper.

Chapter 8 uses Evolutionary Game Theory, which is based upon Fisher's counter–argument against Divine Providence, and Evolutionary psychology as examples to illustrate why researchers need both mathematical models and contextual explanations to address surprisingly phenomena. If the researcher explains a phenomenon by citing a covering statistical law without giving the detail of the causal process, this type of explanation is not qualified to be a causal explanation.

These chapters are adapted from my articles listed below:

Chapter 1: Yu, C. H. (2004, August). *History of science and statistical education: Examples from Fisherian and Pearsonian Schools.* Paper presented at the 2004 Joint Statistical Meeting, Toronto, Canada.

Chapter 2: Yu, C. H. (2001 April). *Misconceived relationships between logical positivism and quantitative methods.* Paper presented at the Annual Meeting of the American Educational Research Association, Seattle, WA (ERIC Document Reproduction Service No. ED 452 266) (also posted on *Research method Forum*, 2003).

Chapter 3: Yu, C. H. (1994, April). *Induction? Deduction? Abduction? Is there a logic of EDA?* Paper presented at the Annual Meeting of American Educational Research Association, New Orleans, LA (ERIC Document Reproduction Service No. ED 376 173).

Chapter 4: Yu, C. H. (2004). Advance in Monte Carlo Simulations and robustness study and their implications for the dispute in philosophy of mathematics. *Minerva, 8,* 62–90.

Chapter 6: Yu, C. H. (2002 April). *A philosophical investigation of causal interpretation in structural equation models.* Paper presented at the Annual Meeting of the American Educational Research Association SIG: Structural Equation Modeling, New Orleans, LA (also posted on *Research Method Forum*, 2001).

Chapter 7: Yu, C. H. (2002, October). *Assumptions and interventions of probabilistic causal models.* Paper presented at the 2002 Annual Meeting of the Arizona Educational Research Association, Tempe, AZ.

I am indebted to Dr. John Behrens, Dr. Samuel Green, Dr. Marilyn Thompson, Dr. Barbara Ohlund, Dr. Keith Markus, Dr. Sharon Osborn–Popp, Dr. Brad Armendt, Dr. Bernard Kobes, Dr. Richard Creath, Dr. Manfred Laubichler, Dr. William Fisher, Ms. Samantha Waselus, Ms. Donna Denning, Dr. Candace Collins, Dr. Trisha Fritz, and the anonymous reviewers for their valuable input to different chapters of this book. Also, I am grateful to Dr. Samuel DiGangi and Dr. Angel Jannasch–Pennell for providing me with various research opportunities. And special thanks to Mr. Chang Kim and Mr. Inhyun Choi for checking the references of this book. Most importantly, thanks God for my supportive wife, Josephine Wong. Without her encouragement my intellectual adventure will end up in a barren field.

Chong Ho Yu, Ph.D.

Chapter 1 Philosophy of the Fisherian and Pearsonian Schools

Introduction

R. A. Fisher and Karl Pearson are considered the two most important figures in statistics as well as influential scholars in evolutionary biology and genetics. While statistical procedures are widely applied by scholars in various disciplines, including the natural and social sciences, statistics is mistakenly regarded as a subject–neutral methodology. It is important to point out that as R. A. Fisher and Karl Pearson developed their statistical schools, both of them were also pre–occupied with biological issues. Nonetheless, some authors have shifted the focus of Fisher–Pearson dispute from biology to statistical methodology or philosophy. Morrison (2002) represents the methodology focus by arguing that philosophy such as Pearson's positivism did not play an active role in the debate between Mendelism and biometry; rather to Pearson "the problem of evolution is a problem of statistics" (p. 47). In contrast, while discussing the difference between Fisher and Pearson with regard to Fisher's synthesis of Mendelism and biometrics, Norton and E. S. Pearson (1976), the son of Karl Pearson, argued that "their common stated objection was largely philosophical" (p. 153). Nonetheless, Norton's framework of analysis (1975) emphasizes the interplay between Pearsonian research on heredity and his philosophy of science.

The complexity of the Fisherian and Pearsonian views might not be adequately approached from a biological, statistical, or philosophical perspective alone. It is important to point out that both Fisher and Pearson were practitioners, not pure mathematicians conducting research on self–contained mathematical systems. In addition, Pearson was versed in German cultural and philosophical studies (Pearson, 1938; Williams et al., 2003). Therefore, it is plausible that the development of their statistical methodologies resulted from their philosophical orientations toward biology. Indeed, contemplation of biology issues played a crucial role in shaping their philosophy of science, and their philosophy of science influenced their statistical modeling. It is not the intention of this article to portray a simplistic view that the influences occur in a linear fashion: biology–philosophy–statistics. Instead, it could be conceived as an iterative process in which biology, philosophy and statistics are interwoven. One may argue that their Pearson's and Fisher's philosophies are an abstraction of their statistical practice. On the other hand, one could also analyze Fisher's and

Pearson's views on biology by tracing the sources of influence back to statistics. The order of "biology–philosophy–statistics" taken by this article is merely for the ease of illustration.

In the following section brief background information, such as the influence of biology on both Fisher and Pearson, the debate between the Schools of Mendelism and Biometrics and the social agenda of Eugenics, will be introduced. Next, it will discuss the relationship between biology and philosophy of science in both Fisherian and Pearsonian Schools. The thesis is that Pearson is pre–occupied with between–group speciation and thus his statistical methods, such as the Chi–squared test, are categorical in nature. On the other hand, variation within species plays a central role in Fisher's framework and thus Fisher's approach, such as partitioning variance, is more quantitative than Pearson's in terms of the measurement scale. In addition, Fisher adopted a philosophy of embracing causal inferences and theoretical entities, such as infinite population and gene, while Pearson disregarded unobservable and insisted upon description of the data at hand. Afterwards, it will illustrate how Fisher disagreed with Pearson in almost every aspect of Pearson's contributions to statistics due to their differences in biology and philosophy. The last part is an attempt to examine the difference between the significance testing approach developed by Fisher and the hypothesis testing approach advocated by Neyman and E. S. Pearson, who were both influenced by Karl Pearson.

Influence of biology on Fisher and Pearson

Pearson and biology

Karl Pearson was a follower of Galton, who is credited as the founder of the biometric school. However, Galton's mathematical approach to biology is coarse; it is Pearson who elevated the statistical approach to biology to a higher level. Thanks to Galton's efforts, in the late 18th century it became commonplace to picture the range of variation of species by a frequency distribution, especially the use of a normal curve. When Galton attempted to find out what happened to the curve if selection affects a population over several generations, he proposed the law of ancestral inheritance. Later Pearson followed up this theme and revised the law of ancestral inheritance with sophisticated statistics (Bowler, 1989).

Besides Galton, the closest colleague of Karl Pearson, W. F. R. Weldon, is also a biologist. Darwinism occupied a central theme in Weldon's research. Collaboration between Pearson and Weldon, needless to say, centered around biological topics. Karl Pearson's interest in biology was manifested in his speeches delivered in the Gresham Lectures from 1891 to 1894. Among those thirty–eight lectures, eight of them are concerned with philosophy of science, and later these papers were revised and published in a book entitled *The grammar of science*. The rest of the lectures are mostly related to biology. Eighteen of those papers were named "Mathematical Contribution to the Theory of Evolution" with different subtitles. In these papers Pearson introduced numerous concepts and procedures that have great impact on quantitative methodology, such as standard error of estimate, use of histograms for numeric illustration, and use of determinantal matrix algebra for biometrical methods. One of Pearson's goals was to develop a mathematical approach to biology. When Pearson started to develop the idea of speciation in terms of asymmetrical distributions, he proudly proclaimed, "For the first time in the history of biology, there was a chance of the science of life becoming an exact, mathematical science" (as cited in Magnello, 1996, p. 59). In some lectures Karl Pearson focused on the research agenda of Weldon. To be specific, Pearson and Weldon needed a criterion to reconstruct the concept of species. This provided the impetus to Pearson's statistical innovation of the Chi–square test of goodness of fit in 1892 (Magnello, 1996). No wonder Magnello (1996) bluntly asserted that "Pearson's statistical innovation was driven by the engine of evolutionary biology fuelled by Weldon" (p. 63).

Fisher and biology

The influences of biology on Fisher could be traced back to as early as Fisher's primary and secondary schooling. According to Joan Fisher–Box (1978), daughter of R. A. Fisher, Fisher excelled at school in biological and physical science as well as mathematics. Some of the books he chose as school prizes, such as his choice of the complete works of Charles Darwin in 1909, indicate his early interest in biology. At that time Fisher read many heavy–duty books on biology such as *A familiar history of birds, Natural history and antiquities of Selnorne, Introduction to zoology,* and *Jelly–fish, starfish, and sea–urchins* Later when Fisher went to Cambridge University, he read three newly published books on evolution and genetics by the Cambridge University Press.

It is a well–known fact that Fisher's 1918 paper on the synthesis of Mendelism and biometrics is considered a milestone in both biology and statistics. Actually, in 1911 Fisher had contemplated this synthesis in an unpublished paper, which was a speech delivered to the Cambridge University's Eugenics Society. At that time biological science was not fully conceptualized in a quantitative manner. In the 1911 paper, Fisher started to recognize the importance of quantitative characters to biological studies. It is also noteworthy that during Fisher's study at Cambridge, Bateson, a Professor of Biology who specialized in genetics, gave Fisher tremendous influences. To Bateson the origin of species is equated to the origin of gradual variation. Henceforth, variation has become a major thread of Fisherian thought. However, in the 1911 paper Fisher departed from Bateson's gradualism and suggested a thorough quantitative study of variation in both Mendelian and Darwinian senses (Bennett, 1983).

From 1915 for about twenty years, Fisher maintained extensive contact with Leonard Darwin, son of Charles Darwin. During much of this time they corresponded with each other one another every few days. Leonard Darwin introduced Fisher to a job in the Eugenics Education Society and encouraged him to pursue biological research topics. In 1916 when one of Fisher's papers was rejected by the Royal Society due to negative comments made by Karl Pearson, Leonard Darwin financed Fisher so that Fisher could pay another journal for printing the paper. That paper, which appeared in 1918, is the one that synthesizes Mendelism and biometrics (Norton, 1983). In exchanging ideas on academic topics, Darwin repeatedly encouraged Fisher to develop a mathematical approach to evolution and genetics. This invitation was well received by Fisher (Bennett, 1983). Indeed, Fisher observed this methodological "gap" in biological scholarship. In 1921 when Fisher reviewed the paper entitled "The relative value of the processes causing evolution," he commented, "The authors evidently lack the statistical knowledge necessary for the adequate treatment" (as cited in Bennett, 1983, p. 11). Throughout his career, Fisher continuously devoted tremendous effort to developing statistical methods for evolution and genetics. Fisher's 1958 book entitled *The genetical theory of natural selection* summarizes his statistical contribution to biology. In brief, it is obvious that the development of Fisherian statistical methodology was driven by his motivation to fill the methodological gap in biological science.

Background of the debate: Evolution and genetics

In the late 19th century, Charles Darwin proposed natural selection, in terms of survival for the fittest, as a driving force of evolution. Francis Galton, a cousin of Darwin, was skeptical of the selection thesis. Galton discovered a statistical phenomenon called *regression to the mean*, which is the precursor of regression analysis. According to regression to the mean, in a population whose general trait remains constant over a period of generations, each trait exhibits some small changes. However, this change does not go on forever and eventually the traits of offspring would approximate those of the ancestors. For example, although we expect that tall parents give birth to tall children, we will not see a super–race consisting of giants after ten generations, because the height of offspring from tall people would gradually regress towards the mean height of the population. According to Darwinism, small improvement in a trait happens across generations, and natural selection, by keeping this enhanced trait, makes evolution possible, but Galton argued that the regression effect counter–balances the selection effect (Gillham, 2001).

The central question of evolution is whether variation of a trait is inheritable. In the late 19th century Mendel gave a definite answer by introducing an elementary form of genetic theory. Mendel's theory was forgotten for a long while but it was re–discovered by de Vries in 1900. In contrast to Darwin's position that evolution is a result of accumulated small changes in traits, biologists who supported Mendel's genetics suggested otherwise: evolution is driven by mutation and thus evolution is discontinuous in nature. By the early 20th century, two opposing schools of thought had developed, namely, biometricians, who supported discontinuous evolution with "sports," and Mendelians, who supported continuous evolution with gradual changes. Although Galton rejected the idea of small changes in traits as an evolutionary force, he was credited as the pioneer of biometrics for his contribution of statistical methods to the topic of biological evolution.

Another important piece of background information is the fashion of Eugenics during the late 19th century and early 20th century. During that period of time many research endeavors were devoted to explaining why Western civilizations were superior to others (e.g., research on intelligence) and how they could preserve their advanced civilizations. According to Darwinism, the fittest species are the strongest ones who could reproduce more descendants. This notion fit the social atmosphere very well, since Darwinism could rationalize the idea that the West is stronger and thus fitter; it has the "mandate destiny" because the nature has selected the superior. Both Fisher and Pearson attempted to provide an answer to a question that was seriously concerned by Western policy makers and scholars. Under the Mendelian–Darwinian–Biometrician synthesis, Fisher suggested that the only way to ensure improvement of the nation was to increase the reproduction of high–quality people (Brenner–Golomb, 1993; Gigerenzer et al., 1989).

According to Howie (2002), during the dispute between Fisher and Pearson in the 1920s regarding evolution and genetics, "Fisher kept up a steady barrage and rarely missed a chance to either attack Pearson directly" (p. 66). Fisher boldly claimed that his method of estimating population parameters was efficient and sufficient, but Pearson's methods were inefficient, insufficient, or inconsistent.

On the other hand, perhaps because Fisher had pre–determined to synthesize evolution and the genetic theory proposed by Mendel, Fisher was very forgiving to Mendel even though he proved that Mendel was not rigorous in interpreting the results of his genetics experiments (Press & Tanur, 2001; Fisher, 1936). Mendel established the notion that physical properties of species are subject to heredity. In accumulating evidence for his views, Mendel conducted a fertilization experiment in which he followed several generations of axial and terminal flowers to observe how specific genes were carried from one generation to another. On subsequent examination of the data using Chi–square tests of association, Fisher (1936) found that Mendel's results were so close to the predicted model that residuals of the size reported would be expected by chance less than once in 10,000 times if the model were true. In spite of this rebuttal, Fisher was surprisingly polite to Mendel. For example, in telling that Mendel omitted details, Fisher wrote, "Mendel was an experienced and successful teacher, and might well have adopted a style of presentation suitable for the lecture–room without feeling under any obligation to complete his story by unessential details" (p. 119). While discussing how Mendel lied about his data, Fisher wrote, "He (Mendel) is taking excessive and unnecessary liberties with the facts" (p. 120). To explain why Mendel was wrong about his results, Fisher wrote, "It remains a possibility among others that Mendel was deceived by some assistant who knew too well what was expected" (p. 132).

Interestingly enough, Fisher treated Darwin in a similar manner, probably due to his strong Darwinian orientation. In the development of his randomization test for paired data, Fisher used Darwin's data on the relative growth rates of cross– and self–fertilized corn to demonstrate the merits of this non–parametric procedure. Although Fisher criticized that Darwin did not randomize the group assignment, he did not criticize other aspects of Darwin's experimental design. After carefully checking Darwin's description of the experiment, Jacquez and Jacquez (2002) found that this experiment indeed did not use true paired comparisons. They argued that although the foundation of Fisher's randomization test is justified, indeed the data do not meet the rigorous criteria for paired data. Jacquez and Jacquez regarded this matter as being of a historical interest without making further implications. However, one may wonder what criticisms Fisher would have made if Pearson were the one who made such experimental errors.

Biology and philosophy in the Pearsonian School

Grammar of science

Classification of facts

Karl Pearson was strongly influenced by Ernst Mach, a scientist who zealously subscribed to the positivist view, which is anti–latent variables and anti–counterfactual. He initially rejected the existence of shock waves caused by bullets going faster than the speed of sound because this could not be directly observed by scientists (as cited in Shipley, 2000). Based on the same reasoning, Mach was opposed to untestable "absolute space" in Newtonian physics (as cited in Greene, 2004). In addition, Mach (1941) said, "The universe is not twice given, with an earth at rest and an earth in motion; but only once, with its relative motions, alone determinate. It is, accordingly, not permitted us to say how things would be if the earth did not rotate" (p. 284).

In 1892 Karl Pearson published a book entitled *The grammar of science*, which manifested his positivist view on science. In Pearson's view scientific methodology is a "classification of facts" (p. 21), and thus causal inferences and explanations are unwarranted. In this book Pearson paid much attention to evolutionary biology, in which "variation," "inheritance," "natural selection," and "sexual selection" were treated as mere description. It may be difficult to determine whether his biological thought influenced his philosophy of science or vice versa. In *The grammar of science*, Pearson declared that his proposed scientific method is subject–free by saying, "The unity of all science consists alone in its method, not in its material…it is not the fact themselves which form science, but the method in which they are dealt with" (p. 16).

Nevertheless, in spite of this claim of "subject–free" methodology, there is an interesting link between the notion of speciation in biology and the notion of science as a classification of facts. Speciation is an evolutionary formation of new biological species, usually by the division of a single species into two or more genetically distinct ones. In later years Pearson employed statistics to divide a non–normal distribution into two normal distributions as a means to describe speciation (Magnello, 1996). In addition, one of the major contributions to statistics by Pearson is the invention of the Chi–squared test, which is a test of goodness of fit using discrete and categorical data. In *The grammar of science* Pearson strongly disapproved of metaphysics, German Hegelianism, and religion for their ambiguity and unanswerable questions. Interestingly enough, rather than promoting science as a methodology of using precise continuous–scaled measurement with ten decimal points following each numeric output, Pearson regarded science as a discrete classification of facts, which fits well with speciation in biology.

Anti–theoretical entity and anti–cause

Pearson's positivist attitude could also be found in his position on anti–theoretical entities. In the first edition of *The grammar of science* (1892/1937), Karl Pearson mocked the theory of atoms. After 1900 the impetus for Mendelian genetics had been revived. However, as late as 1911, Pearson still showed no interest in unobservable entities by asserting, in the Preface to the third edition of *The grammar of science*, that theoretical entities are nothing more than constructs for conveniently describing our experience. Causal explanations, equally hidden and unobservable, were also dissatisfying to Pearson. In the third edition of *The grammar of science*, he added a new chapter entitled "Contingency and Correlation—the Insufficiency of Causation." Pearson strongly objected to using hidden causal forces as an explanation in science. Instead, he proposed using a contingency table, which is a description and classification of data.

His anti–cause position is obviously influenced by Galton's correlational method. In 1889 Pearson wrote, "It was Galton who first freed me from the prejudice that sound mathematics could only be applied to natural phenomena under the category of causation" (Pearson, 1938, p. 19).

Interestingly enough, this anti–cause position is also tied to his crusade against animistic philosophy, such as employing "teleology" and "will," in biology (Pearl, 2000). When Darwinism was proposed as a naturalistic explanation of the origin and evolution of species, the causal mechanism behind evolution was portrayed in the fashion that species are "willing" to evolve towards a teleological consummation. As a scholar who disliked metaphysics and the Hegelian notion that history evolves with an ideal, it is not surprising that Pearson was opposed to casual explanations in biology and favored contingency tables. Nonetheless, Porter (2004) argued that the position of downplaying invisible, hypothetical objects did not play a central role in Pearson's rejection of Mendelian genetics. He was critical of concepts such as "force" and "matter," but not "gene" and "molecule." Rather he charged that the Mendelians defined nature in one and only one approach while indeed natural phenomena could be described in multiple ways. In philosophy of science terminology, there should be more than one way to "save the phenomenon."

The grammar of science was warmly embraced by Pearson's scholarly contemporaries such as Neyman, who later co–developed the Neyman/Pearson hypothesis testing approach with Karl Pearson's son, E. S. Pearson. Neyman said,

> We were a group of young men who had lost our belief in Orthodox religion, not from any sort of reasoning, but because of the stupidity of our priests, [But] we were not freed from dogmatism and were prepared in fact to believe in authority, so far as it was not religious. The reading of *The grammar of science* . . . was striking because . . . it attacked in an uncompromising manner all sorts of authorities. . . . At the first reading it was this aspect that struck us. What could it mean? We had been unused to this tone in any scientific book. Was the work 'de la blague' [something of a hoax] and the author a 'canaille' [scoundrel] on a grand scale . . . ? But our teacher, Bernstein, had recommended the book; we must read it again (as cited in Reid. 1982, pp. 23–24).

Pearsonian School of statistics

Pearsonian methodologies carry unmistakable marks of his philosophy of science. Karl Pearson made four major contributions to statistical methods before the turn of the century: (1) Method of moments (Pearson, 1894), (2) Curve–fitting based on least squares (Pearson, 1895), (3) Correlation (Pearson & Filon, 1898), and (4) Chi–squared test of goodness of fit (Pearson, 1900). These methodologies share two common threads, namely, correlation instead of causation, and description of data at hand instead of idealistic, theoretical modeling.

Method of moments

In 1893–94 Karl Pearson wrote a paper in response to Weldon's request about speciation in terms of breaking up a distribution into two. In this paper Pearson introduced the method of moments as a means of fitting a curve to the data (Pearson, 1928; Magnello, 1996). To be specific, the method of moments was applied to the estimation of a mixture of normal distributions. In a normal distribution, which is symmetrical in shape, only the first and second moments (mean and standard deviation) are matters of concern. In a non–normal distribution, the third and fourth moments (skewness and kurtosis) are essential for describing the distribution. Although Galton is arguably the first scholar to employ statistics in biology, he was so obsessed with normal distributions that he spent his whole life attempting to fit any data to a normal curve. In contrast, Pearson found that symmetrical normality is by no means a universal phenomenon, especially for problems in evolutionary biology. As early as 1900, Pearson was critical to normal curves by maintaining that normal curve possesses no special fitness for describing errors or deviations such as arise either in observing practice or in nature. As a remedy, Pearson introduced the method of moments as a statistical approach of curving fitting for both symmetrical and asymmetrical distributions. To be specific, a bi–modal distribution, also know as a double–humped curve, could be dissected into two normal curves. Its application is to break up a species into two species. When the measure of a trait of a species appears to be non–normally distributed, speciation has occurred.

This notion of "anti–normality" is tied to Pearson's attitude of anti–theoretical entities. Indeed, in subsequent ages many researchers tended to support Pearson. For example, French physicist Lippmann disliked use of normal curves for the circular logic of proving normality: "Everybody believes in the normal approximation, the experimenters because they think it is a mathematical theorem, the mathematicians because they think it is an experimental fact" (as cited in Thompson, 1959, p. 121). In a similar vein to Lippmann, Stigler (1986) criticized the circular logic employed by Gauss. Gauss conceptualized the mean in terms of "least squares": the mean could be used to summarize a data set, because when more observations are closer to the mean and fewer observations are farther from the mean, the sum of squares of the deviation is minimal. The mean is only "most probable" if the errors (deviations) are normally distributed; and the supposition that errors are normally distributed leads back to least squares. In response to the lack of proof of universal normal distributions, Geary (1947) stated that normality could be viewed as a special case of many distributions rather than a universal property. However, since the school of R. A. Fisher became dominant, universal normality has been favored and interest in non–normality has retreated to the background. In conclusion, Geary suggested that future editions of all existing textbooks and new textbooks should include this warning: "Normality is a myth; there never was, and never will be, a normal distribution" (p. 241).

Least square and curve–fitting

The least square method and curve–fitting are built upon the theory of error. When multiple measures were administered in astronomy research, there were always some fluctuations. In the past scientists had tended to dismiss certain unreliable measurements, but later scientists took the average of multiple measures. In this approach, the degrees of the departure from the mean are regarded as errors or residuals. To Pearson the aim of curve–fitting is to minimize the residuals or errors. It is important to point out that this approach is more data–driven than model–driven since it is obvious that errors varying from sample to sample are taken into account. Today the theory of error is in line with the residual analysis that is commonly seen in the school of Exploratory Data Analysis (EDA), since EDA is also more data–driven than model based (Behrens & Yu, 2003).

In addition, curve–fitting as a graphical technique is tied to Pearson's emphasis on the descriptive nature of scientific methodology. During the 1880s Pearson concentrated on graphical methods as his central contributions to engineering education. Later he extended his vision to biometrics, in which the geometrical sense of evolutionary processes was said to be detectable by graphing methods. To be specific, he thought that he could find the effects of natural selection from frequency curves. However, unlike data visualization techniques in modern EDA, Pearson was opposed to curve smoothing because it might blend away double peaks of correlation surfaces (Porter, 2004).

Correlation

Galton invented the concept of correlation and Pearson further expanded this idea by introducing several correlation coefficients such as Product Moment and tetrachoric, as a replacement for causal inferences. In Pearson's view, the ultimate essence of biological knowledge is statistical and there is no room for causal factors. To be specific, if variables A and B are correlated, it does not necessarily imply that A causes B or vice versa. For example, the correlation coefficient derived from a bivariate distribution fitted to the heights of fathers and sons could be used to describe the process of heredity, but one should not specify any biological mechanism in a causal sense. This approach has been applied by both Karl Pearson and W. F. R. Weldon in biological research, but Pearson even went further to use correlation to reject Mendelism. By computing the correlation coefficients of physical traits among relatives sampled from human populations, Pearson concluded that there is no evidence that the variance of height among humans could be explained by heredity, and thus the correlational studies contradicted the Mendelian scheme of inheritance (Norton, 1975; Provine, 2001).

Chi–squared test

The Chi–squared procedure is a test of goodness of fit between the expected and the observed frequency of categorical data in a contingency table. E. S. Pearson (1938), son of Karl Pearson, praised the Chi–squared test as "a powerful new weapon in the hands of one who sought to battle with the myths of a dogmatic world" (p. 31). Pearson presented the Chi–squared distribution in place of the normal distribution to solve the goodness of fit for multinomial distributions. In Pearson's view, there is no "true" chi–square in the Platonic or absolute sense, or the so–called "true" chi–square cannot be estimated even if it exists. The focal point of the Chi–squared test is the exact frequency of the data and thus there is no probabilistic property in the data. To be specific, for Pearson the so–called probabilities associated with the test do not represent a model–based attribute such as the frequency of incorrectly rejecting the hypothesis. Rather, it is just a convenient way to describe the fit between the hypothesis and the data (Baird, 1983). Like the modern Rasch modeling school, Pearson emphasized that the model must fit the data, but not the other way around. When data seemed to contradict calculation, he doubted the mathematics (Porter, 2004).

Biology and philosophy in the Fisherian School

Mendelian genetics and model–based deduction

Unlike Pearson, Fisher did not write any book concerning philosophy of science. In the collected correspondence of Fisher edited by J H. Bennett (1990), only eight pages of Fisher's writing are put under the category of "history and philosophy of science." Moreover, most of these writings are fragmented thoughts rather than systematic inquiry into the history and philosophy of science. Nevertheless, Fisher's philosophical ideas are manifested in his view on biology. Neyman's praise of Pearson, as cited above, indicates the academic atmosphere of the late 19th century. Being skeptical of metaphysics and religion, certain scholars were eager to search for methodologies of high certainty and low ambiguity. To Fisher, Mendelian genetics was a viable means because genetics could potentially explain a large amount of variance among observations (Howie, 2002). Further, Fisher was disinterested in individualistic information, but asserted that biological inferences should be made with reference to an indefinitely large number of Mendelism characteristics, which conforms to his view that statistical inference is based upon comparing the observed statistics with an infinite theoretical sampling distribution. Obviously, this view is in direct opposition to the Pearsonian idea that using large but finite populations, not infinite populations, is the cornerstone of biometric methods (Morrison, 2002). Roughly speaking, the Fisherian approach is a type of model–based deduction, in which data are fitted to a model, while the Pearsonian approach is a kind of data–driven induction, in which a model is constructed to approximate the phenomenon.

Interestingly enough, Fisherian model–based reasoning and Mendelian genetics have some degree of resemblance. Darwinian biometricians such as Pearson and Weldon viewed inheritance in an individualistic fashion, in which blending of characteristics varies from case to case. In contrast, Mendelians maintained that there is a mechanism of heredity, in which genes are simply passed on unchanged to the offspring without blending (Morrison, 2002). Thus, the invariant gene, as a blueprint of a species, could be a metaphor of model. In the former fluctuations in biological traits could be traced back to one abstraction. By the same token, fluctuations among statistical observations in general could also be treated as deriving from a pre–determined invariant model. As mentioned before, Pearson had problems with unobservable constructs owing to his positivist position, and thus Mendelism that emphasizes the role of unobservable genes was flatly rejected. On the other hand, in Fisher's framework unobservable abstraction was never a problem. Rather, Fisher embraced abstract entities such as theoretical distributions and genes. In this perspective, Fisherian philosophy, biology, and statistics are totally aligned.

Moreover, there is evidence that Fisher's interest in infinitely large populations and variances was strongly related to his biological research. In the late

19th century questions concerning how the selection effect, in the sense of continuous evolution, could retain the traits enhancing survival fitness were controversial. According to Fisher, a rare gene resulting from mutation, as Mendelians suggested, could be eliminated by chance in a small population. However, large populations encouraged evolution by keeping up variability. In other words, selection was most effective when it acted on the wide variability of a large population. This proposal addressed the question of evolution in a continuous and unbranching line. In contrast to Pearson, *Fisher ignored the issue of speciation*, splitting of a population into several discrete and distinct branches (Bowler, 1983). Fisher's attempt to theorize selection in terms of "infinitely large populations" clearly demonstrates a link between his research agenda in biology and his later development of statistical inference based upon infinite, theoretical distributions, which will be discussed in a later section. Also, the theme of seeking support for continuous evolution sheds some light on Fisher's orientation towards quantitative thinking in a continuous scale, as opposed to Pearson's discrete thinking, such as the Chi–squared test and the classification of facts.

Fisherian School of statistics

It is not exaggerating to say that Fisher's career, to a certain extent, was built upon his opposition to Pearsonian ideas. Fisher's first paper, "On the absolute criterion for fitting frequency curves" (1912), is considered a rebuttal of Pearson's least squares and curve fitting. The clash between the two giants came to a crescendo in 1918 when Fisher partitioned variances (the precursor of Analysis of Variance) to synthesize Mendelism and Biometry, and hence rejected the Pearsonian idea that Mendelism is incompatible with evolution. But the battle didn't end here. In 1922 Fisher proposed a change in the degree of freedom of the Chi–squared test introduced by Pearson in 1900. Fisher's contributions to statistics and biology go beyond the development of preceding theories, but in terms of confronting Pearsonian notions, his ideas could be summarized as the following: (1) Maximum likelihood estimation as an opposition to least squares; (2) Analysis of variance as an opposition to a–causal description; (3) Modification of Pearsonian Chi–Squared; (4) Randomized experimentation wth counterfactual elements as an opposition to using the data at hand. Each of the above will be discussed below.

Maximum likelihood

Aldrich (1997) asserted that Fisher's 1912 paper is a "very implicit piece of writing, and to make any of it explicit, we have to read outside and guess" (p. 162). In Aldrich's view, although Fisher did not mention Pearson in that paper, the paper reads like a critique of Pearson's theory of curve fitting. In the paper Fisher proposed using the scale–independent absolute criterion as a replacement for the theory of error and the least squared because of their shortcoming in scale–dependence. Later, during Fisher's dispute with Bayesians such as Jeffrey, Fisher further expanded the idea of absolute criterion and eventually developed the maximum likelihood estimation. By applying the maximum likelihood function to gene frequency and recombination frequency estimation, biologists overcame the problems of multiple factors in biology (Piegorsch, 1990).

The main point is that statistical methods could not be confined by individual data sets, whose properties vary from time to time, from place to place, and from person to person; probability should carry *objective and invariant properties* that can be derived from mathematics. As a competent mathematician, Fisher constructed three criteria for desirable properties of estimators to the unknown population, namely, unbiasedness, consistency, and efficiency (Eliason, 1993). A detailed mathematical demonstration of these properties is beyond the scope of this paper; nevertheless, the following brief description of Fisher's approach demonstrates how Fisher elegantly constructed an objective approach to statistics and probability that is effective even if the hypothetical population is unknown in distribution and infinite in size.

If the estimated parameter is the same as the true parameter, this estimation is considered unbiased. However, an estimator has variance or dispersion. The estimator may fall somewhere along the dispersion, nevertheless, the efficient estimator is the one that has achieved the lowest possible variance among all other estimators, and thus it is the most precise one. Moreover, the goodness of the estimation is also tied to the sample size. As the sample size increases, the difference between the estimated and the true parameters should be smaller and smaller. If this criterion is fulfilled, this estimator is said to be consistent. Hence, researchers can make probabilistic inferences to hypothetical populations using these objective criteria. Today some statisticians believe that if the likelihood approach serves as the sole basis for inference, analyzing residuals of data is unnecessary (Nerlove, 1999).

Although the focus of this discussion is concerned with the Fisherian and Pearsonian Schools, it is noteworthy that the quest of *certainty, objectivity, true parameters*, and *invariant statistical properties* constitutes an implicit agenda in Fisher's methodology, and thus it also affected how Fisher viewed other schools of thought besides Pearson. For instance, this agenda explains why Fisher firmly rejected the notion of random genetic drift proposed by Sewall Wright, the biologist who invented the path model (a precursor to structural equation modeling). While Wright proposed that evolution results from both random genetic drift and deterministic natural selection, R. A. Fisher and E. B. Ford insisted that natural selection is the major force to drive the evolutionary process. However, Fisher maintained a single–cause theory and regarded all other random variations as un–intelligible noise. For this reason Fisher and Wright became bitter intellectual enemies (Gould, 1988). The idea of path coefficient as a way of quantify the effect of mating is fundamental to population genetics (Hill, 1996), but when Fisher (1949) wrote about inbreeding, he did not cite a single word from Wright.

Analysis of Variance

In 1916 Karl Pearson, who served as a reviewer of the *Journal of Royal Society*, rejected a paper submitted by Fisher regarding Mendelism and Darwinism. Fisher blamed the rejection on the paper being sent to Pearson, "a mathematician who knew no biology," and another reviewer, a biologist lacking mathematical knowledge (as cited in Morrison, 2002). Two years later, with Leonard Darwin's financial assistance, Fisher paid the *Transactions of the Royal Society of Edinburgh* to publish that paper. In that paper Fisher (1918) bluntly rejected Pearson's assertion that biometrics had refuted Mendelism. Based on the same data set collected by Pearson for denying Mendelism, Fisher demonstrated that the hypothesis of cumulative Mendelian factors seems to fit the data very well. By re–formulating statistical procedures and probabilistic inferences, Fisher concluded that heritable changes in the Mendelian sense could be very small and evolution in the Darwinian sense could be very slow, and that these subtle differences could be detected by Fisher's version of biometrics.

Fisher's 1918 paper is highly regarded as a milestone in both statistics and biology for the introduction of the prototype of Analysis of Variance as well as the synthesis of Mendelism, biometry and evolution (Morran & Smith, 1966). More importantly, it carries important implications for philosophy of science. As mentioned before, Pearson frequently employed descriptive statistics such as correlation coefficients rather than causal inferences. However, in Fisher's methodology variance of traits is partitioned, and therefore it is possible to trace how much variance of a variable is accounted for by the variance of another. Aldrich (1995) praised Fisher's 1918 paper as "the most ambitious piece of scientific inference" (p. 373). Aldrich cited Koopmans and Reiersol (1950) and Cox (1958) to distinguish statistical inference from scientific inference. The former deals with making inferences from a sample to the population whereas the latter addresses the interpretation of the population in terms of a theoretical structurc. This is no doubt revolutionary because Fisher went beyond correlation to causation, beyond description to explanation, and beyond individual observations to the theoretical structure.

It is noteworthy that in the 1918 paper Fisher coined the term "variance" as a means to partition heritable and non–heritable components of species. It is generally agreed that the concept of "variance" revolutionized modern statistical thinking. To be specific, not only are Analysis of Variance and its extended methods, such as Analysis of Covariance (ANCOVA) and Multiple Analysis of Variance (MANOVA), based upon the concept of "variance," but correlational and regression analysis can also be construed in terms of "variance explained" (Keppel & Zedeck, 1989). In addition, in Psychometrics reliability is also conceived as a relationship between the true score variance and the error variance by followers of the True Score Theory (Yu, 2001).

Modified Chi–squared test

Pearson invented the Chi–squared test as a specific materialization of the notion that science is a classification of facts. Fisher was not opposed to the use of Chi–squared; rather he applied this to expose the errors made by Gregor Mendel, the father of genetics (Press & Tanur, 2001; Fisher, 1936). The clash between Fisher and Pearson on Chi–squared happened in 1922 when Fisher introduced "degrees of freedom" to modify the meaning of Chi–squared. Fisher argued that in terms of causal explanation every free parameter reduces one degree of freedom. Pearson, as the inventor of the test, was opposed to Fisher's suggestion (Baird, 1983). In contrast, Fisher's criticism was well–taken by Yule and Greenwood. They attributed Pearson's stubbornness to his personality, an unwillingness to admit errors. But Porter argued that perhaps there is also something in Pearson's attitude that reflects a long standing ideal of curve–fitting, the notion of data over model (Porter, 2004).

Obviously, Pearson was on the wrong side of history. Chi–squared is now applied as Fisher argued it ought to be (Baird, 1983). The degree of freedom, by definition, is the number of pieces of useful information, which is determined by the sample size and also the number of parameters to be estimated (Yu, Lo, & Stockford, 2001). In other words, the degree of freedom is a measure of the informativeness of a hypothesis. Using Chi–squared alone as a measure of fit suffers from a drawback: Chi–squared statistics is a function of sample size. As a remedy today for detecting misfits in Item Response Theory, it is a common practice to divide the Chi–squared by degrees of freedom (Chi–sq/df).

More importantly, Fisher's interpretation of Chi–squared represents a very different philosophy from Pearson's. As mentioned before Pearson did not accept the notion of true Chi–Squared; the meaning of "fit" between the expected and the observed, to him, was nothing more than constructing a convenient model to approximate the observed frequencies in different cells of a contingency table. However, to Fisher a true Chi–squared could be obtained even when expected cell frequencies must be estimated. In this sense, the meaning of "fit" is the closeness to the truth of a hypothesis (Baird, 1983).

Design of experiment

Comparison between Fisherian and Pearsonian statistics indicates that Fisher favored statistical thinking in terms of variance on a continuum while Pearson oriented towards statistical thinking in a discrete mode. Actually their differences go beyond this. As mentioned before, Pearsonian methodology is tied to his philosophy of science, which is a–causal and descriptive in essence. Fisher realized that this approach was a hindrance to biological science because scientists must contemplate a wider domain than the actual observations. For Fisher, the concept of variation or variance is not confined to actual cases, but also applied to theoretical distributions including a wider variation that has no mapping to the empirical world. For instance, biologists would take the existing two sexes for granted; no biologist would be interested in modeling what organisms might experience if there were three or more sexes. However, from a mathematical viewpoint it is logical to consider this question with reference to a system of possibilities infinitely wider than the actual (Fisher–Box, 1978). Today philosophers call this type of reasoning "counterfactual." Counterfactual reasoning leads Fisherians to go beyond mere description of the actual world. Nonetheless, it is interesting to compare Fisher's reasoning with Mach's (1941) that was cited previously: "The universe is not twice given, with an earth at rest and an earth in motion; but only once, with its relative motions, alone determinate. It is, accordingly, not permitted us to say how things would be if the earth did not rotate" (p. 284).

Although Fisher did not develop counterfactual-based methodologies like modal logic in philosophy or path searching algorithms in structural equation modeling, his design of experiments definitely carries certain counterfactual elements. To be specific, the researcher employing design of experiments can go beyond the actual world to counterfactual worlds by creating situations (treatment groups) that did not naturally happen.

Although many researchers know that Fisher is the pioneer of design of experiments, the difference between randomized and controlled experiments is a common subject of confusion. Today "randomized experiment" and "controlled experiment" are often used synonymously. One of the reasons is that usually an experiment consists of a controlled group and treatment group, and group membership is randomly assigned into one of the groups. Since "control" and "randomization" are both perceived as characteristics of an experiment, it is not surprising that in many texts randomized experiment and controlled experiment are either used in an interchangeable fashion or the two terms are combined as one term such as "randomized controlled experiment." Actually, there is a subtle difference between the two.

Fisher invented randomized experiment, not controlled experiment. In Fisher's view, even if there is a significant difference between the control and the treatment group, we may not be able to attribute the difference to the treatment when there are many uncontrollable variables and sampling fluctuations. The objective of randomization is to differentiate between associations due to causal effects of the treatment and associations due to some variable that is a common cause to both the treatment and response variables. If there are influences resulting from uncontrolled variables, by randomization the influences would be randomly distributed across the control and treatment groups even though no control of those variables is made.

On the other hand, the logic of experimentation up to Fisher's time was that of controlled experiment. In a controlled experiment, many variables are experimentally fixed to a constant value. However, Fisher explicitly stated that it is an inferior method, because it is impossible to know what variables should be taken into account. For example, a careful researcher may assign equal numbers of males and females into each group, but she/he may omit the age and educational level of the subjects. In Fisher's view, instead of attempting to put everything under control, the researcher should let randomization take care of the uncontrollable factors. This is not to suggest that Fisher did not advocate controlling for other causes in addition to randomization. Rather he explicitly recommended that the researcher should do as much as control as he can, but he advised that randomization must be employed as "the second line of defense" (Shipley, 2000).

Differences in statistical testing

After Karl Pearson had receded from the stage of statistics, Fisher fought another battle with Karl Pearson's son, E. S. Pearson. Today the widely adopted statistical testing is a fusion between Fisherian significance testing and Neyman/E. S. Pearson's hypothesis testing, which carry many incompatible elements (Lehmann, 1993; Hubbard & Bayarri, 2003). Neyman admired Karl Pearson for the views on philosophy of science expressed in Pearson's book *The grammar of science* (1892/1937). Although E. S. Pearson disagreed with his father on certain issues, basically Karl Pearson's influence on E. S. Pearson is obvious. Not surprisingly, the Neyman/Pearson approach shares many common grounds with Karl's Pearson's philosophy of science. Indeed, when Neyman and E. S. Pearson made amendments to hypothesis testing, Fisher was very displeased. If we keep the above background information concerning biology and philosophy in mind, the differences between R. A. Fisher and E. S. Pearson will be more understandable.

When Fisher introduced his methodology, there was only one hypothesis: Null (i.e., there is no difference between the control group and the treatment group). Following this strategy, the only possible options are whether to reject the null hypothesis or not. Put simply, the conclusion is an either/or answer. To E. S. Pearson, testing a single hypothesis that only yields a simple and dichotomous answer was inadequate. Later Pearson introduced the concept of alternate hypothesis (i.e., there is a difference between the control group and the treatment group). However, the alternate hypothesis is unknown and thereby could be anything (a very huge difference, a large difference, a medium difference, a small difference, a very small difference, etc.). With the presence of alternatives, the conclusion is no longer dichotomous.

Further differences between the two schools can be found in the use of cut–off Alpha level. While Fisher advocated .05 as the standard cut–off Alpha level, Pearson (1933) did not recommend a standard level but suggested instead that researchers look for a balance between Type I and Type II errors. Statistical power is also taken into consideration for computing probabilities and statistics.

Fisherian model

In Figure 1.1, the y–axis is the frequency and the x–axis is the standardized score with the mean as zero and the standard deviation as one. The curve on the left hand side is the null distribution introduced by Fisher. It is important to note that this is the sampling distribution, which appears *in theory only*. It is derived from neither the population nor the sample. In theory, if there is no difference between the control and treatment groups in the population, the subtraction result is zero. However, there are always some sampling fluctuations due to measurement errors and other factors. In a *thought experiment*, if many samples are drawn from the same population, the difference is not exactly zero all the time. On some occasions it is above zero, and in some cases it is below zero. According to the Central Limit Theorem, when these scores are plotted, a bell–shaped distribution is formed regardless of the shape of the population distribution (Yu, Anthony, & Behrens, 1995). In the Fisherian methodology, a pre–determined Alpha level is set to guide the researcher in making a judgment about the observed sample. After the statistical attributes of the observed sample are found, the sample is compared against this theoretical sampling distribution. If the sample is located in the right hand side of the Alpha level, the data are said to be extremely rare, and thus the null hypothesis is rejected. Therefore, the region in the right hand side of the Alpha level is called the "region of rejection."

At first glance, the approach adopted by Fisher seems overly simplistic. Why did Fisher recognize just one null hypothesis? Why did he want only a dichotomous answer? Given Fisher's model–based reasoning and his quest for certainty derived from Mendelian genetics, his use of null hypothesis testing is not surprising.

Figure 1.1. Fusion of Fisher and Pearson models

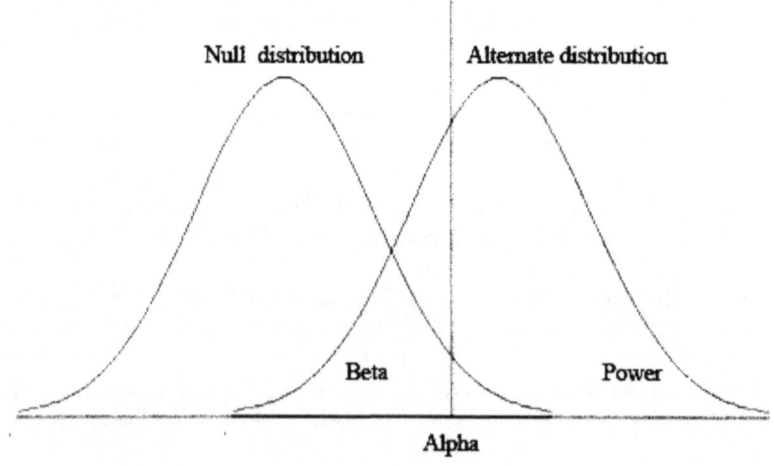

Neyman/Pearson model

Neyman and E. S. Pearson enriched the methodology by introducing the concepts of alternate hypothesis, power, and Type I and Type II errors (Beta). According to Neyman and E. S. Pearson, it is not helpful to conclude that there is either no difference or some difference. If the null hypothesis is false, what is the alternative? The development of Neyman/Pearson's notion of alternate distributions may be partly tied to E. S. Pearson's father's disagreement with Galton on the nature of biological data. Galton believed that all biological data are normally distributed and variations should be confined within certain parameters. As mentioned before, Galton believed in regression to the mean, in which every naturally occurring variable has a fixed mean and all values of the variable should tend to scatter around the mean. On the other hand, Karl Pearson (1896) held a more open–ended view of distributions—the world should have more than one type of distribution. Data could take on a variety of shapes, which could be skewed, asymmetrical, flat, J–shaped, U–shaped, and many others. Skew distributions and skew variations could occur in cases of disease and heredity (Magnello, 1996).

Besides providing an alternate hypothesis, Neyman and Pearson also changed the concept of probability from static and single–faceted to dynamic and multi–faceted. If the difference between the control and the treatment groups is small, it is possible that the researcher is unable to detect the difference when indeed the null hypothesis is false. This is called a Type II error, also known as "Beta" or "miss." On the contrary, the researcher may also reject the null hypothesis when in fact there is no difference. In this case, the researcher makes a Type I error, also known as "false alarm."

Under the frequentist logic of E. S. Pearson, several other probability concepts were introduced: Power, associated with the alternate hypothesis, is the probability that the null hypothesis is correctly rejected (the blue area in Figure 2), whereas Beta is the probability of Type II error. In this dynamic model, power is a function of sample size, Alpha level, and the supposed mean difference between the two groups, which is also known as "effect size."

Why did E. S. Pearson introduce the notions of Type I and Type II errors and power? It seems that these criteria are tied to specific situations. For example, in a research setting where the sample size is small, the statistical power is also small, and as a result, Type II error is inflated. In other words, the Fisherian universal model–based inference is replaced by a type of inference that takes attributes of data sets at hand into account. Indeed, the idea of power could be traced back to the development of the Chi–Squared test by Karl Pearson. As mentioned before, Karl Pearson did not view a test of fit as a measure of the closeness of data to the "truth," but just as a measure of adequacy of some theoretical mathematical model for the observed data. To justify this orientation of "fit," Pearson referred to his test of fit of what we now call the statistical power. His argument is that with a sufficiently large sample the Chi–squared test can suggest whether the hypothesized model could describe the data (Inman, 1994). E. S. Pearson and Karl Pearson were truly in the same vein regarding statistical inferences.

More importantly, E. S. Pearson viewed the interpretation of statistical inference as a purely behavioristic one that refrained from any epistemic interpretation. Unlike Fisherian deductive inference, in which the observed is compared against the model to deduce a dichotomous conclusion, Pearsonian inference was thought to be inductive behavior, not inductive inference (Gigerenzer et al.,

1989). The term "inductive behavior" shows the resemblance between Karl Pearson's and E. S. Pearson's thought. "Induction" indicates that the researcher should focus on collecting individual observations as a basis of drawing conclusions, whereas "behavior" implies that the conclusion has nothing to do with estimating a true parameter based on the sample at hand; rather the behavior is an action taken by the researcher based on the conclusion as if it were true.

Conclusion

By citing the history of Fisher and Pearson, this article attempts to debunk the myth that statistics is a subject–free methodology derived from invariant and timeless mathematical axioms. As discussed above, biological themes and philosophical presumptions drove Karl Pearson and R. A. Fisher to develop their statistical schools. It is fascinating to see that both giants came from the same starting point (developing a mathematical approach in biology), but eventually went in different directions. This chasm got even wider when the Fisherian and Pearsonian philosophies were actualized in hypothesis testing. Today, although many authors realize that current hypothesis testing is a fusion of the Fisher and Pearson/Neyman schools, few recognize the biological and philosophical elements in the origin of this hybrid model. Table 1.1 summarizes the differences between the Fisherian and Pearsonian Schools:

Table 1.1 Difference between Fisherian and Pearson Schools

	Fisherian	**Pearsonian**
Philosophy	Accept causal inferences	Favor a–causal descriptions
	Inference based upon theoretical worlds, such as infinite populations and counterfactual worlds	Inference based on observed data
Biology	Variation is the central theme; ignore speciation Synthesize Mendelism and biometrics	Speciation is the central theme Reject Mendelism
Statistics	Use the Maximum Likelihood Estimation, which is model–based Use variance partitioning Use degree of freedom to amend the Chi–squared test Use randomized experiment	Use Method of Moments, theory of error and least squared, which are data–driven Use correlation and regression Use Chi–squared test of goodness of fit Use observed data

Owing to the contributions by Fisher and Pearson, today statistical thinking continues to be a vibrant component in evolutionary biology. For example, recent scholarship by Walsh (2003) and his colleagues (2002) demonstrated that natural selection could appeal to the statistical structure of populations and sampling error. Interestingly enough, Walsh (2003) didn't view Fisher's integration of statistics, genetics and evolution as a successful one, because to Walsh Darwinian selection is environment–based, forceful, and causal while genetic selection is probabilistic and statistical. Walsh et al. (2002) used the following two experimental setups to illustrate the difference between a dynamical model based upon driving forces and a statistical model based on the population structures. In the first experiment a feather is dropped from certain height. Although the landing location of the feather appears to be random, indeed it could be well–explained by the gravitational force, wind direction and its speed at a certain time. The so–called probabilistic explanation of the outcome is just due to our ignorance of those forces. In the second experiment ten coins are drawn at random out of 1000 coins: half with heads up and head with heads down. In this case, the expected outcome of the coin is not generated by attending to the forces acting on the coins, but by taking into account the structure of the population being sampled.

Discussing whether the Fisherian synthesis of Mendelism, Biometry and Evolution is successful in resolving the difference between a causal and a statistical explanation is beyond the scope of this paper. Indeed, the issue of whether statistical and causal laws are fundamentally different is philosophical in nature (Glymour, 1997). Nonetheless, this example illustrates how biology, philosophy, and statistics are tightly inter–related. Henceforth, statisticians and social scientists are encouraged to be well–informed about the biological and philosophical background of statistical models, while it is also advisable for biologists to be aware of the philosophical aspects of statistical thinking.

Chapter 2 Misconceived links between positivism and quantitative research

Misconceptions of quantitative research

Feldman (1998) observed that while positivism has been universally rejected by philosophers of science over the past fifty years, current textbooks still either associate quantitative methods with positivist ones or cover quantitative methods within a positivist frame of reference. Despite the fact that newer epistemologies and methodologies, such as post–positivism, critical realism, and critical multiplism, have been discussed in numerous books and articles (Cook, 1985, 1991, 1993; Cook & Campbell, 1979; Cook & Shadish, 1994; Phillips, 1987, 1990a, 1990b, 1992, 2000; Phillips & Burbules, 2000), the debate regarding the paradigm of quantitative methods seems to be trapped in a time warp.

The objectives of this chapter are threefold. First, I argue that the dichotomy between the two approaches is misguided due to the popular notion of "paradigm" introduced by Kuhn, which tends to polarize methodological differences and thus leads to epistemological incommensurability. Instead, the problem would be reframed under the notion of "research tradition" advocated by Laudan. Second, historical and theoretical evidence is cited in attempt to break the philosophical ties between quantitative methodology and logical positivism. Logical positivism, which rejects theoretical constructs and causality and emphasizes reductionism, is too restrictive to apply to quantitative methodology, which supports the use of latent constructs, causal inferences, and the iterative process of understanding the data and developing constructs. Last, I argue that when quantitative research departs from logical positivism and methodological differences/similarities are re–conceptualized in research tradition, it widens the door to triangulation with the goals of convergence and completeness.

The misconceived relationships between positivism and quantitative research can still be found in recent textbooks. For example, Berg (2001) explicitly identified quantitative research as a positivistic approach: "Positivists utilize empirical methodologies borrowed from the natural sciences to investigate phenomena. Quantitative strategies serve this positive–science ideal by providing rigorous, reliable, and verifiably large aggregates of data and the statistical testing of empirical hypotheses" (p. 10). Merriam (1998) also related certain "positivist" characteristics to quantitative methods:

> In positivist form of research . . . knowledge gained through scientific and experimental research is objective and quantifiable. . . . on the topic dropping out

> of high school . . . from a positivist perspective you might begin by hypothesizing that students drop out of high school because of low self–esteem. You could then design an intervention program to raise the self–esteem of students at risk. You set up an experiment controlling for as many variables as possible, and then measure the results (p. 4).

Further, in many texts comparing qualitative and quantitative research, the attributes of the latter are often misidentified. The following are some examples: particularistic (quantitative) vs. holistic (qualitative) emphasis, outcome–oriented (quantitative) vs. process–oriented (qualitative), fixed (quantitative) vs. emergent (qualitative) categories, static (quantitative) vs. fluid (qualitative) reality (Huysamen, 1997), mechanical (quantitative) vs. creative (qualitative), formulaic (quantitative) vs. interpretive (qualitative) (Howe, 1988), expansionist (qualitative) vs. reductionist (quantitative), and grounded (qualitative) vs. ungrounded (quantitative) (Reichardt & Cook, 1979).

These comparisons are grounded in the misunderstood relationship between quantitative research and the positivist/logical positivist paradigms. For example, qualitative researchers use the grounded theory (Glaser & Strauss, 1967) to develop "categories" that could fit the data until the categories are saturated. The process is said to be an iterative abstraction grounded on the data. In a similar vein, quantitative researchers employ Exploratory Factor Analysis to develop latent constructs until all dimensions emerge and all observed variables can be properly loaded into the abstracted dimensions. It is difficult to see why the former is said to be grounded while the latter is ungrounded. Probably, this misunderstanding is due to the association between the one–way reductionism endorsed by certain logical positivists and quantitative methods. In addition, quantitative research includes time–series analysis, repeated measures, and other trend–based inquires, and thus it is inaccurate to describe quantitative research as merely orienting towards outcomes and lacking the process orientation. Further, the perception that quantitative research assumes static reality is attributable to the myth that logical positivists are realists. The notion that quantitative researchers are confined by fixed categories results from the omission of the fact that quantitative researchers utilize open concepts and customized instruments in different contexts. In a later section this article will fully discuss the core ideas of logical positivism and point out that the preceding perceived connection is mistaken.

Research tradition vs. Paradigm

One of the sources of the misunderstanding can be traced back to the over-simplification of quantitative research. Usually quantitative research is viewed as Fisherian hypothesis testing, and various statistical procedures are regarded as a unitary approach that can be summarized in a single paradigm. However, at the ontological, epistemological, and methodological levels, the Fisherian School, the Neyman/Pearson School, the Bayesian school, the Resampling

School, and the Exploratory Data Analysis (EDA) school are fundamentally different, and to some extent are incompatible (Lehmann, 1993; Berger, 2001; Behrens, 1997; Behrens & Yu, 2003). Further, in the arena of measurement, the classical test theory and the Item Response Theory are also very different in their premises and assumptions (Embretson & Reise, 2000). According to Kuhn (1962), following a paradigm, all members of a specific scientific community accept a set of commonly agreed exemplars. However, it is doubtful whether the Kuhnian paradigm theory could be applied to such a rich collection of epistemologies and methodologies in quantitative research. Laudan (1977) argued that the paradigm theory does not fit with the history of science. Indeed, it is not uncommon for a number of competing theories based upon incompatible exemplars to coexist. Thus, Laudan proposed the concept of "research tradition" in an attempt to replace "paradigm."

Laudan is not alone. In reaction to the viewing of quantitative research as a positivist approach, Clark (1998) embraced the view that quantitative research is shaped by more than one philosophy. In a similar vein, Cook (1985) doubted that all social and natural scientists have subscribed to all positivist assumptions, that positivism adequately describes scientific practice as it occurs, and that this practice has evolved only from the positivist framework. Rather, Cook asserted that "scientific practice has multiple origins that include trial–and–error behavior of practitioners, selective adaptations from prior philosophies and research" (p. 23). Thus, it would be an oversimplification to treat quantitative methods as a single paradigm. A more appropriate treatment of this issue is to classify different schools of quantitative methods into different research traditions.

Further, in the Kuhnian framework, paradigms are competing worldviews that would inevitably lead to *incommensurability*. Paradigms are said to be so different that in most cases researchers belonging to different camps could not find even a common language in which to conduct a meaningful comparison. Following the Kuhnian view, it is not surprising to see the polarities of "particularistic vs. holistic," and "fixed vs. emergent," as cited in the previous section. Very often researchers express frustrations that some concepts such as reliability and validity, which are taken for granted in the quantitative paradigm, do not have equivalent terms in the qualitative counterpart, and thus mixed methods seem to be in vain. No wonder Phillips (1988) even went so far as to assert that if researchers looked back to the origins of the quantitative and qualitative paradigms, they would never adopt mixed methods.

On the contrary, Laudan emphasized continuity, commensurability, and rationality among research traditions under the common thread of problem–solving. By reviewing the history of science, Laudan gave a detailed and in–depth analysis of how theories are weighted and decisions could be made on the ground of problem–solving effectiveness. Indeed, common threads could be observed in both qualitative and quantitative research traditions. For instance, while introducing qualitative methods, Miles and Huberman (1984) used a metaphor of detective work for illustration. A researcher's role, in their view, is like a detective's: "When the detective amasses fingerprints, hair samples, alibis, eyewitness accounts and the like, a case is being made that presumably fits one suspect far better than others" (p. 234). Interestingly enough, John Tukey (1977, 1980), the quantitative researcher who invented Exploratory Data Analysis (EDA), also related EDA to detective work. In Tukey's view, the role of the EDA researcher is to explore the data in as many ways as possible until a plausible "story" of the data emerges. This common theme shared by both qualitative and quantitative researchers fits Laudan's description of inquiry as problem solving.

When we look for differences among various research traditions, we could easily locate and polarize these differences. Nevertheless, we could also seek continuity and common ground, and conduct integration among different traditions. Take various schools of thought in quantitative methods as examples again. Despite the fact that Fisher, Pearson, and Neyman held different views of probability, their notions of null hypothesis, Alpha level, statistical power, Type I error, and Type two error were synthesized into hypothesis testing. In recent years researchers such as Berger (2000, 2001) and Pawitan (2000, 2001) have been independently devoting effort to fusing Bayesianism and Frequentism.

Laudan's notion of research traditions nonetheless reflects a more realistic picture of the history of scientific inquiry and the current status of quantitative methods. In the following discussion quantitative methodology is portrayed as a collection of different approaches; nevertheless, readers should keep in mind that certain degree of commonalities within various statistical schools still exist. By the same token, although the incompatibility between logical positivism and quantitative methods is highlighted, they still maintain certain overlapped areas, which will be discussed in the section entitled "Links between positivism and quantitative methods."

Major themes of logical positivism

To examine the relationship between quantitative methods and logical positivism, one must define logical positivism. It is important to note that there are differences between classical positivism, introduced by French philosopher August Comte, and logical positivism, which originated in the Vienna Circle, which is composed of a group of European scholars centered around Vienna during the 1920s and 30s, such as M. Schlick, R. Carnap, H. Feigl, P. Frank, K. Gödel, H. Hahn, V. Kraft, O. Neurath, and F. Waismann. In the classical sense, positivism refers to a philosophy that scientific inquiry should be empirical, which led to antirealism and instrumentalism. In the Vienna Circle, besides the emphasis on empirical knowledge, the theme of logical positivism is also centered on the verifiability principle of meaning and logical analysis (Phillips, 2000). In addition, classical positivism was founded by Comte with the goal of systematization of sociology, but logical positivism covers a wide variety of philosophical topics such as philosophy of language, symbolic logic, philosophy of science, and philosophy of mathematics. Further, classical positivism is basically a single movement whereas logical positivism is the result of interactions among several movements, such as analytical philosophy, logical atomism, logical empiricism, and semantics. Table 2.1 highlights the differences between these two schools of thought. Please keep in mind that these are some examples and the list is by no means exhaustive.

Table 2.1. Differences between classical positivism and logical positivism

	Classical positivism	Logical positivism
Emphasized source(s) of knowledge	Empirical	Empirical and logical
Focus areas	Sociology	Philosophy of language Symbolic logic Philosophy of science Philosophy of mathematics
Development	Single movement	Analytical philosophy Logical atomism Logical empiricism Semantics

Werkmeister (1937a, 1937b) identified seven major theses of logical positivism based upon articles and books written by members of the Vienna Circle:

(a) Knowledge is knowledge only because of its form. Content is non–essential.
(b) A proposition is meaningful if only if it can be verified.
(c) There is only empirical knowledge.
(d) Metaphysics are meaningless.
(e) All fields of inquiry are parts of a unitary science: physics.
(f) The propositions of logic are tautologies.
(g) Mathematics can be reduced to logic.

Although Werkmeister's outline captures the essence of logical positivism promoted by the Vienna circle, later logical positivism expanded beyond this community, and some of the Vienna circle's notions are not held by many logical positivists. Moreover, (a), (e), and (f) are not directly related to quantitative methods. Thus, in this article, the definition of logical positivism is adopted from a more recent framework developed by Hacking (1983), which represents the common threads of most logical positivists. This framework will be explained in the following paragraph.

Some logical positivist notions outlined by Hacking are very similar to those of Werkmeister. According to Hacking, there are six major themes of positivism:

(a) an emphasis on verification,
(b) pro–observation,
(c) anti–cause,
(d) downplaying explanation,
(e) anti–theoretical entities, and
(f) anti–metaphysics.

Logical positivism accepts all of the above notions and adds an emphasis on logical analysis. Today, when many authors discuss the relationship between positivism and research methodology, the context is situated in logical positivism rather than classical positivism. For example, Bogdan and Tayler (1975) explicitly contrasted qualitative and quantitative methodologies in the frameworks of phenomenological and logical positivist philosophies. Therefore, in this article the relationship between quantitative methods and logical positivism will be examined. Based upon the preceding notions, logical positivists developed a specific version of frequentist probability theory. Each of these issues will now be discussed individually.

Verification

To logical positivists, the verification criterion is not just a demand for evidence. Verification does not mean that, with other things being equal, a proposition that can be verified is of vastly greater significance than one that cannot. Rather, the verification thesis is much stronger and more restrictive than the above. According to logical positivism, a statement is meaningless if verification is not possible or the criteria for verification are not clear. This notion can be applied in such a radical manner that moral, aesthetic, and religious statements are considered non–verifiable and thus meaningless (Ayer, 1936; Schlick, 1959). In this sense, statements such as "peace is good," "the painting is beautiful," and "God loves the world" are all meaningless. The verification principle can go even further to make statistics meaningless! If the verification criterion is based on empirical evidence, mathematics, including statistics, which cannot be confirmed or disconfirmed by experience, is said to be nonsense by analytic philosopher Ayer (1946). For example, there is no empirical proof to support the claims that "An Eigenvalue is the sum square of factor loadings" and "a logit is the natural log of the odd ratio." To be specific, the verification principle is not an account of the relative importance of propositions, but a definition of meaning. Meaning and verifiability are almost interchangeable (Werkmeister, 1937a).

However, in the tradition of quantitative research, there is no evidence that any major quantitative researchers subscribe to this radical epistemology. For example, Cronbach, the famous statistician who introduced "Cronbach coefficient Alpha" and "construct validity," did not restrict his inquiry to only verifiable materials in the logical positivist sense. When Cronbach contemplated the problem of causal inferences in research, he did not employ LISREL or other quantitative causal modeling techniques. Instead, he looked to the more qualitative methods of the ethnographer, historian, and journalist. He maintained that these methods are more practical and flexible than those of quantitative causal modeling (Cook, 1991).

Further, statistical methods do not provide verification in the logical positivistic sense. The logic of statistical hypothesis testing is not to verify whether the hypothesis is right; rather, the logic is to find the probability of obtaining the sampled data in the long run given that the null hypothesis is true. However, if we put any theory in the perspective of the "long run," nothing can be conclusively verified. We are not able to verify whether a particular penny is a fair coin even if we observe the outcomes of trials in which the coin is tossed. No matter how many times the coin is tossed, the number of trials cannot be equated with the "long run." To rectify the problem, Watkins (1985) framed statistical hypotheses in the Popperian falsificationist spirit (Popper, 1959, 1974). In Popper's view, conclusive verification of hypotheses is not possible, but conclusive falsification is possible within a finite sample. In addition, Popper is explicitly opposed to verificationism (Sanders, 1993). If a theory is claimed to be verified by an observed consequence, the researcher may commit the fallacy of affirming the consequent. A good example of this fallacy is that "if it rains, the floor is wet. If the floor is wet, it rains." By the same token, it is fallacious to claim that "if the treatment is effective, the scores will increase. If the scores increase, the treatment is verified as effective." Although the Popperian notion is controversial and probably carries certain flaws (Howson & Urbach, 1993), it has been considered by some quantitative researchers to be a replacement of the verification logic.

Pro–observation

While verificationism defines the meaning of knowledge, empirical observation is a specific methodology for verification. Schlick (1959) stated that reality refers to experience. However, Schlick (1925/1974) did not maintain that there is a direct path from sense experience to genuine knowledge because immediate contact with the given is both fleeting and subjective. Sense experience comes from particular observations or awareness with reference to a here and now, but empirical laws go beyond such experience. To logical positivists, pro–observation is concerned with empirical laws instead of raw experience (Friedman, 1991; Werkmeister, 1937b).

The debatable issue is Schlick's notion that reality is referred to experience. This notion has been inflated to be a notion that empirical observation implies one objective reality. To be specific, quantitative research is viewed by qualitative researchers as empirical research based on the ontology of an objective reality (Glesne & Peshkin, 1992).

First, pro–observation does not necessarily lead to the position of realism (Phillips & Burbules, 2000). As a matter of fact, logical positivism is viewed as a type of conventionalism, relativism, and subjectivism (Laudan, 1996). Contrary to popular belief, some logical positivists are anti–realists. Even those logical positivists who accept a realist position do not regard the aim of science as finding the objective truth corresponding to the objective reality. Instead, they view inquiry as a convention for conveniences. The most well known brand of conventionalism is Carnap's linguistic conventionalism (Carnap, 1937). From Carnap's standpoint, scientific inquiry allows more than one answer to the question of the meaningfulness of particular sentences. Knowledge claims can only be raised or answered with respect to a particular linguistic convention. Laudan (1996) warned that this relativistic attitude would hinder researchers from bringing academic disputes to a rational closure.

Phillips (1987, 2000) and also Phillips and Burbules (2000) argued that it is fantasy to view positivists as realists and the empirical method as the road to objective truth. To logical positivists, even if there is an ultimate reality, we do not have direct contact with this reality; the only thing that matters is what we are in contact with (observation/experience). Therefore, Phillips and Burbules classified logical positivists as phenomenalists and sensationalists, rather than realists. Phillips (2000) asserted that the beliefs of antirealism, relativism, and subjectivism occurring in some social science research "place them [the researchers] closer to the spirit of logical positivism than they suppose in even their wildest dream" (p. 166).

Second, quantitative research methodology is not necessarily objective, let alone based on one objective reality or aimed at seeking one objective truth. The mainstream Bayesian approach is based upon subjective probability, which represents a degree of belief. Usually a Bayesian starts with an assessment of initial probability that involves some background knowledge. This prior subjective probability would be later corrected by the posterior probability based upon the observed data. According to the frequency and logical theories of probability, probability is objective in nature, and thus when there are two or more estimated probabilities, only one of them could be correct. This notion seems to support the assertion that quantitative researchers seek one objective reality. However, according to the Bayesian theory of probability, the only true probabilities are either one or zero. In a single event, the expected outcome either happened or did not happen. Prior to the event, probability is a degree of belief, and thus it is subjective. Although the iteration process may eventually lead subjective probabilities to some degree of convergence, Bayesians do not claim that they could give sound reasons to substantiate a truth–like conclusion. Rather, they just claim that there are reasons to modify one's belief in the light of new evidence.

Anti–cause

Many educational and psychological researchers incorrectly attribute causal inferences to logical positivism. For example, Erlandson et al. (1993) asserted that "the very structure of our language (and thus our conceptual structure?) heavily depends on the traditional term of positivism. . . . It is particularly hard to expunge from our memories such terms as causality" (p. xii). By the same token, Nation (1997) states that "one precept of logical positivism is that evidence favoring the objective existence of cause and effect can be provided" (p. 68). Surprisingly, even some quantitative researchers improperly make a connection between causality and positivism. For example, Gliner and Morgan (2000) said that in the positivist's view, "every action can be explained as the result of a real cause that precedes the effect temporally" (p. 21).

Actually, the opposite is true. Influenced by Hume's notion that causation is just a perceived regular association and Russell's anti–cause position, quite a few logical positivists do not pursue causal inferences in inquiry. Russell (1913), as a logical atomist, explained relationships in terms of functions. For example, Y=a+bX can be rewritten as X=(Y-a)/b. Thus, X could not be viewed as a cause of Y because the positions of X and Y could be swapped around the equation. By embracing this equation–oriented notion, Russell argued against causation:

> All philosophers imagine that causation is one of the fundamental axioms of science, yet oddly enough, in advanced sciences, the word 'cause' never occurs. . . . The law of causality, I believe, is a relic of bygone age, surviving, like the monarchy, only because it is erroneously supposed to do no harm (as cited in Pearl, 2000, p. 337).

Pearl, the renowned computer scientist who applies causal interpretation into structural equating modeling, objects to Russell's anti–cause attitude: "Fortunately, very few physicists paid attention to Russell's enigma. They continued to write equations in the office and talk cause–effect in the cafeteria; with astonishing success they smashed the atom, invented the transistor and the laser" (p. 338).

In logical positivism, the anti–cause position, the pro–observation thesis, and the anti–theoretical entities notion, which will be discussed in a later section, are inter–related. The meaning of causation has been approached by different schools of thought. One of these approaches believes that causation involves a producing or forcing phenomenon (If X is a cause of Y, a change of X produces or forces a change in Y) (Blalock, 1964). However, this view is incompatible with logical positivism's perspective that "cause," as an invisible force or a theoretical entity, cannot be observed or measured. In brief, according to verificationism, statements that can't be verified had no content. Causal statements are non– verifiable statements (Schuldenfrei, 1972).

Obviously, the anti–cause notion is contradicted by quantitative research in the context of randomization experiments, latent construct theory, Structural Equation Modeling (SEM), and meta–analysis (see Chapter 6 and 7) . In evaluating the counterfactual logic, Glymour (1986) said, "One of the principal goals of statistics has always been the determination of causal relations from both experimental and nonexperimental data" (p. 966). The cause and effect relationship is still undetermined even if X occurs when Y occurs. An experienced researcher would question whether X still occurs in spite of Y or regardless of Y. This doubt would lead to a counterfactual question: What would have happened to X if Y were not present? Some researchers apply randomized or controlled experiments in attempt to answer this counterfactual question. By introducing a control group (~X), a causal inference can be asserted based upon counterfactual logic: If X is true, then Y is true. If X is not true, Y is not true. Thus, Y is said to be causally responsible for X. In addition to drawing causal inferences from randomized experiments, Cook (1991) went even further to interpret results of quasi–experiments in a causal fashion. Interestingly enough, some concepts about experimental design are explicitly related to causation. For example, "internal validity" is also known as "local molar causal validity," and "external validity" is concerned with causal generalization (Cook, 1991, 1993).

In the latent construct theory (see Chapter 5), also known as the measurement model, the relationship between the latent factor and the observed item is considered a cause and effect relationship (Borsboom, Mellenbergh, & van Heerden, 2003). Although operationalists view the latent construct as nothing more than a numeric trick to simplify the observations (condensing many observed items into one factor), Borsboom et al. assert that operationalism and the latent construct theory are fundamentally incompatible. If a latent construct is just for operational convenience, then there should be a distinct latent factor for every single test researchers construct. However, since it is assumed that observed items that are loaded into a factor constitute a single dimension, theoretical constructs are implied to be causally responsible for observed phenomena.

Factor analysis is one of the most popular applications of the latent factor theory. Abbott (1998) argued that early psychometricians viewed factor analysis as a mathematical convenience to reduce complex data to simple forms in order to reconcile quantitative data with intuitive categories, and thus it ignored causality altogether. This view seems to be concurred by Laudan (1977). Laudan classified psychometrics in the early 20th century as a "non–standard research tradition" because it does not have a strong ontology or metaphysics. Instead, its assumption is "little more than the conviction that mental phenomena could be mathematically represented" (p. 105). However, Laudan also asserted that, unlike what Thomas Kuhn described in the paradigm theory, a research tradition is hardly uniform. Rather, competing and incompatible views could coexist within the same research tradition at the same time, and the ontology and metaphysics could change drastically within the tradition over time. Indeed, it is arguable whether early psychometricians were a–causal. While discussing the origin and development of factor analysis, Vincent (1953) asserted that factor analysis is an attempt to identify the causes that are operating to produce the variance and to evaluate the contribution of each cause. In his view, the argument among early psychometricians was concerned with whether one common cause or multiple causes were appropriate. Further, modern scholars view factor analysis as an application of the principle of common cause (e.g., Glymour, 1982; Glymour, Scheines, Spirtes, & Kelly, 1987). Factor analysis has been incorporated into the Structural Equation Model, which blatantly allows for causal inferences.

Structural Equation Modeling, which entails factor models and structural models, definitely specifies cause and effect relationships (Hoyle, 1995). In SEM, a factor model depicts relationships between indicators and underlying factors (Kline, 1998). Experimental design aims at strengthening causal inferences, which are weak or missing in quasi–experiments and non–experiments (Christensen, 1988; Cook & Campbell, 1979; Luker et al., 1998). Usually SEM requires a very large sample size. It is difficult, but not impossible, to recruit thousands of subjects for laboratory experimental studies. Not surprisingly, most data in SEM are observational or quasi–experimental rather than experimental. Nonetheless, Glymour, Scheines, Spirtes, and Kelly (1987) argued that causal inferences could be drawn from SEM based on non–experimental data. Because after the heuristic algorithm computes thousands of possible ways to fit the data with the model a unique solution is found, a causal inference is plausible.

Further, Cook (1993) regarded meta–analysis as a tool for seeking causal generalizations. According to Cronbach (1982), the two major themes of causal generalization in experimental research involve using sample data to make generalizations to the target population and across different populations. Cook claimed that meta–analysis probes both of Cronbach's types of causal generalizations because it synthesizes effect sizes across different studies using different samples and populations. Nonetheless, it is important to note that not all quantitative researchers who employ meta–analysis interpret the results in terms of causation.

Hoyle (1995) asserted that at least three criteria need to be fulfilled to validate a causal inference:

1. *Directionality*: The independent variable affects the dependent variable.
2. *Isolation*: Extraneous noise and measurement errors must be isolated from the study so that the observed relationship cannot be explained by something other than the proposed theory.
3. *Association*: The independent variable and the dependent variable are mathematically correlated.

To establish the direction of variables, the researcher can apply logic (e.g., physical height cannot cause test performance), theory (e.g. collaboration affects group performance), and most powerfully, research design (e.g., other competing explanations are ruled out from the experiment). To meet the criterion of isolation, careful measurement should be implemented to establish validity and reliability and to reduce measurement errors. In addition, extraneous variance, also known as threats against experimental validity, must be controlled for in the design of the experiment. Lastly, statistical methods are used to calculate the mathematical association among variables. However, in spite of a strong mathematical association, the causal inference may not make sense at all if directionality and isolation are not established. In short, all three components of quantitative research, i.e., experimental design, measurement, and statistical analysis, work together to establish the validity of cause and effect inferences. In brief, the anti–cause notion of logical positivism is incompatible with many branches of quantitative methods such as randomized experiments, quasi–experiments, latent construct theory, Structural Equation Modeling, and, arguably, meta–analysis.

Downplaying explanation

It is not surprising that explanation, along with causality, is misidentified as a link between logical positivism and quantitative research. For instance, Langenbach et al. (1994) asserted that quantitative research, which is based on a positivist philosophy, seeks to explain the cause of changes in social facts. On the contrary, positivists such as Schlick maintain that inquiry of knowledge describes what happens, but does not explain or prescribe it. While the spirit of quantitative research is to seek explanation, it demonstrates complex relationships among variables/constructs, rather than merely describing what happens. According to Bredo and Feinberg (1982), researchers who hold a realist position do not accept the positivist account of explanation as adequate. To the realist, an adequate explanation is one that can explain the phenomenon in terms of causal necessity, not just lawful regularity.

The covering law model, introduced by Hempel (1965), illustrates how positivists seek explanation in terms of regularity. In Hempel's view, to explain an event (S), a law (L) is applied and some particular facts (F) are observed to link S and L. This deductive approach is descriptive in nature and thus does not generate any new knowledge. For example,

L: Human behaviors are rational.
F: One of several options is more efficient in achieving the goal.
S: A rational human takes the option, which directs him to achieve his goal. (Anderson, 1990)

In this case, "rationality" is the term to describe the phenomenon that humans choose more efficient options. Interestingly enough, the descriptive approach of positivism is more compatible with phenomenological–oriented qualitative research than quantitative research. Quantitative researchers have a different view of explanation. In quantitative research, explanation implies a theoretical formulation about the nature of the relationship among the variables (Pedhazur, 1982). Within some theoretical frameworks it may be meaningful to compute semipartial correlations, whereas in others such statistics are not meaningful. In other words, the explanation in quantitative research is not entirely descriptive.

Explanation is tied to statistical modeling in SEM. According to Kelley (1998), very often there is a gap between the explanandum (that which is to be explained) and the explanation (hypothesis); a good explanation is capable of bridging the gap. Kelley pointed out that a gap exists in such a simple explanation as "a person is sad (explanandum) because her cat is dead (explanation)."

Between the preceding explanandum and the explanation, one must prove that the person is emotionally attached to the cat. In research this gap is even wider, and that is why statistical modeling is necessary. For example, let's evaluate this statement: Children from Protestant families have better performance in school because of Protestant work ethics. To validate this explanation, many other statements/variables are needed to fill the gap:

X1: Protestant work ethics motivate people to work hard.
X2: Working hard accumulates more money.
X3: Parents who have more money will buy resources such as books and computers for their child's education.
X4: Children who grow up in a Protestant family study harder.
X5: Hard–working children who are exposed to rich educational resources learn better.
Y: Children from Protestant families have better performance in school.

Assuming that we can re–express all of the above statements into measurable variables, a statistical model can be drawn as shown in Figure 2.1.

Figure 2.1. Relationships between the explanandum and explanation

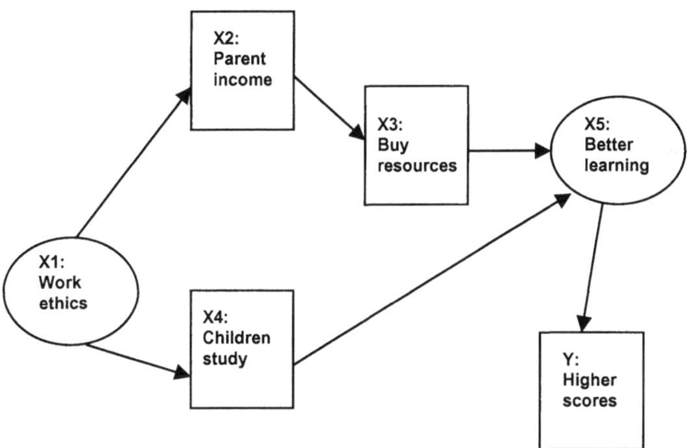

In brief, statistical modeling plays the role of filling the gap between the explanandum and the explanation. Quantitative research definitely seeks explanation and thus does not subscribe to the positivist notion of downplaying explanation.

Anti–theoretical entities

As mentioned before, logical positivists restrict reality to the observable, reject causal inferences, and downplay explanation. Therefore, logical positivists are skeptical of unobservable and theoretical entities such as latent variables, or factors. Some qualitative researchers drew an association between quantitative research and logical positivism, which is synonymous with the scientific paradigm. Indeed, logical positivism is not the modern scientific paradigm because modern scientists have turned away from the logical positivist position of anti–theoretical entities. For example, in a discussion of the existence of a nucleus inside an electron, Schlick (1959) explicitly rejected unobservable theoretical entities. Obviously, this approach hinders scientists from exploring the subatomic world. No wonder Weinberg (1992) argued that the development of 20th century physics was delayed by physicists who took positivism seriously and thus could not believe in atoms, let alone electrons or smaller particles. Meehl (1986) also pointed out that "it [logical positivism] is not an accurate picture of the structure of advanced sciences, such as physics; and it is grossly inadequate as a reconstruction of empirical history of science" (p. 315).

As a matter of fact, many quantitative researchers in the social sciences assert abstract theoretical constructs. Campbell (1995) maintained that factor analysis and multi–dimensional scaling must be theory–driven. In psychometrics, latent constructs such as self–esteem and intrinsic motivation are always hypothesized. Although Cronbach (1989) and Cronbach and Meehl (1955), who developed the concept of construct validity, had accepted the definitional operationalism, construct validity could be viewed as a product of a feedback loop between hypothetical, theoretical constructs and observable data. If the notion of anti–theoretical entities was imposed on quantitative research, a large portion of quantitative research regarding latent constructs would be impossible.

Anti–metaphysics

Logical positivists deny the existence of metaphysical and transcendental reality (Ayer, 1934; Carnap, 1959). Although both metaphysics and theoretical entities are unobservable, there is a difference between them. In the viewpoint of logical positivism, theoretical entities such as electronics belong to the physical world. As Schlick (1959) said, the world of science is the same as the world of our everyday life where memories, desires, ideas, stars, clouds, plants and animals exist. In philosophy, the metaphysical world is "the other world" beyond this physical realm. Logical positivism denies this metaphysical world.

On the other hand, many quantitative researchers do not necessarily reject the metaphysical existence. Mathematicians have developed a world of distributions and theorems. Essentially, statistical testing is a comparison between the observed statistic and theoretical distributions. Although statistical methods are considered empirical, Fisher (1956) asserted that theoretical sampling distributions could not be empirically reproduced. Actually, sampling distributions involve not only theoretical entities, but also mathematical reality, which has been a debatable topic in philosophy (Devitt, 1991; Drozdek & Keagy, 1994; Gonzalez, 1991; Penrose, 1989; Russell, 1919; Tieszen, 1992, 1995; Whitehead & Russell, 1950). On one hand, many mathematicians, statisticians, and quantitative researchers subscribe to the view that theoretical distributions are non–empirical but not metaphysical, and that they involve mathematical and logical truths. On the other hand, many view theoretical distributions and the broader mathematical realm as metaphysical (see Chapter 4).

Logical analysis and reductionism

Logical positivism adds an emphasis on logical analysis of language into positivism. According to Russell's logical atomism (1959), complex phenomena could be expressed in terms of mathematics, and mathematics could be further reduced to logic. This idea was embraced by logical positivists such as Carnap (Coffa, 1991). Inspired by mathematical/logical reductionism, logical positivists went further to develop methods based upon analytic reductionism. In analytic reductionism, an observed relationship is broken down into the components that are necessary and sufficient for a relationship to occur (Cook, 1985). At first glance, this notion describes the practice of quantitative research, and thus certain researchers explicitly charged that quantitative research is mechanistic and reductionistic (e.g. Dootson, 1995). In quantitative research, the complexity of events is expressed in terms of manageable variables, numbers, and mathematical equations; statistical analysis is viewed as a process of data reduction. However, the link between reductionism and quantitative methods is questionable when one examines the issue carefully.

Although the previous section mentioned that quantitative researchers embrace theoretical constructs, quantitative research is by no means a one–way reduction from events to numeric data to mathematical models. Instead, events, data, and theory form a positive feedback loop. For example, when Cronbach and Meehl (1955) proposed the concept of construct validity, they maintained that hypothetical constructs drive the nature of data collection. In turn, the data resulting from the administration of the instrument are then used to revise the theory itself.

Unlike the positive loop in quantitative research, Russell's mathematical model is a formal analysis of a closed system. Russell is not concerned with what the reality is and whether geometric objects exist. The mission of mathematicians is to discover the logical relationships among objects. An axiom is considered valid just because Y logically entails X.

This line of thinking can be found among some quantitative researchers. For example, there is an old saying that "a statistical model is neither right nor wrong." This approach treats a mathematical model as a closed logical system; therefore empirical data does not constitute evidence to prove or disprove a model. Nonetheless, the belief that "all models are false" has become more popular (Bernardo & Smith, 1994; MacCallum, 1995). In this view, no data can fit any model perfectly, and thus all models are wrong to some degree. This saying indicated that quantitative research is an interaction between data and theory, rather than a one–way reduction from events to a logical–mathematical system.

Frequentist probability

Probability theory is considered a specific application of logical positivism to quantitative methods. Fisherian hypothesis testing is based upon relative frequency in the long run. Since a version of the frequentist view of probability was developed by positivists Reichenbach (1938) and von Mises (1964), the two schools of thought seem to share a common thread. However, this is not necessarily true. Both Fisherian and positivist frequency theory were proposed in opposition to the classical Laplacean theory of probability. In the Laplacean perspective, probability is deductive and theoretical. To be specific, this probability is deduced from theoretical principles and assumptions in the absence of verification by empirical data. Assuming that every member of a set has equal probability to occur (the principle of indifference), probability is treated as a ratio between the desired event and all possible events. This probability, derived from the fairness assumption, is made before any events occur.

Reichenbach and von Mises maintained that a very large number of empirical outcomes should be observed to form a reference class. Probability is the ratio of the frequency of desired outcome to the reference class. Indeed, the empirical probability hardly concurs with the theoretical probability in the classical sense. For example, when a die is thrown, in theory the probability of the occurrence of number "one" should be 1/6. But even in a million simulations, the actual probability of the occurrence of "one" is not exactly one out of six times. It appears that von Mises's frequency theory is more valid than the classical one. However, the usefulness of this actual, finite, relative frequency theory is limited, for it is difficult to tell how large the reference class must be to be considered large enough.

Fisher (1930) argued that Laplace's theory is incompatible with the inductive nature of science. However, unlike the logical positivists' empirical–based theory, Fisher's is a hypothetical, infinite relative frequency theory. In the Fisherian school, various theoretical sampling distributions are constructed as references for comparing the observed. Fisher and Reichenbach developed their frequency theories independently. In the beginning of the 20th century, von Mises was not widely cited in statistics texts or debates of the Royal Statistical Society, in which Fisher was active (Howie, 2002). On the other hand, Salmon (1967), who is a student of Reichenbach, credited Reichenbach as the developer of the frequency theory without a single word about Fisher.

Although von Mises (1928/1957) mentioned Fisher's work in his book entitled *Probability, statistics, and truth,* his discussion about the Fisherian notion of likelihood is negative:

> I do not understand the many beautiful words used by Fisher and his followers in support of the likelihood theory. The main argument, namely, that p is not a variable but an "unknown constant," does not mean anything to me. It is interesting to note that some philosophers have already begun to expound "likelihood" as a new kind of probability which would not depend on relative frequencies (p. 158).

It is important to point out that probability, in Fisher's sense, is hypothesis–oriented, while in the positivist's view probability is empirically based. In Fisher's view, likelihood is not the same as probability. Likelihood is the probability of the observed outcome (O) given the hypothesis (H) is true P(O|H). In contrast, positivists view probability as the possibility that the hypothesis is true given the observed data P(H|O). It is obvious that the frequentist positions taken by Fisher and von Mises are quite different.

Further, backed by thorough historical research, Hacking (1990) asserted that "to identify frequency theories with the rise of positivism (and thereby badmouth frequencies, since "positivism" has become distasteful) is to forget why frequentism arose when it did, namely when there are a lot of known frequencies" (p. 452).

Links between positivism and quantitative methods

To be fair, in history there are several links between quantitative research and positivism, including the classical and the logical versions. For instance, Stevens, the originator of the representation theory of measurement, adopted the ideas of logical positivism and operationalism (Michell, 1997). Cronbach and Meehl (1955), who developed construct validity, also accepted operationalism within the positivist framework. One of the most obvious links between positivism and quantitative methods could be found in Karl Pearson. Pearson, the inventor of the correlation coefficient, was a follower of Comte's positivism (Peirce, 1954; also see Chapter 1). According to Pearl (2000), Pearson denied any need for an independent concept of causation beyond correlation. Nevertheless, although Pearson downplayed causal explanation, his view should not be equated with the logical positivists' anti–cause notion. Pearson admitted that correlation analysis might be misleading because of spurious correlation. In other words, behind the two highly correlated variables, there might be other variables acting as common causes. The ultimate objective of research was to find evidence of an "organic relationship," which was "causal or semi–causal" (Aldrich, 1995). Harold Jeffreys, who endorsed Bayesian methods in probabilistic inferences, was influenced by Pearson's epistemology. However, later Jeffreys became skeptical to Pearson's anti–cause view. Jeffreys believed that the data he collected in astronomy could be used to infer causes (Howie, 2002).

Further, the development of Cronbach's construct validity has been moving away from operationalism to multi–operationism (Cook, 1985). The modern concept of construct validity is in sharp contrast to the classical sense of operationalism. In classical operationalism, every term is narrowly defined by a specific set of operations, which become its sole empirical referent. In modern construct validity, a measure is taken to be one of an extensive set of indicators of the theoretical construct. In this spirit, multiple items are loaded into a latent factor using factor analysis. Because the sets of indicators are extensible and often probabilistically related to the theoretical construct as well as to each other, constructs are not "operationally" defined, but are more like "open concepts" (Salvucci, Walter, Conley, Fink, & Saba, 1997). More importantly, as mentioned before, in causal inferences Cronbach did not adopt the narrow view of positivist epistemology, in which only verifiable statements are considered meaningful. Constructs could be generated through qualitative methods (Cook, 1991).

Implications for triangulation

Beyond positivism

The above discussion is devoted to stressing the view of continuity in research traditions rather than the notion of incommensurability in paradigms, and also to unlinking logical positivism and current quantitative methodology. Both of these ideas have important implications for researchers. When quantitative research does not aim at using fixed categories and discovering one objective reality, it opens the door to a richer interpretation of research findings even though there is more than one answer. To be specific, statisticians would not be embarrassed by different probabilities yielded from Bayesian inferences and the frequentist approach; by the same token, measurement experts could allow psychometric attributes returned from classical item analysis, Rasch models, two–parameter models, and three–parameter models to coexist. Also, open concepts and modified instruments are encouraged in varying contexts.

At first glance, this seems to be a dangerous notion of relativism that could hinder research endeavors from reaching a conclusive closure. But it is not. Different methods are tied to different contexts such as the properties of the sample/population and the assumptions imposed on the research methods. Woodward (1998, 1999, 2000, 2001, 2003) and Hausman and Woodward (1999) asserted that statistical findings are not universal. Rather, they could be just invariant and robust within a limited range of circumstances. Moreover, the nature of probabilistic and statistical approaches could be interpreted in Bohr's conception of experimentation. One can answer questions of the form: "If the experiment is performed, what are the possible results and their probabilities?" One should not answer any question in this form: "What is really happening when . . . ?" (as cited in Jaynes, 1995, p. 1012). If seeking a single answer is not the goal of quantitative research, mixing various qualitative and quantitative methods for triangulation could be promising.

Post–positivism, critical realism, and critical multiplism

If logical positivism is not the underlying philosophy of quantitative methodology, then what philosophy can it fit into? As mentioned in the beginning, several philosophical foundations such as critical realism, critical multiplism, and post–positivism have currently been proposed. Post–positivism and critical realism are classified under the same umbrella by Letourneau and Allen (1999). However, this classification may be questionable. Post–positivism is a philosophy that views theories as socially constructed linguistic systems, which are ultimately underdetermined; and truths are also ultimately unknowable. Following the direction of post–positivism, research endeavors should be devoted to translation and comparison of various "languages" in the hope of reaching warranted assertions (Laudan, 1996). Out of frustration with this under–determination thesis, Laudan (1996) used the phrase "the sins of the fathers" (p. 3) to criticize that post–positivism inherits this problematic feature from logical positivism. Critical realism, on the other hand, accepts the existence of an objective reality, but asserts that claims about reality must go through critical examinations (Guba & Lincoln, 2000). Nonetheless, through critical examinations knowledge about this objective world is possible (Patomaki & Wight, 2000). Although critical realism is said to be epistemological relative, its ontology is by no means relative. In other words, in critical realism the first part (critical) is about epistemology and methodology while the second part (realism) is concerned with ontology. Obviously, tensions exist between post–positivism and critical realism. Post–positivism tends to pull researchers away from asserting an objective reality while critical realism tends to push researchers towards the assertion of a real world. Nevertheless, critical multiplism does not necessarily view the world as a linguistic description or a reality that is independent of our language.

Furthermore, like logical positivism, several post–positivists maintain that metaphysics is still outside the boundary of science (Bronowski, 1965/1972). On the contrary, critical realists perceive that the reality consists of unobservable elements beyond our empirical realm, but they are still reachable by scientific inquiry (Clark, 1998). In the section regarding major theses of logical positivism, it has been pointed out that some quantitative researchers do accept metaphysical notions such as infinite distributions and mathematical axioms. In this sense, post–positivism and quantitative methodology may not be fully compatible.

Certain critical realists assert that while experimentation is possible in natural sciences, it is impossible in social sciences because in the former manipulation is conducted in a closed system, but in the latter social activities occur only in an open system. Further, social sciences deal with meanings and concepts that can only be understood, but not measured (Warner, 2001). This notion may alienate critical realism from the majority of quantitative researchers. It is a well–known fact that many quantitative researchers do believe that experimentation could be implemented in social sciences and concepts could be measured by numeric means. Taking all of the above into consideration, it may be better not to put post–positivism and critical realism together as the supporting philosophies for quantitative methodology.

Various schools in quantitative research, such as Bayesianism, Fisherianism, Exploratory Data Analysis, Confirmatory Data Analysis, and so on, carry different philosophical assumptions, and could be treated as independent research traditions. Nevertheless, given the richness and diversity of various quantitative methodologies, it is the author's belief that critical multiplism could be a meta–research–tradition for unifying quantitative methodologies. More importantly, critical multiplism, a philosophy that encourages using multiple sources of data and research techniques, provides a logical path to triangulation.

Triangulation

There are two major goals of triangulation, namely, *convergence* and *completeness*. The notion of scientific convergence could be traced back to American philosopher Charles Sanders Peirce. According to Peirce (1934/1960), academic inquiry is a self–correcting and "limiting" process contributed by the research community. The notion of "limiting" may be counterintuitive. In this context "limiting" does not mean the limitations or drawbacks of research methodologies. Rather, it should be comprehended as a mathematical concept. For example, according to the Central Limit Theorem, the variance of sample statistics would be reduced as more samples are drawn. This notion, in Peirce's view, could be well–applied to research endeavors. In spite of short–run variances and discrepancies, long–run convergence might be resulted from the multitude and variety of different inquiries. This form of convergence acts as a "cable" for linking various arguments and evidence.

In recent years, mixed methods have been proposed by certain researchers (e.g. Johnson & Onwuegbuzie, 2004; Webb et al., 1981) in attempt to reach convergent validity or a more warranted assertion. While the mixed method approach aims to synthesize quantitative and qualitative research traditions, within the quantitative arena methodological pluralism is also encouraged by quantitative researchers, such as allowing diverse views to causal inferences in structural equating modeling (Markus, 2004). On the other hand, other researchers (e.g. Jick, 1983) countered that different results yielded from various methods should not be used to validate each other; rather, these differences should be retained so that a more complete picture of the phenomenon under investigation could be seen. For example, Fielding & Fielding (1996) asserted that "We should combine theories and methods carefully and purposefully with the intention of adding breadth and depth to our analysis, but not for the purpose of pursuing objective truth" (p. 33).

Actually, convergence and completeness might not be contradictory. It is important to point out that seeking convergence is not the same as looking for one single answer representing an objective truth. Clearly, this notion has been rejected in the previous discussion. Rather, convergence shows a *pattern* of different research results while retaining the residuals departing from the pattern. Take regression as an example. It is extremely rare to obtain a straight line going through all data points in a scattergram. Instead, data points scatter around the plot and each point carries a different degree of residuals. The regression line summarizes the pattern of the data; at the same time, the data points and the residuals depict the complexity and the fitness of the model. By the same token, different results obtained by different methods based upon different research traditions are like data points in a scatterplot, and the smoothed regression line is like the converged pattern in a mixed method study. Using the cable metaphor introduced by Peirce again, a regression line is a "cable" linking all points within a single data set within the same research approach, while triangulation is a "cable" tying together all results from different research traditions. Completeness and convergence, indeed, could go hand in hand.

Conclusion

In the early 20th century, logical positivism was popular in both natural and social sciences, and thus experimental methods were developed under the influence of logical positivism. However, cultures, including the academic culture, receive influences from multiple sources. For example, several impressionists drew ideas from photography and Japanese printing, yet an art history professor would not stretch to claim that impressionism is based upon Japanese art or photography. By the same token, the statement that quantitative research is based on logical positivism ignores the dynamic complexity of the academic culture, in which multiple research traditions could interact and compete with each other. Also, the academic culture is evolving. As mentioned in the beginning, many philosophers of science have rejected logical positivism. Relating an outdated philosophy to quantitative research may discourage social science researchers from using this research approach, and also lead to misguided dispute between quantitative and qualitative researchers (e.g., McLaughlin, 1991; Rennie, 1999). What is needed is to encourage researchers to keep an open mind to different methodologies by allowing research methods being driven by research questions (Leech & Onwuegbuzie, 2004; Onwuegbuzie & Leech, 2005), while retaining skepticism to examine their philosophical assumptions of various research methodologies instead of unquestioningly accepting popular myths.

As mentioned in the beginning, newer epistemologies and methodologies that allow for rival theories and methods to be integrated, such as critical multiplism and triangulation, have emerged. In the spirit of critical multiplism and triangulation, researchers should be encouraged to employ mixed methods, including qualitative and quantitative approaches. Within the quantitative school, different approaches, such as hypothesis testing, meta–analysis, EDA, Bayesian inference, Structural Equation Modeling, and many others, should be considered based upon the research question and the data structure.

Chapter 3 Logics of Abduction, Deduction, and Induction

Introduction

Fisher (1935, 1955) considered significance testing as "inductive inference" and argued that this approach is the source of all knowledge. On the other hand, Neyman (1928, 1933a, 1933b) maintained that only deductive inference was appropriate in statistics as shown in his school of hypothesis testing tradition. However, both deductive and inductive methods have been criticized for various limitations such as their tendency to explain away details that should be better understood and their incapability of generating new knowledge (Hempel, 1965; Josephson & Josephson, 1994; Thagard & Shelley, 1997). In the view of the logical system introduced by Charles Sanders Peirce (1839–1914) a century ago, one may say the logic of abduction and deduction contribute to our conceptual understanding of a phenomena (Hausman, 1993), while the logic of induction provides empirical support to conceptual knowledge. In other words, abduction, deduction, and induction work together to explore, refine and substantiate research questions.

Although abduction is central in the Peircean logical system, Peirce by no means downplayed the role of deduction and induction in inquiry. Peirce had studied the history of philosophy thoroughly and was influenced by a multitude of schools of logic (Hoffmann, 1997). Peirce explained these three logical processes (1934/1960) as, "Deduction proves something must be. Induction shows that something actually is operative; abduction merely suggests that something may be" (Vol. 5, p. 171). Put another way: Abduction plays the role of generating new ideas or hypotheses; deduction functions as evaluating the hypotheses; and induction is justifying the hypothesis with empirical data (Staat, 1993).

This chapter attempts to apply abduction to offer a more comprehensive logical system of research methodology. Therefore, I will evaluate the strengths and weaknesses of the preceding three logical processes under Peircean direction, and point to implications for the use of Exploratory Data Analysis (EDA) and quantitative research within this philosophical paradigm.

It is important to note that the focus of this article is to extend and apply Peircean ideas into research methodologies in an epistemological fashion, not to analyze the original meanings of Peircean ideas in the manner of historical study. Almder (1980) contended that Peirce wrote in a style that could lead to confusion. Not surprisingly, many scholars could not agree on whether Peircean philosophy is a coherent system or a collection of disconnected thoughts (Anderson, 1987). In response to Weiss (1940) who charged some philosophers with distorting and dismembering the Peircean philosophy, Buchler (1940) contended that cumulative growth of philosophy results from the partial or limited acceptance of a given philosopher's work through discriminating selection. One obvious example of extending the Pericean school is the "inference to the best explanation" (IBE) proposed by Harman (1965) based upon the Peircean idea of abduction. While the "classical" abduction is considered a logic of discovery, IBE is viewed as a logic of justification (Lipton, 1991; Minnameier, 2004). But in the context of debating realism and anti–realism, de Regt (1994) criticized that Peircean philosophy was mis–used to the extent that the "inference to the *best* explanation" had become the "inference to the *only* explanation." This article is concerned with neither history of philosophy nor discernment of various interpretations of the Peircean system; rather I adopted the position suggested by Buchler, and thus Peircean ideas on abduction, deduction, and induction are discussed through discriminating selection.

Abduction

Premise of abduction

Before discussing the logic of abduction and its application, it is important to point out its premises. In the first half of the 20th century, verificationism derived from positivism dominated the scientific community. For positivists unverifiable beliefs should be rejected. However, according to Peirce, researchers must start from somewhere, even though the starting point is an unproven or unverifiable assumption. This starting point of scientific consciousness is private fancy a flash of thought, or a wild hypothesis. But it is the seed of creativity (Wright, 1999). This approach is very different from positivism and opens more opportunities for inquirers (Callaway, 1999). In the essay *The Fixation of Belief*, (1877) Peirce said that we are satisfied with stable beliefs rather than doubts. Although knowledge is fallible in nature, and in our limited lifetime we cannot discover the ultimate truth, we will still fix our beliefs at certain points. At the same time, Peirce did not encourage us to relax our mind and not pursue further inquiry. Instead, he saw seeking knowledge as interplay between doubts and beliefs, though he did not explicitly use the Hegelian term "dialectic."

In addition, for Peirce the degree of believing could be conceptualized and quantified in terms of *the ratio of favorable to unfavorable cases* (Linacre, 2000). Today psychometricians use a similar approach to Peirce's in Rasch modeling. For example, if the pass rate of an item is one of out five candidates, the favorable outcome is passing the item (1 count) and the unfavorable outcome is failing the question (4 counts). In this case, we can compute the odd ratio as (favorable:unfavorable) = 1:4 = 0.25. But psychometricians go even further to transform the odd ratio into the logit, which is the natural logarithmic scale of the odd ratio (Logit = Log(Odd ratio)). Linacre was amazed by the fact that Peirce proposed the crude idea of the odd ratio over a century before its re–invention by Ben Wright et al. (Wright & Masters, 1982; Wright & Stone, 1979). Explaining the logistic Rasch model is beyond the scope of this chapter. Nevertheless, it is noteworthy that in the Peircean system of philosophy fixing a belief is something more than a mere feeling or intuition; rather it is backed up by rigorous reasoning.

The logic of abduction

Grounded in the fixation of beliefs, the function of abduction is to look for a pattern in a surprising phenomenon and to suggest a plausible hypothesis. The following example illustrates the function of abduction:

The surprising phenomenon, B, is observed.
But if A were true, B would be a matter of course.
Hence there is a reason to suspect that A might be true.

By the standard of deductive logic, the preceding reasoning is clearly unacceptable for it is incompatible with a basic rule of inference in deduction, namely, *Modus Poenes*. Following this rule, the legitimate form of reasoning takes the route as follows:

A is observed.
If A, then B.
Hence, B is accepted.

Modus Ponens is commonly applied in the context of conducting a series of deduction for complicated scientific problems. For example, A; (A → B); B; (B → C); C; (C → D); D . . . etc. However, Peirce started from the other end:

B is observed.
If A, then B.
Hence, A can be accepted.

Logicians following deductive reasoning call this *the fallacy of affirming the consequent*. Consider this example. It is logical to assert that "It rains; if it rains, the floor is wet; hence, the floor is wet." But any reasonable person can see the problem in making statements like: "The floor is wet; if it rains, the floor is wet; hence, it rained." Nevertheless, in Peirce's logical framework this abductive form of argument is entirely valid, especially when the research goal is to discover plausible explanations for further inquiry (de Regt, 1994). In order to make inferences to the best explanation, the researcher must need a set of plausible explanations, and thus, abduction is usually formulated in the following mode:

The surprising phenomenon, X, is observed.
Among hypotheses A, B, and C, A is capable of explaining X.
Hence, there is a reason to pursue A.

At first glance, abduction is an educated guess among existing hypotheses. Thagard and Shelley (1999) clarified this misconception. They explained that unifying conceptions were an important part of abduction, and it would be unfortunate if our understanding of abduction were limited to more mundane cases where hypotheses are simply assembled. Abduction does not occur in the context of a fixed language, since the formation of new hypotheses often goes hand in hand with the development of new theoretical terms such as "quark," and "gene." Indeed, Peirce (1934/1960) emphasized that abduction is the only logical operation that introduces new ideas.

Some philosophers of science such as Popper (1968) and Hempel (1966) suggested that there is no logic of discovery because discovery relies on creative imagination. Hempel used Kekule's discovery of the hexagonal ring as an example. The chemist Kekule failed to devise a structural formula for the benzene molecule in spite of many trials. One evening he found the solution to the problem while watching the dance of fire in his fireplace. Gazing into the flames, he seemed to see atoms dancing in snakelike arrays and suddenly related this to the molecular structure of benzene. This is how the hexagonal ring was discovered. However, it is doubtful whether this story supports the notion that there is no logic of discovery. Why didn't other people make a scientific breakthrough by observing the fireplace? Does the background knowledge that had been accumulated by Kekule throughout his professional career play a more important role to the discovery of the hexagonal ring than a brief moment in front of a fireplace? The dance of fire may serve as an analogy to the molecular structure that Kekule had contemplated. Without the deep knowledge of chemistry, it is unlikely that anyone could draw inspiration by the dance of fire.

For Peirce, progress in science depends on the observation of the right facts by minds furnished with appropriate ideas (Tursman, 1987). Definitely, the intuitive judgment made by an intellectual is different from that made by a high school student. Peirce cited several examples of remarkable correct guesses. All success is not simply luck. Instead, the opportunity was taken by the people who were prepared:

(a) Bacon's guess that heat was a mode of motion;
(b) Young's guess that the primary colors were violet, green and red;
(c) Dalton's guess that there were chemical atoms before the invention of microscope (as cited in Tursman, 1987).

By the same token to continue the last example, the cosmological view that "atom" is the fundamental element of the universe, introduced by ancient philosophers Leucippus and Democritus, revived by Epicurus, and confirmed by modern physicists, did not result from a lucky guess. Besides the atomist theory, there were numerous other cosmological views such as the Milesian school, which proposed that the basic elements were water, air, fire, earth . . . etc. Atomists were familiar with them and provided answers to existing questions based on the existing framework (Trundle, 1994).

Peirce stated that classification plays a major role in making a hypothesis, which is the characters of a phenomenon are placed into certain categories (Peirce, 1878b). Although Peirce is not a Kantian (Feibleman 1945), Peirce endorsed Kant's categories in *Critique of Pure Reason* (Kant, 1781/1969) to help us to make judgments of the phenomenal world. According to Kant, human thought and enlightenment are dependent on a limited number of a priori perceptual forms and ideational categories, such as causality, quality, time and space. Also, Peirce agreed with Kant that things have internal structure of meaning. Abductive activities are not empirical hypotheses based on our sensory experience, but rather the very structure of the meanings themselves (Rosenthal, 1993). Based on the Kantian framework, Peirce (1867/1960) later developed his "New list of categories." For Peirce all cognition, ranging from perception to logical reasoning, is mediated by "elements of generality" (Peirce, 1934/1960). Based upon the notion of categorizing general elements, Hoffman (1997) viewed abduction as a search for a mode of perception while facing surprising facts.

Applications of abduction

Abduction can be well applied to quantitative research, especially Exploratory Data Analysis (EDA) and Exploratory statistics (ES), such as factor rotation in Exploratory Factor Analysis and path searching in Structural Equation Modeling (Glymour, Scheines, Spirtes, & Kelly, 1987; Glymour & Cooper, 1999). Josephson and Josephson (1994) argued that the whole notion of a controlled experiment is covertly based on the logic of abduction. In a controlled experiment, the researchers control alternate explanations and test the condition generated from the most plausible hypothesis. However, abduction shares more common ground with EDA than with controlled experiments. In EDA, after observing some surprising facts, we exploit them and check the predicted values against the observed values and residuals (Behrens, 1997; Behrens & Yu, 2003). Although there may be more than one convincing pattern, we "abduct" only those that are more plausible for subsequent randomized or controlled experimentation. Since experimentation is hypothesis–driven and EDA is data–driven, the logics behind them are quite different. The abductive reasoning of EDA goes from data to hypotheses while inductive reasoning of experimentation goes from hypothesis to expected data. By the same token, in Exploratory Factor Analysis and Structural Equation Modeling, there might be more than one possible way to achieve a fit between the data and the model; again, the researcher must "abduct" a plausible set of variables and paths for modeling building.

Shank (1991), Josephson and Josephson (1994), and Ottens and Shank (1995) related abductive reasoning to detective work. Detectives collect related "facts" about people and circumstances. These facts follow from shrewd guesses or hypotheses based on keen powers of observation. In this vein, the logic of abduction is in line with EDA. In fact, Tukey (1977, 1980) often related EDA to detective work. In EDA, the role of the researcher is to explore the data in as many ways as possible until a plausible "story" of the data emerges. EDA is *not* "fishing" significant results from all possible angles during research: it is not trying out everything.

Rescher (1978) interpreted abduction as an opposition to Popper's falsification (1963). There are millions of possible explanations of a phenomenon. Due to the economy of research, we cannot afford to falsify every possibility. As mentioned before, we don't have to know everything to know something. By the same token, we don't have to screen every false thing to dig out the authentic one. During the process of abduction, the researcher should be guided by the elements of generality to extract a proper mode of perception.

Summary

In short, abduction can be interpreted as conjecturing the world with appropriate categories, which arise from the internal structure of meanings. The implications of abduction for researchers as practiced in EDA and ES are that the use of EDA and ES is neither exhausting all possibilities nor making hasty decisions. Researchers must be well equipped with proper categories in order to sort out the invariant features and patterns of phenomena (See Chapter 1 about how classification plays a central role in the Pearsonian School). Quantitative research, in this sense, is not number crunching, but a thoughtful way of dissecting data.

Deduction

Premise of deduction

Aristotle is credited as the inventor of deduction (Trundle, 1994) though the pre–Socratics had used rudimentary deductive logics. Deduction presupposes the existence of truth and falsity. Quine (1982) stated that the mission of logic is the pursuit of truth, which is the endeavor to sort out the true statements from the false statements. Hoffmann (1997) further elaborated this point by saying that the task of deductive logic is to define the validity of one truth as it leads to another truth. It is important to note that the meaning of truth in this context does not refer to the ontological, ultimate reality. Peirce made a distinction between truth and reality: Truth is the understanding of reality through a self–corrective inquiry process conducted by the whole intellectual community across time (See Chapter 5 about inter–subjectivity discussed by Stanley Mulaik). On the other hand, the existence of reality is independent of human inquiry (Wiener, 1969). In terms of ontology, there is one reality. In regard to methodology and epistemology, there is more than one approach and one source of knowledge. Reality is "what is" while truth is "what would be." Deduction is possible because even without relating to reality, propositions can be judged as true or false within a logical and conceptual system.

Logic of deduction

Deduction involves drawing logical consequences from premises. An inference is endorsed as deductionaly valid when the truth of all premises guarantees the truth of conclusion. For instance,

First premise: All the beans from the bag are white (True).
Second premise: These beans are from this bag (True).
Conclusion: Therefore, these beans are white (True) (Peirce, 1986).

According to Peirce, deduction is a form of analytic inference and inferences of this sort are all mathematical demonstrations (1986).

Limitations of deduction

Tendency to dichotomy, certainty, and infallibility

There are several limitations of deductive logic. First, deductive logic confines the conclusion to a dichotomous answer (True/False). A typical example is the rejection or failure of rejection of the null hypothesis. This narrowness of thinking is not endorsed by the Peircean philosophical system, which emphasizes the search for a deeper insight of a surprising fact. Using the deductive approach, the researcher have to follow the Boolean logic, as shown in the Truth Table (See Table 3.1), to draw a binary conclusion.

Table 3.1. Truth table

First premise	Second premise	Conclusion
True	True	True
True	False	False
False	True	True
False	False	True

In the context of statistical testing, the preceding logic can be translated into the following fashion:

All observed statistics beyond the .05 cutoff are significant (True).
This observed statistic is beyond the .05 cutoff (True).
Significant; reject the null hypothesis (True).

All observed statistics beyond the 0.05 cutoff are significant (True).
This observed statistic is *not* beyond the .05 cutoff (False).
Not significant; not to reject the null hypothesis (False).

However, what will a researcher conclude if neither the proposition "all observed statistics beyond the 0.05 cutoff are significant" nor the statement "this observed statistic is beyond the .05 cutoff" is true? Consider these example: "If 3 is a perfect square, then 3 is not prime;" "If Congress passes serious campaign finance reform, then I am the Pope!" In both cases, the first and second sentences are false but following the rule of material implication, the two false antecedents create a true conditional (F ^ F → T) (Suber, 1997). Now back to the statistical example: If the Alpha level is not the correct cutoff for determining the significance of an observed statistic and the observed statistics does not fall into the rejection region, it is absurd to claim that this logical flow leads to a certain answer (True).

Based upon the necessity of logical flow, some researchers associate the binary conclusion with certainty. It may be exaggerating to blame the naïve quest of certainty on deductive logic and mathematics (statistics). Although it is true that in the Fisherian school of statistics the quest of certainty and the deductive nature of mathematics seem to lead the researcher to either accept the hypothesis or reject it, a dichotomous answer contradicts the very definition of probabilistic inference, which indicates *uncertainty*. In an attempt to amend this problem, Pearson (1955) admitted that the terms "acceptance" and "rejection" in statistical conclusions, which carry a connotation of absolute certainty or infallibility, were unfortunately chosen. Rao's (1992) assessment of Fisher's work is helpful to clarify several misconceptions of dichotomous decisions in statistical testing:

> The decision (reject/not reject the null) is based on the logical disjunction. . . . Such a prescription was, perhaps, necessary at a time when statistical concepts were not fully understood and the exact level of significance attained by a test statistic could not be calculated due to the lack of computational power. . . . Fisher gives a limited role to tests of significance in statistical inference, only useful in situations where alternative hypotheses are not specified. . . . Fisher's emphasis on testing of null hypotheses in his earlier writings has probably misled the statistical practitioners in the interpretation of significance tests in research work (p. 46).

Rao is entirely correct in his assessment of Fisher's work. In his later career, Fisher started to realize the weaknesses of his methodology. First, he disapproved of the use of any standard Alpha level, though he once supported it. He wrote, "No scientific worker has a fixed level of significance from year to year, and in all circumstances, he rejects hypothesis; he rather gives his mind to each particular case in the light of his evidence and ideas" (as cited in Upton, 1992, p. 397). Fisher (1956) emphasized that the purpose of research is to gain a better understanding of the experimental material and of the problem it presents. Unfortunately, up to the present day most researchers could not distinguish Fisher's early view on probability and statistics from his later view. As a counter–measure, today some researchers de–emphasize the dichotomous character of hypothesis testing by asserting that the proper language of concluding a hypothesis testing should be "failed to reject the hypothesis" rather than "accepting the hypothesis" or "proving the hypothesis" (Cohen, 1990; Parkhurst, 1985, 1990). In short, the association between the deductive logic and testing of the null hypothesis and the tendency of yielding a binary conclusion may not be an inherent feature of deduction. Let alone the Fisherian school and hypothesis testing.

Incapability of new discovery and insightful explanation

Moreover, deductive reasoning cannot lead to the discovery of knowledge that is not already embedded in the premise (Peirce, 1934/1960). Certain premises in the deductive method are simply covering laws, but Ruben (1998) argued that if the researcher explains L by citing a higher law L*, such that L is treated as a special case of L*, indeed the researcher does not offer any *causal* explanation at all. I would go even further to argue that if the researcher explains a phenomenon by citing a covering law without giving the detail of the causal process, this type of explanation is also not qualified to be a causal explanation.

For example, based upon evolutionary game theory, philosopher of science Brian Skyrms (1996, 2000a, 2003) developed Monte Carlo simulation–based models to explain how certain behaviors and population structures (e.g., the concept of fairness, social networks) could eventually emerge after many generations regardless of what the initial conditions are. First, his theory focuses on the structures of topology and population, but takes no account of genetic bases for behavioral dispositions as suggested by evolutionary biologists. Second, in contrast to evolutionary psychology, which emphasizes particular psychological factors of human behaviors, the Skyrmsian approach omits the psychological mechanisms or the evolutionary histories from which humans emerge. To compensate for the lack of detail in describing psychological mechanisms and to add weight to the explanatory power of the Skyrmsian explanation, mathematical properties such as robustness are introduced to establish some kind of law–like certainty. Although social scientists can cite Evolutionary Game Theory to explain many social pheonomena, it is doubtful whether it can be treated as a *causal* explanation. The above example may be too remote for many readers. The following are simplified examples, but please keep in mind that they are not related to Skyrms' theory:

All organic entities that receive energy are subject to the principle of self–organizing tendency.
X is organic and receives energy.
The order of X is a result of its self–organizing tendency.

Consider another example:

All entities in a closed system are subject to Entropy (the second law of Thermodynamic, which is a statistical law).
X is an entity in a closed system.
The chaos of X results from the second law of Thermodynamic.

The following is a similar example:

All entities in the universe are subject to the law of equilibrium between Entropy and self–organizing tendency.
X is an entity in the universe.
The condition of X results from the law of equilibrium.

Obviously, the preceding form of covering–law reasoning fails to give an insightful explanation for it tends to invoke the "statistical God of the gaps" argument (see Chapter 8). In some cases found in social sciences, the premise may even be tautological—true by definition. Brown (1963) illustrated this weakness by using an example in economics: An entrepreneur seeks maximization of profits. The maximum profits will be earned when marginal revenue equals marginal cost. An entrepreneur will operate the business at the equilibrium between marginal cost and marginal revenue. Put it another way, the maximum profits will be gained when marginal revenue exceeds marginal cost. An entrepreneur will reduce marginal cost and increase marginal revenue as far as this can be sustained over the long run.

The above deduction simply tells you that a rational man would like to make more money. There is a similar example in cognitive psychology:

Human behaviors are rational.
One of several options is more efficient in achieving the goal.
A rational human will take the option that efficiently achieves the goal (Anderson, 1990).

The above two deductive inferences simply provide examples that a rational person will do rational things. The specific rational behaviors have been included in the bigger set of generic rational behaviors. Since deduction facilitates analysis based upon existing knowledge rather than generating new knowledge, Josephson and Josephson (1994) viewed deduction as truth preserving and abduction as truth producing.

Absence of a self–sufficient logical–mathematical system

Third, deduction is incomplete as we cannot logically prove that all the premises are true. Russell and Whitehead (1910) attempted to develop a self–sufficient logical–mathematical system. In their view, not only can mathematics be reduced to logic, but also logic is the foundation of mathematics. However, Gödel (1944, 1947/1986) showed that we cannot even establish all mathematics by deductive proof. To be specific, it is impossible to have a self–sufficient system as Russell and Whitehead postulated. Any lower order theorem or premise needs a higher order theorem or premise for substantiation; and no system can be complete and consistent at the same time. Deduction alone is clearly incapable of establishing the empirical knowledge we seek.

Peirce reviewed Russell's book *Principles of Mathematics* in 1903, but he only wrote a short paragraph with vague comments. Nonetheless, based on Peirce's other writings on logic and mathematics, Haack (1993) concluded that Peirce would be opposed to Russell and Whitehead's notion that the epistemological foundations of mathematics lie in logic. It is questionable whether the logic or the mathematics can fully justify deductive knowledge. No matter how logical a hypothesis is, it is only sufficient within the system; it is still tentative and requires further investigation with external proof.

This line of thought posed a serious challenge to researchers who are confident in the logical structure of statistics. Mathematical logic relies on many unproven premises and assumptions. Statistical conclusions are considered true only given that all premises and assumptions that are applied are true. But as a matter of fact, these so–called invariant assumptions or premises are subject to revision (see Chapter 4) In recent years many Monte Carlo simulations have been conducted to determine how robust certain tests are, and which statistics should be favored. The reference and criteria of all these studies are within logical–mathematical systems without any worldly concerns. For instance, the Fisher protected t–test is considered inferior to the Ryan test and the Tukey test because it cannot control the inflated Type I error very well (Toothaker, 1993), not because any psychologists or educators made a terribly wrong decision based upon the Fisher protected t–test. The Pillai–Bartlett statistic is considered superior to Wilk's Lambda and Hotelling–Lawley Trace because of much greater robustness against unequal covariance matrices (Olson, 1976), not because any significant scientific breakthroughs are made with the use of Pillai–Bartlett statistic. For Peirce this kind of self–referential deduction cannot lead to progress in knowledge. Knowing is an activity which is by definition involvement with the real world (Burrell, 1968).

As a matter of fact, the inventor of deductive syllogisms, Aristotle, did not isolate formal logic from external reality and he repeatedly admitted the importance of induction. It is not enough that a conclusion is deduced correctly according to the formal laws of logic. Aristotle assumes that the conclusion is verified in reality. Also, he devoted attention to the question: How do we know the first premises from which deduction must start? (Copleston, 1946/85; Russell, 1945/72)

Certain developments in quantitative research methodology are not restricted by logic. Actually, statistics is by no means pure mathematics without interactions with the real world (see Chapter 4). Gauss discovered the Gaussian distribution through astronomical observations. Fisher built his theories from applications of biometrics and agriculture. Survival analysis or the hazard model is the fruit of medical and sociological research. Differential item functioning (DIF) was developed to address the issue of reducing test bias.

Under–determination

Last but not least, for several decades philosophers of science have been debating the issue of under–determination, a problematic situation in which several rival theories are empirically equivalent but logically incompatible (de Regt, 1994; Psillos, 1999). Under–determination is no stranger to quantitative researchers, who constantly face model equivalency in factor analysis and Structural Equation Modeling. Under–determination, according to Leplin (1997), is a problem rooted in the limitations of the hypothetico–deductive methodology, which is disconfirmatory in nature.

For instance, the widely adopted hypothesis testing is based on the logic of computing the probability of obtaining the observed data (D) given that the theory or the hypothesis (H) is true (P(D|H)). At most this mode of inquiry can inform us when to reject a theory, but not when to accept one. Thus, quantitative researchers usually draw a conclusion using the language in this fashion: "Reject the hypothesis" or "fail to reject the hypothesis," but not "accept the hypothesis" or "fail to accept the hypothesis." Passing a test is not confirmatory if the test is one that even a false theory would be expected to pass.

At first glance it may be strange to say that a false theory could lead to passing of a test, but that is how under–determination occurs. Whenever a theory is proposed for predicting or explaining a phenomenon, it has a deductive structure. What is deduced may be an empirical regularity that holds only statistically, and thus, the answer by deduction works well for the true theory as for the false ones.

Summary

For Peirce, deduction alone is a necessary condition, but not a sufficient condition of knowledge. Peirce (1934/1960) warned that deduction is applicable only to the ideal state of things. In other words, deduction alone can be applied to a well–defined problem, but not an ill–defined problem, which is more likely to be encountered by researchers. Nevertheless, deduction performs the function of clarifying the relation of logical implications. When well–defined categories result from abduction, premises can be generated for deductive reasoning.

Induction

Premise of induction

For Peirce, induction is founded on the premise that inquiry is a self–corrective process by the whole intellectual community across time. Peirce stressed the continuity of knowledge and the collective nature of inquiry by saying "No mind can take one step without the aid of other minds" (1934/1960, p. 398). First, knowledge does not emerge out of pure logic. Instead, it is a historical and social product. Second, Peirce disregarded the Cartesian skepticism of doubting everything (DesCartes, 1641/1964). To some extent we have to fix our beliefs on those positions that are widely accepted by the intellectual community (Peirce, 1877).

Peirce considered knowledge to be continuous and cumulative through induction. Rescher (1978) used the geographical–exploration model as a metaphor to illustrate Peirce's idea: The replacement of a flat–world view with a global–world view is a change in conceptual understanding. After we have discovered all the continents and oceans, measuring the height of Mount Everest and the depth of the Nile River is adding details to our conceptual knowledge.

Logic of induction

Induction introduced by Francis Bacon is a direct revolt against deduction. Bacon (1620/1960) found that people who use deductive reasoning rely on the authority of antiquity (premises made by masters), and the tendency of the mind to construct knowledge within the mind itself. Bacon criticized deductive users as spiders for they make a web of knowledge out of their own substance. Although the meaning of deductive knowledge is entirely self–referent, deductive users tend to take those propositions as assertions. Propositions and assertions are not the same level of knowledge. For Peirce, abduction and deduction only give propositions, however, self–correcting induction provides empirical support to assertions.

Inductive logic is often based upon the notion that probability is the relative frequency in long run and a general law can be concluded based on numerous cases. For examples,

A1, A2, A3 . . . A100 are B.
Hence, all As are B.

Nonetheless, the above is by no mean the only way of understanding induction. Induction could also take the form of prediction:

A1, A2, A3 . . . A100 are B.
Thus, A101 will be B.

Limitations of induction

Humean challenge: The future may not resemble the past

Hume (1777/1912) argued that things are inconclusive by induction because in infinity there are always new cases and new evidence. Induction can be justified, if and only if, instances of which we have no experience resemble those of which we have experience. Thus, the problem of induction is also known as "the skeptical problem about the future" (Hacking, 1975). Take the previous argument as an example. If A101 is not B, the statement "All As are B" can become questionable. However, it is important to note that one anomalous case cannot constitute a total refutation of an established theory. In statistics we call that non–conforming observation "outlier" and in measurement we call that "misfit." But if A102, A103, A104, and many other subsequent cases are not B, then it may be alarming enough for the researcher to question the existing theory. But, how many are many? How one can determine a cut–off for distinguishing outliers from non–outliers and how many anomalous cases are considered adequate to overthrow a theory continue to be crucial questions in both statistics and philosophy of science.

Further, we never know when a regression line will turn flat, go down, or go up. Even inductive reasoning using numerous accurate data and high power computing can go wrong, because predictions are made only under certain specified conditions (Samuelson, 1967). For instance, based on the case studies in the 19th century, sociologist Max Weber (1904/1976) argued that capitalism could be developed in Europe because of the Protestant work ethic; other cultures like the Chinese Confucianism are by essence incompatible with capitalism. However, after World War II, the emergence of Asian economic powers such as Taiwan, South Korea, Hong Kong, and Singapore challenged the Weberian hypothesis.

Take the modern economy as another example. Due to American economic problems in the early 1980s, quite a few reputable economists made gloomy predictions about the U.S. economy such as the takeover of American economic and technological throne by Japan. By the end of the decade, Roberts (1989) concluded that those economists were wrong; contrary to those forecasts, in the 1980s the U.S. enjoyed the longest economic expansion in its history. In the 1990s, the economic positions of the two nations changed: Japan experienced recession while America experienced expansion.

Goodman: New riddle of induction

"The skeptical problem about the future" is also known as "the old riddle of induction." In a similar vein to the old riddle, Goodman (1954/1983) introduced the "new riddle of induction," in which conceptualization of kinds plays an important role. Goodman demonstrated that whenever we reach a conclusion based upon inductive reasoning, we could use the same rules of inference, but different criteria of classification, to draw an opposite conclusion. Goodman's example is: We could conclude that all emeralds are green given that 1000 observed emeralds are green. But what would happen if we re–classify "green" objects as "blue" and "blue" as "green" in the year 2020? We can say that something is "grue" if it was considered "green" before 2020 and it would be treated as "blue" after 2020. We can also say that something is "bleen" if it was counted as a "blue" object before 2020 and it would be regarded as "green" after 2020. Thus, the new riddle is also known as "the grue problem."

In addition, Hacking (1999) cited the example of child abuse, a construct that has been taken for granted by many Americans, to demonstrate this riddle. He pointed out that the concept of "child abuse" in the current form did not exist in other cultures. Cruelty to children just emerged as a social issue during the Victorian period, but "child abuse" as a social science concept was formulated in America around 1960. To this extent, Victorians viewed cruelty to children as a matter of poor people harming their children, but to Americans child abuse was a classless phenomenon. When the construct "child abuse" became more and more popular, many American adults recollected childhood trauma during psychotherapy sessions, but authenticity of these child abuse cases was highly questionable. Hacking proposed that child abuse is a typical example of how re–conceptualization in the future alters our evaluations of the past.

Another main theme of the new riddle focuses on the problem of projectibility. Whether an "observed pattern" is projectible depends on how we conceptualize the pattern. Skyrms (1975) used a mathematical example to illustrate this problem: If this series of digits (1, 2, 3, 4, 5) is shown, what is the next projected number? Without any doubt, for most people the intuitive answer is simply "6." Skyrms argued that this seemingly straight–forward numeric sequence could be populated by this generating function: (A–1)(A–2)(A–3)(A–4)(A–5)+A. Let's step through this example using an Excel spreadsheet (see Table 3.2).

Table 3.2. Generating function for a sequence of numbers

	A	B	
1	1	1	*Fx*(B1) =(A1–1)*(A1–2)*(A1–3)*(A1–4)*(A1–5)+A1
2	2	2	*Fx*(B2) =(A2–1)*(A2–2)*(A2–3)*(A2–4)*(A2–5)+A2
3	3	3	*Fx*(B3) =(A3–1)*(A3–2)*(A3–3)*(A3–4)*(A3–5)+A3
4	4	4	*Fx*(B4) =(A4–1)*(A4–2)*(A4–3)*(A4–4)*(A4–5)+A4
5	5	5	*Fx*(B5) =(A5–1)*(A5–2)*(A5–3)*(A5–4)*(A5–5)+A5
6	6	126	*Fx*(B6) =(A6–1)*(A6–2)*(A6–3)*(A6–4)*(A6–5)+A6
7	7	727	*Fx*(B7) =(A7–1)*(A7–2)*(A7–3)*(A7–4)*(A7–5)+A7
8	8	2528	*Fx*(B8) =(A8–1)*(A8–2)*(A8–3)*(A8–4)*(A8–5)+A8
9	9	6729	*Fx*(B9) =(A9–1)*(A9–2)*(A9–3)*(A9–4)*(A9–5)+A9
10	10	15310	*Fx*(B10)=(A10–1)*(A10–2)*(A10–3)*(A10–4)*(A10–5)+A10

In Cell A1 to A10 of the Excel spreadsheet, enter 1–10, respectively. Next, in Cell B1 enter the function "=(A1–1)*(A1–2)*(A1–3)*(A1–4)*(A1–5)+A1" and this function will yield "1." Afterwards, select Cell B1 and drag the cursor downwards to Cell B10; it will copy the same function to B2, B3, B4...B10. As a result, (B1 to B5) will correspond to (A1 to A10), which are (1, 2, 3, 4, 5). However, the sixth number in Column B, which is 126, substantively deviates from the intuitive projection. All numbers in the cells below B6 are also surprising. Skyrms pointed out that whatever number we want to predict for the sixth number of the series, there is always a generating function that can fit the given members of the sequence and that will yield the projection we want. This indeterminacy of projection is a mathematical fact.

Furthermore, the new riddle, which is considered an instantiation of the general problem of under–determination in epistemology, is germane to quantitative researchers in the context of "model equivalency" and "factor indeterminacy" (DeVito, 1997; Forster, 1999; Forster & Sober, 1994; Kieseppa, 2001; Muliak, 1996; Turney, 1999). Specifically, the new riddle and other philosophical notions of under–determination illustrate that all scientific theories are under–determined by the limited evidence in the sense that the same phenomenon can be equally well–explained by rival models that are logically incompatible. In factor analysis, for example, whether adopting a one–factor or a two–factor model may have tremendous impact on subsequent inferences. In curving–fitting problem, whether using the Akaike's Information Criterion or the Bayesian Information Criterion is crucial in the sense that these two criteria could lead to different conclusions. Hence, the preceding problem of model selection criteria in quantitative–based research is analogous to the problem of re–conceptualization of "child abuse" and the problem of projectibility based upon generating functions. At the present time, there are no commonly agreed solutions to either the new riddle or the model selection criteria.

Indefinability in a single case

Further, induction suggests the possible outcome in relation to events in long run. This is not definable for an individual event. To make a judgment for a single event based on probability like "your chance to survive this surgery is 75 percent" is nonsense. In actuality, the patient will either live or die. In a single event, not only the probability is indefinable, but also the explanatory power is absent. Induction yields a general statement that explains the event of observing, but not the facts observed. Josephson and Josephson (1994) gave this example: "Suppose I choose a ball at random (arbitrarily) from a large hat containing colored balls. The ball I choose is red. Does the fact that all of the balls in the hat are red explain why this particular ball is red? No…All 'As are Bs' cannot explain why 'this A is a B' because it does not say anything about how its being an A is connected with its being a B" (p. 20).

As mentioned before, induction also suggests probability as a relative frequency. In the discussion of probability of induction, Peirce (1986) raised his skepticism to this idea: "The relative probability . . . is something which we should have a right to talk about if universes were as plenty as blackberries, if we could put a quantity of them in a bag, shake them well up, draw out a sample, and examine them to see what proportion of them had one arrangement and what proportion another" (pp. 300–301). Peirce is not alone in this matter. To many statisticians, other types of interpretations of probability, such as the subjective interpretation and the propensity interpretation, should be considered.

Theoretical laws vs. empirical laws

Carnap, as an inductive logician, knew the limitation of induction. Carnap (1952) argued that induction might lead to the generalization of empirical laws but not theoretical laws. For instance, even if we observe thousands of stones, trees and flowers, we never reach a point at which we observe a molecule. After we heat many iron bars, we can conclude the empirical fact that metals will bend when they are heated. But we will never discover the physics of expansion coefficients in this way.

Indeed, superficial empirical–based induction could lead to wrong conclusions. For example, by repeated observations, it seems that heavy bodies (e.g. metal, stone) fall faster than lighter bodies (paper, feather). This Aristotelian belief had misled European scientists for over a thousand years. Galileo argued that indeed both heavy and light objects fall at the same speed. There is a popular myth that Galileo conducted an experiment in the Tower of Pisa to prove his point. Probably he never performed this experiment. Actually this experiment was performed by one of Galileo's critics and the result supported Aristotle's notion. Galileo did not get the law from observation, but by a chain of logical arguments (Kuhn, 1985). Again, superficial induction runs the risk of superficial and even incorrect conclusions.

Quantitative researchers have been warned that high correlations among variables may not be meaningful. For example, if one plots GNP, educational level, or anything against time, one may see some significant but meaningless correlation (Yule, 1926). As Peirce (1934/1960) pointed out, induction cannot furnish us with new ideas because observations or sensory data only lead us to superficial conclusions but not the "bottom of things" (p. 878).

Circularity and psychological disposition

Last but not least, induction as the sole source of reliable knowledge was never inductively concluded. An Eighteenth century British moral philosopher Thomas Reid embraced the conviction that the Baconian philosophy or the inductive method could be extended from the realm of natural science to mind, society, and morality. He firmly believed that through an inductive analysis of the faculties and powers by which the mind knows, feels, and wills, moral philosophers could eventually establish the scientific foundations for morality. However, some form of circularity was inevitable in his argument when *induction was validated by induction*. Reid and his associates counter–measured this challenge by arguing that the human mental structure was designed explicitly and solely for an inductive means of inquiry (as cited in Bozeman, 1977). Today the issue of inductive circularity remains unsettled because psychologists still could not reach a consent pertaining to the human reasoning process. While some psychologists found that the frequency approach appears to be more natural to learners in the context of quantitative reasoning (Gigerenzer, 2003; Hoffrage, Gigerenzer, & Martignon, 2002), some other psychologists revealed that humans have conducted inquiry in the form of Bayesian network by the age of five (Gopnik & Schulz, 2004). Proclaiming a particular reasoning mode as *the* human mind structure in a hegemonic tone, needless to say, would lead to immediate protest.

Summary

For Peirce induction still has validity. Contrary to Hume's notion that our perception of events is devoid of generality, Peirce argued that the existence we perceive must share generality with other things in existence. Peirce's metaphysical system resolves the problem of induction by asserting that perceptual data are not reducible to discrete, logically and ontologically independent events (Sullivan, 1991). In addition, for Peirce all empirical reasoning is essentially making inferences from a sample to a population; the conclusion is merely approximately true (O'Neill, 1993). Forster (1993) justified this view with the Law of Large Numbers. On one hand, we don't know the real probability due to our finite existence. However, given a large number of cases, we can approximate the actual probability. We don't have to know everything to know something. Also, we don't have to know every case to get an approximation. This approximation is sufficient to fix our beliefs and lead us to further inquiry.

Conclusion

In summary, abduction, deduction and induction have different merits and shortcomings. Yet the combination of all three reasoning approaches provides researchers a powerful tool of inquiry. For Peirce a reasoner should apply abduction, deduction and induction altogether in order to achieve a comprehensive inquiry. Abduction and deduction are the conceptual understanding of phenomena, and induction is the quantitative verification. At the stage of abduction, the goals are to explore available data, to find out a pattern, and to suggest a plausible hypothesis or a cluster of hypotheses with the use of proper categories; deduction builds a logical and testable hypothesis based upon other plausible premises; and induction is the approximation of truth and fixing our beliefs en route to further inquiry. In short, abduction creates, deduction explicates, and induction verifies.

A good example of their application can be found in the use of the Bayesian Inference Network (BIN) in psychometrics (Mislevy, 1994). According to Mislevy, the BIN builds around deductive reasoning to support subsequent inductive reasoning from realized data to probabilities of states. Yet abductive reasoning is vital to the process in two aspects. First, abductive reasoning suggests the framework for inductive reasoning. Second, the BIN as a tool for reasoning deductively and inductively within the posited structure requires abduction to reason about the structure.

Ward, Vertue, and Haig (1999) also employed the inductive, abductive, and deductive methods together in clinical assessment. According to Ward et al., the fist phrase of the clinical reasoning process aims to formulate a *descriptive hypothesis* by inductively inferring from diverse data to the existence of a coherent phenomenon. In the second phrase, research endeavors are devoted to uncover the causal mechanisms and thus to produce an explanatory hypothesis by abduction. In the third stage, the phenomena under study, the causal mechanisms, and the factors that contribute to the development of these mechanisms are put together into an integrated theory. Finally, this hypothetico–deductive theory is subject to rigorous testing according to explanatory coherence.

Another example can be found in the mixed methodology developed by Johnson and Onwuegbuzie (2004). Research employing mixed methods (quantitative and qualitative methods) makes use of all three modes of reasoning. To be specific, its logic of inquiry includes the use of induction in pattern recognition, which is commonly used in thematic analysis in qualitative methods, the use of deduction, which is concerned with quantitative testing of theories and hypotheses, and abduction, which is about inferences to the best explanation based on a set of available alternate explanations.

It is important to note that researchers do not have to follow a specific order in using abduction, deduction, and induction. In Johnson and Onwuegbuzie's framework, abduction is a tool of justifying the results at the end rather than generating a hypothesis at the beginning of a study. In the clinical assessment process conducted by Ward et al., abduction plays a central role in the second stage as a reasoning tool for discovering causal mechanisms. More importantly, the order of the three modes of reasoning does not matter. Minnameier (2004) argued that the Peircean triad (abduction, deduction, induction) as a whole is a *recursive* process that it is not just a sequence of inferences that "ends" with induction. Rather, it leads to a projection of the theoretical qualities onto all relevant cases and stimulate further inquiries. Hence, it is not inconsistent to arrange abduction, deduction, and induction into different orders, because any combination may be a "snapshot" of an ongoing self–correcting process. For example,

Study 1: Abduction, deduction, induction
Study 2: Induction, abduction, deduction
Study 3: Deduction, induction, abduction (Figure 3.1)

Figure 3.1. Different snapshots of an ongoing self–correcting process

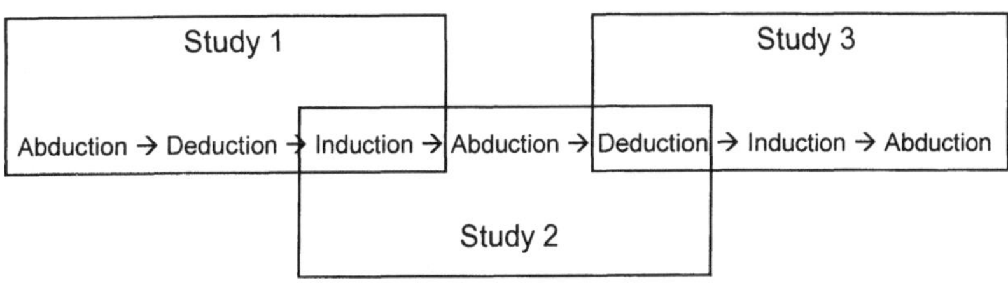

One of the goals of this chapter is to illustrate a tight integration among different modes of inquiry, and its implication to exploratory and confirmatory analyzes. Consider this counter–example. Glymour (2001) viewed widespread applications of factor analysis as a sign of system–wide failure in social sciences in terms of causal interpretations. As a strong advocate of Structural Equation Modeling, Glymour is very critical of this exploratory factor modeling approach. By reviewing the history of psychometrics, Glymour stated that reliability (a stable factor structure) was never a goal of early psychometricians. Thurstone faced the problem that there were many competing factor models that were statistically equivalent. In order to "save the phenomena" (to uniquely determining the factor loadings), he developed the criterion of the simple structure, which has no special measure–theoretic virtue or special stability properties. In addition, on finite samples, factor analysis may fail to recover the true causal structure because of statistical or algorithmic artifacts. On the contrary, Glymour et al. (2005) developed path–searching algorithms for model building, in which huge data sets are collected; automated methods are employed to search for regularities in the data; hypotheses are generated and tested as they go along (see Chapter 6). The last point is especially important because for Glymour there is no sharp distinction between the exploratory and confirmatory steps.

However, even if path–searching algorithms are capable of conducting hypothesis generation and testing altogether, it is doubtful whether the process is totally confirmatory and nothing exploratory. In a strict sense, even CFA is a mixture of exploratory and confirmatory techniques, in which the end product is derived in part from theory and in part from a re–specification based on the analysis of the fitness indices. The same argument is well applied to path–searching. According to Peirce, in the long run scientific inquiry is a self–correcting process; earlier theories will inevitably be revised or rejected by later theories. In this sense, all causal conclusions, no matter how confirmatory they are, must be exploratory in nature because these confirmed conclusions are subject to further investigations. A product resulted from induction may be a starting point for another abduction. In short, it is the author's belief that integration among abduction, induction, and deduction, as well as between exploratory and confirmatory analyses, could enable researchers to conduct a thorough investigation.

Chapter 4 Philosophy of mathematics and quantitative research

Beyond mathematical realism

Researchers who employ statistics always apply theoretical distributions to determine the significance of a test statistic. There is an implicit assumption that mathematical objects, such as theoretical distributions, are "real" entities. However, Sir R. A. Fisher, the founder of statistical hypothesis testing, asserted that theoretical distributions against which observed effects are tested have no objective reality "being exclusively products of the statistician's imagination through the hypothesis which he has decided to test" (Fisher, 1956, p. 81). In other words, he did not view distributions as outcomes of empirical replications that might actually be conducted. In a similar fashion, Lord (1980) dissociated the statistical world from the real world:

> A statistician doing an Analysis of Variance does not try to define the model parameters as if they existed in the real world. A statistical model is chosen, expressed in mathematical terms undefined in the real world. The question of whether the real world corresponds to the model is a separate question to be answered as best we can (p. 6).

Mathematicians have developed a world of distributions and theorems. Essentially, statistical testing is a comparison between the observed statistic and theoretical distributions to decide which hypothesis should be retained, based upon the central limit theorem. Questions regarding the basis of statistical testing lead directly to its philosophical foundations. To be specific, how could we justify collecting empirical observations and using a non–empirical reference to make an inference? Are the t–, F–, Chi–square, and many other distributions just from a convention imposed by authorities, or do they exist independently from the human world? Alternatively, mathematical reality is proposed as a foundation to justify mathematical–based methodologies such as statistical testing.

It is important to note that this chapter focuses on theorems and distributions rather than certain "cut–off" decisions, which are defined and determined by human intuition and convention. For instance, in regard to statistical significance, there is a well–known saying that "God loves the .06 nearly as much as the .05." for debunking the myth of Alpha level (Rosnow & Rosethal, 1989; Cohen, 1990). One and a half of the inter–quartile range (IRQ) as the criterion for classifying outliers and non–outliers is another good example. When Paul

Velleman asked John Tukey, the father of Exploratory Data Analysis who invented the boxplot and the 1.5*IQR Rule, "Why 1.5?" Tukey replied, "Because 1 is too small and 2 is too large" (Cook, 1999). By the same token, the classification of low, medium, and high effect size and power are also arbitrary conventions. Issues of this kind do not fall into any philosophical discussion.

Reality, by definition, is an objective existence which is independent from human perception (Devitt, 1991). Mathematical realism, which assumes that mathematical entities exist independently of human cognition, dates back to the era of Plato. Thus, mathematical realism is often associated with Platonism. It was popular in the late 19th century. However, it lost popularity in the 20th century with the emergence of non–Euclidean geometries and set theory. Instead, formalism became the dominant force. Those who adhere to formalism view mathematical formulas as just formulas, a set of rules for convenience. In fact, this view is shared by statisticians who believe statistical modeling is nothing more than a convenient way for description and prediction; the model is not intrinsic to the phenomenon itself. Nonetheless, support for mathematical realism has been revived recently (Drozdek & Keagy, 1994).

Realism and anti–realism has been an ongoing debate in philosophy, and unfortunately, any attempt to give a final solution to this matter seems to be futile. Searle (1998) asserted that realism is not a theory at all, rather it is the *default position,* in which things are taken for granted as the way they really are; and anti–realism is motivated by certain non–intellectual sentiments.

It might be too demanding for statisticians and social scientists to adopt a fully justified philosophical view to mathematical objects or theoretical distributions in conducting quantitative research. But on the other hand, quantitative researchers might keep facing unsettling tensions between two polarities: "If mathematical objects are regarded as real entities in the ontological sense, am I naively seeking for objective truths based upon the blind faith that mathematical truths are invariant? If mathematics is nothing more than a formal system of symbols that is subject to human revision, would probabilistic inferences become arbitrary and groundless?" This dichotomy is not necessary. The central question should not be about whether mathematical objects are real entities because as mentioned before, this inquiry might lead to a black hole that absorbs all energies. Rather, the focal concern should be whether mathematics can be revised based upon our empirical studies no matter whether one holds a realist or an anti–realist position. In the following this issue will be thoroughly discussed in the context of Carnap's and Quine's philosophy of mathematics.

Carnap and Quine made tremendous contributions to numerous areas of modern philosophy, including the philosophy of mathematics. Carnap endorsed the dichotomy between analytic and synthetic knowledge and classified certain mathematical questions as internal questions appealing to logic and convention. In addition, he regarded the ontological question about the reality of mathematical objects as a pseudo–question. On the contrary, Quine made an ontological commitment to mathematical entities by asserting that mathematical objects are on a par with physical objects. However, readers should be cautious to interpret this notion because Quine (1951) stated that his acceptance of the existence of the particles of atomic physics is on a par with the acceptance of the existence of Homer's God. Nonetheless, the assertion that mathematical objects are on a par with physical objects is tied to his belief that there is no first philosophy prior to natural science. In addition, Quine was opposed to the analytic–synthetic distinction and promoted a holistic view of scientific inquiry. On one hand, Quine recognized that there are differences between logic/mathematics and physical sciences. On the other hand, Quine maintained that it is a mistake to hold a dualistic view. For Quine logic and mathematics are essentially empirically–based and they are subject to revision according to new evidence. The purpose of this paper is to argue that in light of the recent advancement of experimental mathematics such as Monte Carlo simulations, limiting mathematical inquiry to the domain of logic is unjustified. Robustness studies implemented in Monte Carlo Studies demonstrate that mathematics is on a par with other experimental–based sciences.

Quine (1966/1976) wrote, "Carnap more than anyone else was the embodiment of logical positivism, logical empiricism, the Vienna circle" (p. 40). To discuss Carnap's philosophy of mathematics, it is essential to illustrate the ideas of the Vienna circle, as well as how members of the Vienna circle adopted and rejected other ideas. In the following, the theories of Frege, Russell, Whitehead and Gödel will be briefly introduced. These are by no means the only ones who are related to the formulation of Carnap's and the Vienna Circle's notions. Nonetheless, since this article concentrates on the argument against the logical view of mathematics endorsed by Carnap, discussion of Frege, Russell, Whitehead and Gödel is germane to the topic.

Different views on the philosophy of mathematics

The Vienna circle

Logical positivism, which originated with the Vienna circle, embraced verificationism as the criterion for obtaining meaningful knowledge. The verification criterion is not just a demand for evidence. Verification does not mean that, with other things being equal, a proposition that can be verified is of vastly greater significance than one that cannot. Rather, the verification thesis is much more restrictive than the above. According to logical positivism, a statement is meaningless if verification is not possible or the criteria for verification are not clear (Ayer, 1936; Schlick, 1959). To be specific, the verification principle is not an account of the relative importance of propositions, but a definition of meaning. Meaning and verifiability are almost interchangeable (Werkmeister, 1937). The principle of verification was used by the Vienna Circle as a tool to counteract metaphysics by enforcing adherence to empiricism. However, one may then ask how we can substantiate mathematical knowledge when mathematics is considered by many to be a form of knowledge that cannot be verified by sensory input. Following the strict criterion of verifictionism, the analytic philosopher

Ayer (1946) has said that mathematics is nonsense. In his view, mathematics says nothing about the world. What it can accomplish is to enlighten us how to manipulate symbols.

Russell and Whitehead

In order to make sense out of mathematics, logical positivists adopted a view of mathematics in the Frege–Russell–Whitehead tradition. This tradition took care of logic and mathematics, and thus left a separate epistemological problem of non–logical and non–mathematical discourse (Isaacson, 2000). According to Frege (1884/1960), logical and mathematical truths are true by virtue of the nature of thought. This notion is further expanded by Russell, and also by collaboration between Russell and Whitehead.

In Russell's view (1919), in order to uncover the underlying structures of mathematical objects, mathematics should be reduced to a more basic element, namely, logic. Thus, his approach is termed logical atomism. Russell's philosophy of mathematics is mainly concerned with geometry. At the time of Russell, the existence of geometric objects and the epistemology of geometry could not be answered by empiricists. In geometry a line can be broken down infinitely to a smaller line. We can neither see nor feel a mathematical line or a mathematical point. Thus, it seems that geometric objects are not objects of empirical perception (sense experience). If this is true, how could conceptions of such objects and their properties be derived from experience as an empiricist would require? Russell's answer is that although geometric objects are theoretical objects, we can still understand geometric structures by applying logic to the study of relationships among those objects: "What matters in mathematics, and to a very great extent in physical science, is not the intrinsic nature of our terms, but the logical nature of their inter–relations" (1919, p. 59).

Whitehead and Russell's work on *Principia Mathematica* (1910/1950) is a bold attempt to develop a fully self–sufficient mathematical system through logical relationships. For Russell and Whitehead, mathematics is a purely formal science. The existence of mathematical objects is conditional upon structures. If a certain structure or system exists, then there also exist some other structures or systems whose existence follows logically from the existence of the former. In their view, mathematics could be reduced to logical relationships within the logical system without external references. The Frege–Russell–Whitehead tradition is considered the logical approach to mathematics. This approach is said to be a solution to infinite regress or circular proof. Nonetheless, today cognitive scientists dispute this logical view to mathematics by showing that logic is not the foundation of all other reasoning modes, including mathematical reasoning (Lakoff & Nunez, 2000).

Gödel

However, the proposal by Whitehead and Russell is seriously challenged by Gödel. Gödel (1944, 1947/1986) proposed that a complete and consistent mathematical system is inherently impossible, and within any consistent mathematical system there are propositions that cannot be proved or disproved on the basis of the axioms within that system. Thus, the consequences drawn from mathematical axioms have meaning only in a hypothetical sense. In addition, mathematical propositions cannot be proved by using combinations of symbols without introducing more abstract elements. In Gödel's sense, logicism in mathematics does not solve the problem of infinite regress or circular proof.

In rejecting the logical approach, Gödel took an "intuitionistic" position to mathematics. Unlike Russell, who asserted mathematical structures exist in terms of relationships, Gödel maintained that it is not a question of whether there are some real objects "out there". Rather, our sequences of acts construct our perceptions of so–called "reality" (Tieszen, 1992). According to Gödel, "despite their remoteness from sense experience, we do have something like a perception also of the objects of set theory. . . . I don't see any reason why we should have less confidence in this kind of perception, i.e. in mathematical intuition, than in sense perception" (as cited in Lindstrom, 2000, p. 123). Indeed, there are followers of Gödel's even in the late 20th century. Jaffe and Quinn (1993) observed that there is "a trend toward basing mathematics on intuitive reasoning without proof" (p. 1).

Carnap

Carnap disliked ontology and metaphysics. For Carnap intuition is a kind of mysterious and unreliable access to matters of independent fact. Creath (1990a, 1990b) argued that anti–intuition is one of the primary motives of Carnap's philosophy. Carnap was firmly opposed to the Platonic tradition of accepting "truths" based upon "supposed direct metaphysical insight or grasp of objects or features of things independent of ourselves but inaccessible to ordinary sensory observation." (p. 4) Creath (1900b) pointed out,

> Carnap's proposal, then, is to treat the basic axioms of mathematics, of logic, and of the theory of knowledge itself, as well as the sundry other special sentences, as an implicit definition of the terms they contain. The upshot of this is that simultaneously the basic terms are understood with enough meaning for the purpose of mathematics, logic and so on, and the basic claims thereof need no further justification, for we have so chosen our language as to make these particular claims true. . . . On Carnap's proposal the basic claims are in some sense truths of their own making. It is not that we make objects and features thereof, rather we construct our language in such a way that those claims are true (p. 6).

Following Poincaré and Hilbert's assertion that the axioms of mathematics can be constructed as implicit definitions of the terms they contain, Carnap viewed numbers as logical objects and rejected the intuitionist approach to mathematics. Although Gödel's theorem brought arguably insurmountable difficulties to the Russell–Whitehead project, Carnap still adopted Russell's logico–analytic method of philosophy, including philosophy of mathematics. By working on logical syntax, Carnap attempted to make philosophy into a normal science in a logical, but not empirical, sense (Wang, 1986). Carnap accepted Russell and Whitehead's thesis that mathematics can be reduced to logic. Further, Carnap asserted that logic is based on convention and thus it is true by convention. In his essay entitled "Foundations of logic and mathematics" (1971, originally published in 1939), Carnap clearly explained his position on logic and convention:

> It is important to be aware of the conventional components in the construction of a language system. This view leads to an unprejudiced investigation of the various forms of new logical systems which differ more or less from the customary form (e.g. the intuitionist logic constructed by Brouwer and Heyting, the systems of logic of modalities as constructed by Lewis and others, the systems of plurivalued logic as constructed by Lukasiewicz and Taski, etc.), and it encourages the construction of further new forms. The task is not to decide which of the different systems is the right logic, but to examine their formal properties and the possibilities for their interpretation and application in science (pp. 170–171).

The preceding approach is called linguistic conventionalism, in which things can make sense with reference to particular linguistic frameworks. Once we learn the rules of a certain logical and mathematical framework, we have everything we need for knowledge of the required mathematical propositions. In this sense, like the Russell–Whitehead approach, a linguistic framework is a self–contained system.

As mentioned earlier, the verification criterion of logical positivism might face certain difficulties in the context of mathematical proof. Carnap supported a distinction between synthetic and analytical knowledge as a way to delimit the range of application of the verification principle (Isaacson, 2000). To be specific, Carnap (1956) distinguished analytic knowledge from synthetic knowledge, and also internal questions from external questions. An external question is concerned with the existence or reality of the system of entities as a whole. A typical example is, "Is there a white piece of paper on my desk?" This question can be answered by empirical investigation. A question like "Do normal distributions exist?" is also an external question, but for Carnap, it is a pseudo–question that cannot be meaningfully answered at all.

On the other hand, an internal question is about the existence of certain entities within a given framework. Mathematical truths, such as 1+1=2, or a set theoretic truth, are tautology in the sense that they are verified by meanings within a given frame of reference; any revision may lead to a change of meanings. In Carnap's view it is meaningful to ask a question like "Is there a theoretical sampling t–distribution in the Fisherian significance testing?" In other words, to be real in logic and mathematics is to be an element of the system. Logic and mathematics do not rely on empirical substantiation, because they are empty of empirical content.

Quine

Unlike Carnap, Quine did not reject the ontological question of the realness of mathematical entities. Instead, for Quine the existence of mathematical entities should be justified in the way that one justifies the postulation of theoretical entities in physics (Quine, 1957). However, this notion is misunderstood by some mathematicians such as Hersh (1997), and thus needs clarification. Hersh argued that physics depends on machines that accept only finite decimals. No computer can use real numbers that are written in infinite decimals; the microprocessor would be trapped in an infinite process. For example, pi (3.14159...) exists conceptually, but not physically and computationally. While electrons and protons are measurable and accessible, mathematical objects are not. Thus, Hersh was opposed to Quine's ontological position. Hersh was confused here because he was equating measurability and representation to existence. In the realist sense, the existence of an object does not require that it be known and measured by humans in an exact and precise manner. While the numeric representation of pi does not exist, one could not assert that π also does not exist. Actually, the ontological commitment made by Quine, in which mathematical objects are considered on par with physical objects, is strongly related to his holistic view of epistemology. While Quine asserted that logic/mathematics and physical sciences are different in many aspects, drawing a sharp distinction between them, such as placing logic/mathematics in the analytic camp and putting physical science on the synthetic side, is erroneous. In his well–known paper *Two dogmas of empiricism*, Quine (1951) bluntly rejected not only this dualism, but also reductionism, which will be discussed next.

Quine (1966/1976, originally published in 1936) challenged Carnap's notion that mathematics is reduced to logic and that logic is true by convention. Quine asserted that logic cannot be reduced to convention, because to derive anything from conventions one still needs logic. Carnap viewed logical and mathematical syntax as a formalization of meaning, but for Quine a formal system must be a formalization of some already meaningful discourse. Moreover, in rejecting the analytic–synthetic dichotomy, Quine rejected the notion that mathematics and logical truths are true definitions and we can construct a logical language through the selection of meaning. A definition is only a form of notation to express one term in form of others. Nothing of significance can follow from a definition itself. For example, in the regression equation, y=a+bx+e, where y is the outcome variable, x is the regressor, a is the slope, b is the beta weight, and e is the error term, these symbols cannot not help us to find truths; they are nothing more than a shorthand to express a wordy and complicated relationship. For Quine, meaning is a phenomenon of human agency. There is no meaning apart from what we can learn from interaction with the human community. In this sense, logical truths are not purely analytical; rather, constructing logic can be viewed as a type of empirical inquiry (Isaacson, 2000).

Quine (1951) asserted that there are no purely internal questions. Our commitment to a certain framework is never absolute, and no issue is entirely isolated from pragmatic concerns about the possible effects of the revisions of the framework. In Putnam's (1995) interpretation, Quine's doctrine implies that even so–called logical truths are subject to revision. This doctrine of revisibility is strongly tied to the holistic theme in Quine's philosophy. To be specific, the issue of what logic to accept is a matter of what logic, as a part of our actual science, fits the truth that we are establishing in the science that we engaged in (Isaacson, 2000). Logics are open to revision in light of new experience, background knowledge, and a web of theories. According to Quine's holism, mathematics, like logic, has to be viewed not by itself, but as a part of all–embracing conceptual scheme. In this sense, even so–called mathematical truths are subject to revision, too.

It is essential to further discuss two Quineian notions: revisability of terms and holism, because viewing these Quineian notions as opposition to Carnapian views is a mistake. According to Friedman (2002), criticism of Carnap by Quine is based on Quine's "misleading" assumption that analytic statements are said to be unrevisable. However, Carnap did not equate analyiticity to unrevisability. It is true that in Carnap's linguistic conventionalism logical and mathematical principles play a constitutive role. Nevertheless, even if we stay within the same framework, terms can be revised but their meanings would be changed. Further, we could move from one framework to another, whicn contains a different set of principles. Consequently, terms are revised in the process of framework migration.

According to Creath (1991), the holist view that Quine embraced in Quine's earlier career might be called radical holism. In Quine's view it is the totality of our beliefs which meets experience or not at all. French scientist Duhem was cited in defense of this holism, but Duhem's argument was not that extreme. In the Duhemian thesis, scientists do not test a single theory; instead, the test involves a web of hypotheses such as auxiliary assumptions associated with the main hypothesis. On the other hand, radical holism states that in theory testing the matter is concerned with whether the totality of our beliefs meets the experience. Creath (1991) criticized that if that is the case, then all our beliefs are equally well confirmed by experience and also are equally disposed to give up as another.

In Quine's later career (1990/1992), he modified his holist position to a moderate one, in which we test theories againist a critical mass rather than a totality. A critical mass is a big enough subset of science to imply what to expect from some observation or experiment. The size of this critical mass will vary from case to case. According to Friedman (2002), Carnap explicitly embraced certain portions of holism such as the Duhemian thesis. For Carnap, a linguistic framework is wholly predicated on the idea that logical principles, just like empirical ones, can be revised in light of a web of empirical science. In this sense, the philosophies of Quine and Carnap share the common ground based on the Duhemian thesis.

According to Pyle (1999), Quine viewed moderate holism as an answer to certain questions in philosophy of mathematics, which are central to Carnapian philosophy. Carnap asserted that mathematics is analytic and thus mathematics can be meaningful without empirical context. Moderate holism's answer is that mathematics absorbs the shared empirical content of the critical masses to which it contributes. In addition, Carnap's analytic position to mathematics makes mathematical truth necessary rather than contingent. Moderate holism's answer is that when a critical mass of sentences jointly implies a false prediction, we could choose what component sentence to revoke. On the other hand, we employ a maxim of "minimum mutilation" (conversativism) to guide our revision, and this accounts for mathematical necessity. Nevertheless, Carnap might not have objections to this, because as mentioned before, Carnap accepted revision of beliefs in light of empirical science. Indeed, moderate holism, as the guiding principle of mathematical and other scientific inquiries, is more reasonable and practical than radical holism.

Implications

Carnap's views on logic and mathematics, such as distinguishing between analytic–synthetic knowledge, reducing mathematics to logic and basing logic on convention, are problematic. Indeed, Quine has deeper insight than Carnap because he asserted that logic and mathematics are based on empirical input in the human community; and thus they are subject to revision.

Statistical theories and empirical evidence

There are many examples of mathematical theories that have been substantively revised in light of new evidence. How the newer Item Response Theory amends Classical True Score Theory is a good example. In the article "New rules of measurement," prominent statisticians Embretson and Reise (2000) explained why the conventional rules of measurement are inadequate and proposed another set of new rules, which are theoretically better and empirically substantiated. For example, the conventional theory states that the standard error of measurement applies to all scores in a particular population, but Embretson found that the standard error of measurement differs across scores but generalizes across populations.

In addition, R. A. Fisher criticized Neyman's statistical theory because Fisher asserted that mathematical abstraction to the neglect of scientific applications was useless. He mocked that Neyman was misled by algebraic symbolism (Howie, 2002). Interestingly enough, on some occasion Fisher was also confined by mathematical abstraction and algebraic symbolism. In the theory of maximum likelihood estimation, Fisher suggested that as sample size increases, the estimated parameter gets closer to closer to the true parameter (Eliason, 1993). But in the actual world, the data quality may decrease as the sample size increases. To be specific, when measurement instruments are exposed to the public, the pass rate would rise regardless of the examinee's ability. In this case the estimation might be farther away from the true parameter! Statisticians could not blindly trust the mathematical properties postulated in the Fisherian theorems.

Someone may argue that the preceding examples have too much "application," that they are concerned with the relation between a measurement theory and observations, not a "pure" relation among mathematical entities. Nevertheless, on some occasions, even the functional relationship among mathematical entities is not totally immune from empirical influence. For example, the Logit function, by definition, is the natural log of the odd ratio, which is the ratio between the success rate and the failure rate. However, in the context that the rate of failure is the focal interest of the model, the odd ratio can be reversed.

Putting statistical findings in the arena of "applied mathematics" seems to be an acceptable approach to dismissing the argument that mathematics is subject to revisions. Actually, the distinction between pure and applied mathematics is another form of dualism that attempts to place certain mathematics in the logical domain. In the following I argue that there is no sharp demarcation point between them, and mathematics, like the physical sciences, is subject to empirical verification. Empirically verifying mathematical theories does not mean using a mapping approach to draw correspondence between mathematical and physical objects. Counting two apples on the right hand side and two on the left is not a proof that 2+2=4. Instead, empirical verification in mathematics is implemented in computer–based Monte Carlo simulations, in which "behaviors" of numbers and equations are investigated.

Distinction between pure and applied mathematics

Conventionally speaking, mathematics is divided into pure mathematics and applied mathematics. There is a widespread belief that some branches of mathematics, such as statistics, orient toward application and thus are considered applied mathematics. Interestingly enough, in discussion of the philosophy of mathematics, philosophers tend to cite examples from "theoretical mathematics" such as geometry and algebra, but not "applied" mathematics such as statistics. Although I hesitate to totally tear down the demarcation between pure and applied mathematics, I doubt whether being so–called "pure" or "applied" is the "property" or "essence" of the discipline. As a matter of fact, geometry could be applied to architecture and civil engineering, while statistics can be studied without any reference to empirical measurement. To be specific, a t–test can be asked in an applied manner, such as "Does the IQ mean of Chinese people in Phoenix, Arizona significantly higher than that of Japanese people in the same city?" However, a t–test–related question can be reframed as "Can the mean difference between set A and set B be detected given that the Alpha level is 0.5, the power level is 0.75, both sets have unequal variances and numbers in each set are not normally distributed?" A research question could be directed to the t–test itself: "Would the actual Type I error rate equal the assumed Type I error rate when the Welch's t–test is applied to a non–normal sample of 30?"

A mathematician can study the last two preceding questions without assigning numbers to any measurement scale or formulating a hypothesis related to mental constructs, social events, or physical objects. He/she could generate numbers in computer to conduct a mathematical experiment. There is another widespread belief that computer–based experimental mathematics is applied mathematics while traditional mathematics is pure. A century ago our ancestors who had no computers relied on paper and pencil to construct theorems, equations, and procedures. Afterwards, they plugged in some numbers for verification. Today these tasks are performed in a more precise and efficient fashion with the aid of computers. However, it is strange to say that mathematics using pencil and paper is pure mathematics while that employing computers is applied.

In brief, I argue that the line between pure and applied mathematics is blurred. Conventional criteria for this demarcation are highly questionable; the subject matter (geometry or statistics) and the tool (pencil or computer) cannot establish the nature of mathematics (pure or applied). In the following discussion I will discuss how mathematicians use Monte Carlo simulations to support my argument that mathematics is not purely logical but rather has empirical elements. Next, I will use an example of a robustness study to demonstrate how traditional claims on certain statistical theories are revised by findings in simulations.

Computer–based experimental mathematics

With the advancement of high–powered computers, computer simulation is often employed by mathematicians and statisticians as a research methodology. This school is termed "experimental mathematics" and a journal entitled *Journal of Experimental Mathematics* is specifically devoted to this inquiry (Bailey & Borwein, 2001). Chaitin (1998), a supporter of experimental mathematics, asserted that it is a mistake to regard mathematical axioms as self–evident truths; rather the behaviors of numbers should be verified by computer–based experiments. It is important to differentiate the goal of experimentation in psychology, sociology, and engineering from that of experimental mathematics. In the former, the objective is to draw conclusions about mental constructs and physical objects, such as the treatment effectiveness of a counseling program or the efficiency of a microprocessor. In these inquiries, mathematical theories are the frame of reference for making inferences. But in the latter, the research question is directed to the mathematical theories themselves.

Both of them are considered "experiments" because conventional experimental criteria, such as random sampling, random assignment of group membership, manipulation of experimental variables, and control of non–experimental variables, are applied (Cook & Campbell, 1979). Interestingly enough, in terms of the degree of fulfillment of these experimental criteria, experimental mathematics has even more experimental elements than randomized or controlled experiments in the social sciences. Consider random sampling first. In social sciences, it is difficult, if not impossible, to collect true random samples. Usually the sample obtained by social scientists is just a convenient sample. For example, a researcher at Arizona State University may recruit participants in the Greater Phoenix area, but he/she rarely obtains subjects from Los Angeles, New York, Dallas, etc., let alone Hong Kong, Beijing, or Seoul. In terms of controlling extraneous variables or conditions that might have an impact on dependent variables, again social sciences face inherent limitations. Human subjects carry multiple dimensions such as personality, family background, religious beliefs, cultural context, etc. It is definitely impossible that the experimenter could isolate or control all other sources of influences outside the experimental setting. On the other hand, computer–based experiments achieve random sampling by using a random number generator. It is argued that some random number generators are not truly random, but the technology has become more and more sophisticated. Actually, even a slightly flawed random number generator could yield a more random sample than one collected in the human community. Also, computer–based experimental mathematics does not suffer the problem of lacking experimental control, because numbers and equations do not have psychological, social, political, religious or cultural dimensions. In brief, the preceding argument is to establish the notion that experimental mathematics is experimental in every traditional sense.

Monte Carlo simulations and robustness study

Traditional parametric tests, such as t–test and ANOVA, require certain parametric assumptions. Typical parametric assumptions are homogeneity of variances, which means the spread of distributions in each group do not significantly differ from each other, and normal distributions, which means the shape of the sample distribution is like a bell–curve. Traditional statistical theories state that the t–test is robust against mild violations of these assumptions; the Satterthwaite t–test is even more resistant against assumption violations; and the F–test in ANOVA is also robust if the sample size is large (please note that in these theories the sample can be composed of observations from humans or a set of numbers without any measurement unit). The test of homogeneity of variance is one the preliminary tests for examining whether assumption violations occur. Since conventional theories state that the preceding tests are robust, Box (1953) mocked the idea of testing the variances prior to applying an F–test: "To make a preliminary test on variances is rather like putting to sea in a rowing boat to find out whether conditions are sufficiently calm for an ocean liner to leave port!" (p. 333)

However, in recent years statisticians have been skeptical of the conventional theories. Different statisticians have proposed their own theories to counteract the problem of assumption violations (Yu, 2002). For instance,

(1) Some researchers construct non–parametric procedures to evade the problem of parametric test assumptions. As the name implies, non–parametric tests do not require parametric assumptions because interval data are converted to rank–ordered data. Examples of non–parametric tests are the Wilcoxon signed rank test and the Mann–Whitney–Wilcoxon test. Some version of non–parametric method is known as order statistics for its focus on using rank–ordered data. A typical example of it is Cliff's statistics (Cliff, 1996).

(2) To address the violation problem, some statisticians introduce robust calculations such as Trimmed means and Winsorized means. The trimmed mean approach is to exclude outliers in the two tails of the distribution while the Winsorized mean method "pulls" extreme cases toward the center of the distribution. The Winsorized method is based upon Winsor's principle: All observed distributions are Gaussian in the middle. Other robust procedures such as robust regression involve differential weighting to different observations. In the trimmed mean approach outliers are given a zero weighting while robust regression may assign a "lighter" count, say 0.5, to outliers. Cliff (1996), who endorsed order statistics, was skeptical of the differential weighting of robust procedures. He argued that data analysis should follow the principle of "one observation, one vote." Mallows and Tukey (1982) also argued against Winsor's principle. In their view, since this approach pays too much attention to the very center of the distribution, it is highly misleading. Instead, Tukey (1986) strongly recommended using data re–expression procedures, which will be discussed next.

(3) In data re–expression, linear or non–linear equations are applied to the data. When the normality assumption is violated, the distribution could be normalized through re–expression. If the variances of two groups are unequal, certain transformation techniques can be used to stabilize the variances. In the case of non–linearity, this technique can be applied to linearize the data. However, Cliff (1996) argued that data transformation confines the conclusion to the arbitrary version of the variables.

(4) Resampling techniques such as the randomization exact test, jackknife, and bootstrap are proposed by some other statisticians as a counter measure against parametric assumption violations (Diaconis & Efron, 1983; Edgington, 1995; Efron & Tibshirani, 1993; Ludbrook & Dudley, 1998; Yu, 2003). Robust procedures recognize the threat of parametric assumption violations and make adjustments to work around the problem. Data re–expression converts data in order to conform to the parametric assumptions. Resampling is very different from the above remedies, for it is not under the framework of theoretical distributions imposed by classical parametric procedures. For example, in bootstrapping, the sample is duplicated many times and treated as a virtual population. Then samples are drawn from this virtual population to construct an empirical sampling distribution. In short, the resampling school replaces theoretical distributions with empirical distributions. In reaction against resampling, Stephen E. Fienberg criticized that "you're trying to get something for nothing. You use the

same numbers over and over again until you get an answer that you can't get any other way. In order to do that, you have to assume something, and you may live to regret that hidden assumption later on" (as cited in Peterson, 1991, p. 57).

It is obvious that statisticians such as Winsor, Tukey, Cliff, and Fienberg do not agree with each other on the assumption violation and robustness reinforcement issues. If different mathematical systems, as Russell and Whitehead suggested, are self–contained systems, and if mathematics, as Carnap maintained, is reduced to logic that is based on different conventions, these disputes would never come to a conclusive closure. Within the system of Winsor's school, the Gaussian distribution is the ideal and all other associated theorems tend to support Winsor's principle. Within the Tukey's convention, the logic of re–expression fits well with the notions of distribution normalization, variance stabilization, and trend linearization.

It is important to note that these disputes are not about how well those statistical theories could be applied to particular subject matters such as psychology and physics. Rather, these statistical questions could be asked without reference to measurement, and this is the core argument of the school of data re–expression. For example, researchers who argue against data re–expression complain that it would be absurd to obtain a measurement of people's IQ and then transform the data like [new variable = 1/(square root of IQ)]. They argue that we could conclude that the average IQ of the Chinese people in Phoenix is significantly higher than that of the Japanese, but it makes no sense to say anything about the difference in terms of 1/(square root of IQ). However, researchers supporting data re–expression argue that the so–called IQ is just a way of obtaining certain numbers, just like using meters or feet to express height. Numbers can be manipulated in their own right without being mapped onto physical measurement units. In a sense non–parametric statistics and order statistics are forms of data re–expression. For example, when we obtain a vector of scores such as [15, 13, 11, 8, 6], we can order the scalars within the vector as [1, 2, 3, 4, 5]. This "transformation" no doubt alters the measurement and, indeed, loses the precision of the original measurement. Nevertheless, these examples demonstrate that statistical questions can be studied regardless of the measurement units, or even without any measurements. Monte Carlo simulation is a typical example of studying statistics without measurement.

As you may notice in the section regarding bootstrapping, statisticians do not even need empirical data obtained from observations to conduct a test; they could "duplicate" data by manipulating existing observations. In bootstrapping, number generation is still based on empirical observations, whereas in Monte Carlo simulations all numbers could be generated in computer only. In recent years, robustness studies using Monte Carlo simulations have been widely employed to evaluate the soundness of mathematical procedures in terms of their departure from idealization and robustness against assumption violations. In Monte Carlo simulations, mathematicians make up strange data (e.g. extremely unequal variances, non–normality) to observe how well those mathematical procedures are robust against the violations. Box is right that we cannot row a boat to test the condition for an ocean liner. But using computers to simulate multi–million cases under hundreds scenarios is really the other way around—now we are testing the weather condition with an ocean liner to tell us whether rowing a boat is safe. Through computer simulations we learn that traditional claims concerning the robustness of certain procedures are either invalid or require additional constraints.

There are numerous Monte Carlo studies in the field of statistics. A recent thorough Monte Carlo study (Thompson, Green, Stockford, Chen, & Lo, 2002; Stockford, Thompson, Lo, Chen, Green, & Yu, 2001) demonstrates how experimental mathematics could refute, or at least challenge, the conventional claims in statistical theories. This study investigates the Type I error rate and statistical power of the various statistical procedures. The Type I error rate is the probability of falsely rejecting the null hypothesis, whereas the statistical power is the probability of correctly rejecting the null hypothesis. In this study, statistical procedures under investigation include the conventional independent–samples t–test, the Satterthwaite t–test, the Mann–Whitney–Wilcoxon test (non–parametric test), the test for the difference in trimmed means (robust procedure), and the bootstrap test of the difference in trimmed means (resampling and robust methods). Four factors were manipulated to create 180 conditions: form of the population distribution, variance heterogeneity, sample size, and mean differences. Manipulation of these factors is entirely under the control of the experimenters. No other non–experimental factors could sneak into the computer and affect the conditions. The researchers concluded that the conventional t–test, the Satterthwaite t–test, and the Mann–Whitney–Wilcoxon test produce either poor Type I error rates or loss of power when the assumptions underlying them are violated. The tests of trimmed means and the bootstrap test appear to have fewer difficulties across the range of conditions evaluated. This experimental study indicates that the robustness claims by two versions of the t–test and one of the non–parametric procedures are invalid. On the other hand, one of the robust methods and one of the resampling methods are proved to be true in terms of robustness. Although the scope of this study is narrowed to one of each statistical school, the same approach can be applied to various versions of parametric tests, non–parametric tests, robust procedures, data re–expression methods, and resampling.

Conclusion

The above findings are not achieved by the methods suggested by Russell and Carnap, such as the study of logical relationships, truth by definitions or truth by convention. Rather, the claims result from experimental study. When Quine introduced his philosophical theory on logic and mathematics, computer technology and the Monte Carlo method were not available. Nonetheless, his insight is highly compatible with recent development in experimental mathematics. I strongly believe that if researchers put aside the analytic–synthetic distinction by adopting Quine's moderate holistic view to scientific inquiry, many disputes could come to a conclusive closure. Indeed, a holistic approach has been beneficial to statistics. Although Fisher was a statistician, he was also versed in biology and agriculture science, and indeed most of his theorems were derived from such empirical fields. Winsor's principle is based on the Gaussian distribution, but Gauss discovered the Gaussian distribution through astronomical observations. Survival analysis or the hazard model is the fruit of medical and sociological research. As discussed before, Embretson and Reise, as psychologists, used the psychometric approach to revise traditional measurement theories. The example of robustness study demonstrates how social scientists employed Monte Carlo studies to challenge traditional claims in mathematics and statistics. As Quine's holism proposed, logic, mathematics, observation, and a web of scientific theories are strongly linked to each other.

Chapter 5 Philosophical issues of factor analysis

Factor model as measurement model

Many people equate quantitative research with statistical analysis. In reality, statistics is only a subset of data analysis, and data analysis is only one of three components of quantitative research, namely, research design, measurement, and data analysis. Discussion of research design is beyond the scope of this chapter. The focus here is on factor analysis as a measurement model. Generally speaking, measurement is a process of assigning numbers to the attributes and properties of some observable entity or event. Bond and Fox (2001) asserted the importance of measurement by saying that although psychologists and other researchers in human sciences have been effective in applying sophisticated statistical procedures to their data, there is no way to compensate for bad measurement with good statistical procedures. Factor analysis plays an indispensable role in measurement because of its ability to verify construct validity, which pertains to whether the instrument measures the construct that it is supposed to measure. The history of factor analysis can be traced back as far as the early 20th century. Although this long history of development would arguably facilitate the maturation of factor analysis, debates about controversial issues of this methodology, some philosophical and some non–philosophical, are ongoing. This chapter will concentrate on the philosophical aspect. It does not attempt to resolve all of these ontological, epistemological, and methodological issues; rather, the goal is to outline these issues in order to stimulate readers toward further inquiry.

The factor model is also known as the latent construct model, the latent variable model, or the measurement model. The term “latent variable model” may be misleading since “variables” usually refer to observed items while “factors” and “constructs” refer to theoretical entities that can not be directly observed. Thus, throughout this chapter the term “latent factor” or “latent construct” is used instead.

A measurement model, as its name implies, is about measurement and data collection. A factor model identifies the relationship between observed items and latent factors. For example, when a psychologist wants to study the causal relationships between anxiety and job performance, first he/she has to define the constructs “anxiety” and “job performance.” To accomplish this step, about the psychologist needs to develop items that measure the defined construct. Next, the psychologist employs Cronbach's alpha to evaluate the internal consistency of observed items (Yu, 2001), and also applies factor analysis to extract latent constructs from these consistent observed variables. If the factor structure indicates that the observed items cluster around one eigenvector, which is the graphical representation of factors in subject space, the construct is said to be unidimensional.

The relationship between factors and observed variables is indicated in Figure 5.1. The ellipse represents a latent construct, and the rectangles represent observed variables, which are individual items in a scale. The circles denote measurement errors.

Figure 5.1. Factor model

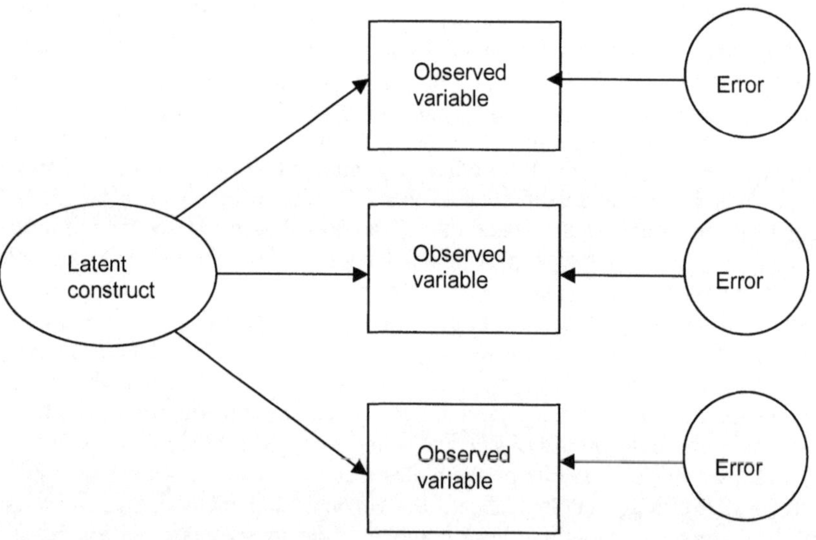

It is important to note that every measurement includes some degree of measurement error. The purpose of Cronbach Alpha is to estimate the test score reliability (r) in terms of the measurement error (e). In other words, reliability and measurement error are in a "see–saw" relationship (r = 1 – e). Factor analysis is a form of triangulation that attempts to minimize measurement error. For example, if an instructor gives a test with only one question and judges whether the student is competent based on the response to this single item, even someone who does not have any statistical training could tell that this assessment is unfair. By giving more items in a test, however, the measurement errors might cancel each other out, and thus the test score would become more reliable.

CFA and EFA: Friend or foe?

It is important for researchers to distinguish Exploratory Factor Analysis (EFA) from Confirmatory Factor Analysis(CFA) (Thompson, 2004). EFA is a data–driven procedure developed in the early 20th century that aims to find common threads among variables (Thurstone, 1947), while CFA, developed in the late 1960s and the 1970s (Joreskog, 1969, 1970, 1971, 1974, 1980; Joreskog & Sorbom, 1979), is a procedure to verify the already identified relationships between constructs and observed variables. CFA can be viewed as a subset of SEM. Indeed, usually CFA is computed by software applications for SEM, such as LISREL, EQS, and PROC CALIS in SAS. In CFA the researcher has no room to explore the data. One must specify a factor structure in advance; the goal of CFA is to evaluate the fit between the data and the pre–constructed factor model. Thus, CFA results do not need rotation to enhance interpretation. It is also noteworthy that the term "confirmatory" should not be taken literally, otherwise, it may mislead users to think that CFA can prove the truth of a model. Actually, what CFA does is to indicate the fit between the model and the data. It is not uncommon for a researcher to use a collection of data sets for EFA in developing a factor model and then use another collection of data sets to confirm the claimed factor structure (Kieffer, 1999).

Philosopher of science Glymour (2001) expressed severe criticism of factor analysis. To be specific, he regarded widespread application of factor analysis as a sign of system–wide failure in the social sciences in terms of causal interpretations. Strangely enough, as a strong advocate of Structural Equation Modeling, an extension of CFA, Glymour is very critical of this latent construct approach. By reviewing the history of psychometrics, Glymour concluded that reliability (a stable factor structure) was never a goal of early psychometricians. Thurstone faced the problem that there were many competing factor models that were statistically equivalent. For the purpose of "saving the phenomena" (uniquely determining the factor loadings), he developed the criterion of the simple structure, which has no special measure–theoretic virtue or special stability properties. In addition, Glymour stated that with finite samples, factor analysis may fail to recover the true causal structure because of statistical or algorithmic artifacts. Moreover, factor analysis, as a latent construct approach, assumes local independence, which means that the response to one item is independent of that to another. This is always violated to some degree, however, since the responses given to earlier questions may influence the responses given to later questions.

Glymour is not alone. Several other scholars have criticized factor analysis using a historical approach. For example, Abbott (1998) argued that early psychometricians viewed factor analysis as a mathematical convenience to reduce complex data to simple forms in order to reconcile quantitative data with intuitive categories. Laudan (1977) also classified psychometrics in the early 20th century as a "non–standard research tradition" because it did not have a strong ontology and metaphysics. Rather, he asserted, its assumption is "little more than the conviction that mental phenomena could be mathematically represented" (p. 105).

It is true that Thurstone sometimes referred to theoretical entities as "convenient postulates," but he did not deny the possibility of some degree of correspondence between constructs and reality. While discussing the origin and development of factor analysis, Vincent (1953) asserted that factor analysis is an attempt to identify the causes that are operating to produce the variance and to evaluate the contribution of each cause. In his view, the argument among early psychometricians was concerned with whether one common cause or multiple causes were appropriate.

Even if factor analysis was a–causal, a–ontological, or a–theoretical at its early stage of development, this doesn't necessary imply that factor analysis today should continue to be interpreted in a non–causal fashion. If someone denies factor analysis just because their ideas depart from those of the approach's founding fathers, it is like rejecting the design of a V–8 engine just because it violates the idea of Henry Ford's Model T.

The problems cited by Glymour are not insurmountable. Measurement errors due to dependent items could be rectified by randomizing the order of items for each subject. The issues of factor indeterminacy and statistical artifacts will be covered in detail in a later section about the debate between Maraun and Mulaik. Nonetheless, Glymour is not the first to question the value of factor analysis. Back in 1980 Liska said,

> Apparently, it is easy to find semantic scales which seem relevant to (information) sources, so easy to name or describe potential/hypothetical sources, so easy to capture college students to use the scales to rate the sources, so easy to submit those ratings to factor analysis, so much fun to name the factors when one's research assistant returns with the computer printout, and so rewarding to have a guaranteed publication with no fear of non–significant results that researchers, once exposed to the pleasures of the factor analytic approach, rapidly become addicted (as cited in Thompson, 2004, p. 6).

Thompson correctly pointed out that these criticisms apply more to EFA than to CFA, because the major shortcoming in EFA is that factors are undetermined and thus cannot be clearly interpreted. But CFA presumes the specifications of an expected factor structure, with the possibility that the pre–determined theory does not fit the data, in which case the researcher would not have the freedom to extract anything out of the computer printouts.

Nevertheless, it is important for us to distinguish a bad researcher who arbitrarily misuses the methodology from a bad methodology. Even though EFA could potentially be misused, it is still an indispensable tool. In spite of the alleged shortcomings of EFA, quite a few researchers have still employed both EFA and CFA in a complimentary fashion. For example, Thompson developed a hybrid method that integrates both EFA and CFA (1992). Moreover, through Monte Carlo simulations, Gerbing and Hamilton (1996) re–affirmed the merits of EFA. For them, when the underlying factor structure is not well–understood,

EFA's lack of prior specifications is a strength rather than a weakness. In a strict sense, even CFA is a mixture of exploratory and confirmatory techniques in the sense that the end product is derived in part from theory and in part from a re–specification based on the analysis of the fitness indices. Gerbing and Hamilton yielded findings that may seem surprising to many people: many EFA techniques, such as orthogonal varimax rotation and oblique promax rotation, can recover the correct factor structure except in small sample sizes with relatively high correlated factors. Thus, they concluded that EFA is a useful tool to aid the researcher in recovering an underlying measurement model that can be subsequently evaluated with CFA.

At first glance, the weaknesses of EFA appear to be so serious that they render EFA an ineffective methodology. However, problems of EFA also occur in CFA in one way or the other, though the degree of these problems may be smaller. Take the violation of independence cited by Glymour as an example. It is very true that item responses may be interrelated, but the same problem also applies to CFA. This inherent measurement error would not go away even if the researcher analyzed the data in a confirmatory mode.

Factor indeterminacy poses a serious challenge to modelers who employ EFA for generating hypotheses. Nonetheless, CFA also suffers from another type of indeterminacy, namely, model equivalency. Contrary to the popular belief that there are only a finite number of models equivalent to a hypothesized covariance structure model, Raykov and Marcoulides (2001) illustrated that there could be infinitely many models in a hypothesized model. Bartholomew (2002) gave a concrete example: a latent construct model with one factor was fitted to the data set collected from the Law School Admissions Test (LSAT); however, a two–factor model was also fitted to the same data, and the results for the two models were virtually indistinguishable. In short, CFA is not immune to the problem of indeterminacy. Uncertainty is an integral part of all scientific inquiries, and so conducting research with a more sophisticated tool in a confirmatory fashion does not mean that the researcher will yield true causal inferences. In the next section, the issue of ambiguity and factor indeterminacy will be addressed.

EFA as information–transformation instrument

Descriptive and incorrigible data for corrigible inquiry

EFA and CFA seem to work harmoniously hand in hand if the former is viewed as a mechanism of construct extraction or model generation while the latter is used to confirm the findings output by the former. Debate would stop here if common consent on the epistemological status of EFA and CFA could be reached. However, this is hardly the case. For example, Baird (1987) argued that EFA is merely an information–transformation or data reexpression operation, like summarizing the correlational data in a linear equation or loading variables into a simple structure. What it produces is not knowledge or a hypothesis, but only condensed data that may or may not be useful. To be specific, Baird summarized the characteristics of information–transformation instruments produced by EFA as the following:

1. *Hypotheses not output.* Instruments do not produce or test hypothesis. Take the output of an imaging device as a metaphor. An image produced by a microscope is not a hypothesis; rather, it is just information represented through an optical process. Also, consider descriptive statistics. The United States Bureau of the Census informs us that the population of South Carolina in 1930 was 1,739,000 and that this state occupied 30,495 square miles. These two pieces of information can be re–expressed by stating that there were 57 people per square mile in South Carolina, but there is nothing theoretical or hypothetical about this population density. Factor structure yielded from EFA should be treated in the same manner.

2. *Instruments summarize information.* EFA, as a data reduction process, may lose or distort some information, but this is not a criticism of EFA. Take optical imaging as a metaphor again. Telescopes also ignore information outside the visible spectrum.

3. *Instruments can produce artifacts.* Instruments can produce measurement artifacts that may not have any significant meaning related to the subject matter under investigation, just as early microscopes were plagued by many sources of distortion, such as chromatic and spherical aberrations.

4. *Instruments are best used interactively.* We come to understand and trust the output of an instrument as we manipulate it during study. Baird made this point in order to emphasize that the mathematical structure yielded from EFA should not be treated as invariant truth; rather, the meaning and usefulness of the factor model may vary from context to context [try to provide an imaging example for consistency, since an example is used in the other five points].

5. *Preparation of input.* Input to an instrument must be specifically selected. To be specific, instruments summarize data by focusing only on certain kinds of properties in the input. For instance, to get useful information about cells from a microscope, the cells need to be colored in order to enhance the appearance of its distinct features. By the same token, factor structure may not stand out unless certain rotation schemes for the Eigenvectors are applied.

6. *Theory of the instrument differs from theory using the instrument.* Making and refining a microscope belongs to the domain of optical science. A biologist does not need to know the mechanics of the lenses to successfully extract information from microscopic observation.

All of the above points to a coherent thesis: EFA is nothing more than an instrument that describes summarized data. Baird argued that the process of *interpreting* the factor structure is extrinsic to the process of factor analysis. In other words, this type of interpretation is not based upon the intrinsic mathematical properties of the factor model. The usefulness of the instrument is a matter to be determined at the level of application, not instrumentation. In the geometric space, no one can argue about how the linear equation is computed or how the sum of squares of factor loadings equals the Eigenvalue, but one can argue about what it means in the psychological territory. Thus, the EFA provides incorrigible data which could be treated as evidence to test or suggest a corrigible hypothesis.

Foundationalist epistemology

However, these points were not convincing to Mulaik (1991). For Mulaik these six theses fail to provide an adequate account of how information–transformation instruments are to be used in science. Moreover, Mulaik argued that these points rest on the outmoded foundationalist epistemology.

First, Mulaik criticized that Baird mistakenly reduced EFA to a process of running algorithms using correlation or covariance matrix. Indeed, EFA should be taken holistically by including both computation and interpretation. In other words, the end output of EFA is not just the number of factors and the factor loadings for each variable, but also the corresponding latent constructs in sociological or psychological domains. I concur with Mulaik's holistic view of EFA. Some output that is mathematically sound may not have meaningful sociological or psychological implications. In Baird's terms, the output may be nothing more than some mathematical artifact. Consider this case: a test developer authored items to measure both verbal and logical intelligence, but it turns out that some items meant to measure verbal skills are loaded into the logical factor, or all items, regardless of content, are loaded into one single factor. What would the test developer do? A responsible test developer would carefully examine the content and the wording of those problematic items. An iterative process of rewriting, dropping, and inserting items and re–running EFA is inevitable. As Baird suggested in thesis four, instruments must be used in an interactive fashion. It is hard to imagine that any researcher could demarcate data reexpression and data interpretation. In short, it seems that Baird created an unnecessary dichotomy between computation and interpretation while in practice the two are interwoven.

Further, Mulaik criticized that Baird's view on EFA echoes the Pearsonian philosophy of science, in which statistical methodology is regarded as merely descriptive (see Chapter 1), as well as foundationalism, which maintains that our knowledge must be based on some incorrigible foundation, such as objective mathematical structures. As a counter argument to Baird, Mulaik took the position that science is a normative practice embedded in a social context. A normative practice is like a game, in which activities are bound by rules. Rules do not intrinsically cause or determine action in the sense that one is free not to follow rules. However, there are external rewarding systems that guide our action. Scientists are trained in certain ways of making observations and using instruments. A layman may look through the microscope a thousand times but never "see" any outstanding features of a cell. In contrast, a trained biologist, using the same instrument, can identify certain cellular structures because he/she has a specific way of seeing things. Put bluntly, that is a normative practice. Factor analysis is not an exception. Assigning variables to certain factors is not a purely computational matter; rather, it is a normative process.

Again, I side with Mulaik in this point. Choosing between orthogonal and oblique rotations is a good example. When we have sound reason to believe that all factors should be independent, an orthogonal rotation seems to be a wise choice. However, in the social sciences there is always some degree of correlation among factors, and thus an oblique rotation is more appropriate. Obviously, choosing a mathematical procedure to summarize the data requires knowledge that is *external* to data structures and mathematical axioms. It is a normative process based upon how the data are related to the worldly matter under study.

Reichenbach's common cause principle

Reichenbach's (1956) common cause principle (CCP) is said to be the philosophical justification for factor modeling. The idea of CCP is that simultaneous correlated events must have prior common causes. When X, Y, and Z are correlated but actually A is the common cause of X, Y, and Z, A is said to be the screener that screens off the pseudo causal relations among X, Y, and Z. This reasoning can be applied effectively to factor analysis for inferring the existence of a latent cause (Glymour, Scheines, Spirtes, & Kelly, 1987). Oddly enough, the argument *for* the intersections of mathematics and interpretation can be approached from the perspective of arguments *against* Reichenbach's CCP. Arntzenius (2005, 1992) argued that CCP does not appear to be universally valid because, given any finite set of correlations in a classical event structure, one can always say that the correlation is due to some common or hidden cause. The following cases are some of the counter–examples:

1. *Law of evolution.* The bread prices in the United Kingdom have been gradually going up over the last few centuries. During the same period of time, the water levels in Venice have also been rising. Although there is a statistical relationship between bread prices in Britain and sea levels in Venice, using common sense or empirical evidence we can assert that there is presumably no direct causation involved, nor is there a common cause. Moreover, Elliot Sober (1988) suggested that similar laws of evolution of independent quantities can lead to correlations for which no common cause exists. In other words, evolutions of species are a temporal–based correlation that could happen independently.

2. *Macroscopic event.* Cleopatra wants to sacrifice fifty slaves to appease the gods during a party. In spite of her unchallenged power, it is difficult for her to simply order slaves to kill themselves. To show her fairness, she decides to give them a chance. She has obtained a very strong poison that can kill a person with only one molecule of it. Then she puts this poison in each of a hundred goblets of wine for one hundred slaves. If one consumes the poison, death is

preceded by an ominous reddening of both hands. In this case, the molecule being in the consumed half of the wine glass will be a *prior screener off* of the correlation between left hand and right hand reddening. Since death occurs in the exact cases in which the poison is swallowed, death will be a *posterior screener off.* If one restricts oneself to macroscopic events, there will only be a posterior screener off. If death is not strictly determined by the swallowing or non–swallowing of the poison, there will be no macroscopic screener off at any time. Thus, if microscopic events can have such macroscopic consequences, a common cause principle cannot hold for macroscopic events.

3. *Statespace correlation*. There is a list of pairs of observed values for two observables, each with possible values 1 and 0. If the value of one of the observations is 1, the other is always 0, and vice versa. This constitutes a perfect correlation and thus suggests a common cause or a latent factor. But actually, this phenomenon is a particle bouncing around in a closed system. The particle always positions either in the left or the right side of the system. This statespace correlation has neither a common cause nor a latent factor.

4. *Equilibrium state*. In a city there is a statistical relationship between the take–off time of airplanes and the time clothes take to dry in residences near the airport. By CCP the probable explanation is that high humidity causes both long drying times and long take–off times. This explanation assumes that the humidity at the airport and at nearby houses is actually related, but it is not true that the humidity in one area directly causes the humidity in another area. Rather, the explanation for this statistical relationship is that when the total system is in an equilibrium state, the humidity in different areas is almost identical. Indeed this type of equilibrium state is ubiquitous in the world and thus an explanation by specific common causes is unnecessary.

5. *Markovian indeterministic process*. Suppose that water in a tea cup is stirred in one direction and there is a ball inside the cup. The surface of the water is divided into four sections, namely S1, S2, S3, and S4. The flow in the tea cup is circular but quite turbulent; consequently the motion of the ball is irregular. Suppose that in about half the cases this ball crosses the boundary between two sections in the forward direction, and in half the cases it crosses no boundaries; it very rarely crosses a boundary in the backward direction or crosses more than one boundary in the forward direction. Taking all these into account, one can conclude a statistical relationship between the ball being in S1 and being in S2, being in S2 and being S3, being S3 and being in S4. This phenomenon is considered a Markovian indeterministic process, but obviously there is no common cause.

6. *Order out of chaos*. When one lowers the temperature of certain minerals, the spins of all atoms of the minerals will line up in the same direction. If one selects any two atoms in this structure, one can observe that their spins are correlated. However, it is not the case that lowering the temperature is the common cause. Actually, lowering the temperature determines that the orientations of atoms will be correlated, but not the directions in which they will line up. A similar example is a fluid in a box in thermodynamic equilibrium. Originally the

directions of motion of nearby modules are uncorrelated. But after heating one end of the box and cooling the other end, convection currents occur; the directions of the motions of nearby modules are highly correlated. However, there is no common cause that screens the motions of nearby modules from each other. The external constraints cause some change in the module motion, but they cannot determine how the motions will turn out. These are classical examples of order out of chaos that do not necessitate CCP.

7. *Law of coexistence*. In all frames of reference, Maxwell's equations imply simultaneous relations between charge distributions and electromagnetic fields. In other words, electromagnetism implies that there is a simultaneous correlation between the state of the field on a particular surface and the charge distribution in the region contained by that surface. This correlation must hold even on the space–like boundary at the beginning of the universe, but obviously this type of coexistence law cannot be explained by CCP. In a broader sense, Newtonian gravitation and Pauli's exclusion principle can also be regarded as coexistence laws that violate CCP.

Arntzenius cited these examples to support the notion that CCP is not universally valid. This is correct. Glymour (1999a) pointed out a widespread misconception that scientific laws are universal, but indeed even laws in physics are not valid in all situations. Take the law of the Pendulum as an example. It is not a law of physics in any unconditioned sense. On the contrary, it assumes an endless array of conditions: gravity does not change in the meantime, the length of the pendulum rod remains constant, friction is absent, there is no interference with the motion of the pendulum, etc. Likewise, Woodward (2003) also argued that scientific laws are not universal by citing the example that Coulomb's law holds in the classic regime, but fails to hold in the realm of quantum mechanics. Like CCP, one can cite numerous cases to invalidate the law of the pendulum or Coulomb's law and other scientific laws. Thus, certain counter examples can limit the applications of a principle or a law, but do not entirely invalidate it. The main point here is that Arntzenius used empirical examples to demonstrate how a mathematical relationship, no matter how strong it is, does not necessarily lead to a sensible conclusion (common cause, latent factor). Interestingly enough, the preceding counter–examples against CCP and its application, factor analysis, can be turned around to argue for the merit of factor analysis in the fashion of Mulaik's implementation. Arntzenius's counter–examples warn us against treating EFA as a matter of pure mathematics. Whether there is a common cause or a latent factor requires careful examination of the scenario under study.

Statistical artifact

Mulaik criticized the inadequacy of Baird's definition of "artifact," which confines the meaning of artifact to measurement errors or noise alone. To Mulaik artifact has a further meaning: even an "objective" statistical description without measurement errors can be treated as an artifact if the ontological status of this description is misinterpreted. For example, in the 18th century Quetelet computed a sample of Scottish men and hence introduced the notion of "average man." Terminology of statistics reflects this kind of "average man" thinking by naming a bell–shaped distribution as the "normal" distribution and those who deviate from the norm as "errors." Mulaik treated the "average man fallacy," which regards the average value of a population of measurements as having an objective reality, as a form of statistical artifact. Mulaik cited another example of artifact in the history of factor analysis: during the early development of factor analysis, Spearman proposed the general factor, also known as the G factor, along with the centroid method, whereas Hotelling endorsed the application of the principal component. But Thurstone rejected both Spearman's and Hotelling's methods in favor of the simple structure because those methods are defined in terms of idealized test vectors and thus can produce mathematical artifacts. In brief, artifactuality is no longer associated with flawed measurement; it could result from subjective interpretation of descriptive mathematics.

In Mulaik's theoretical framework, artifactuality is closely related to the idea of *subjectivity with objectivity*. At first glance, the term "subjectivity with objectivity" is an oxymoron, but Mulaik argued that objectivity essentially arises out of the conditions under which one has subjective experience of an object. In other words, one cannot have a concept of an object without the concept of a subject, of their distinctness and of their inter–relationship. Again, objectivity should be viewed as a normative, regulative idea according to the rules set by the intellectual community. So–called "objective knowledge" is not knowledge about how things are independent of experience or some incorrigible description of the world. Rather, it is a *functional* concept. Even in experimental science, our experience of physical objects is mediated by a complex web of theory–laden instruments. In the context of EFA, it is inevitable that the mathematical structure is functionally mapped to the psychological or sociological domain because one cannot report something without making interpretations, as illustrated in the examples that a test developer must go through an iterative process of revising items and re–running EFA, and a researcher must choose between orthogonal and oblique factor rotations according to prior knowledge of the subject matter.

Factor indeterminacy in EFA

Mathematico–grammatical issue

Due to its exploratory nature, sometimes EFA leads to ambiguous results that may be open to interpretation, and in some cases observed variables could be loaded into more than one factor, which thus generates the problem of factor indeterminacy. Although Mulaik saw computation and interpretation as inseparable in EFA, Maraun (1996) argued that resolving indeterminacy in EFA through interpretation is problematic. The central thesis of Maraun's view on factor indeterminacy is that it is a mathematico–grammatical issue. Subscribing to Wittgenstein's position that meaning in language is fixed by rules, Maraun asserted that the claim "X is a latent common factor to Y" is justified by the criterion of mathematical rules. Usually social scientists present "factors" in the form of "underlying factors," "causal factors," or "hypothesized factors," which have certain empirical, psychological, or sociological connotations. But there is no translation rule to bridge the mathematical and the empirical rules. So–called "underlying factors," "causal factors," or "hypothesized factors" are nothing more than metaphors, but unfortunately these metaphors are taken as "myths." To Maraun factor analysis cannot act as a litmus test for the presence or absence of latent constructs. At first glance Maraun's position is like the demarcation of computation and interpretation proposed by Baird (1987), but Maraun went further to claim that there is no solution to factor indeterminacy because it is a grammatical property of the model: that is, it is a result of the very formulation of the model. In this sense Maraun's position seems to be more radical than Baird's. At least Baird viewed EFA as a tool for producing incorrigible and descriptive data for corrigible scientific inquiry. In Maraun's framework, results yielded from mathematical rules or a linguistic convention can hardly be "incorrigible" or "descriptive," especially when factor indeterminacy is viewed as insurmountable within the grammatical system.

Underdetermination and inductive fallacy

In response to the notion that factor indeterminacy is irresolvable, Mulaik contended that underdetermination of concepts is tied to some forms of indeterminacy, such as Goodman's (1954/1983) "new riddle of induction" (See Chapter 3). Factor indeterminacy is just another variant of the indeterminacy of induction. Perceptual experience plays a partial role in determining objective percepts and concepts, thus leaving room for indeterminacy, yet this kind of indeterminacy can be reduced by social agreement on rules. Long before this debate occurred, Mulaik (1987) had asserted that data by themselves are never sufficient to determine theories for generalizing inductively beyond the data. Inductive methods of generating theory always have an indeterminate element in them. Failure to recognize this limitation leads to inductive fallacy.

Grammar by convention

Mulaik's (1996a, 1996b) other counter arguments against the mathematical–grammatical view of Maraun are similar to his arguments against Baird. Indeed, his standpoint can be summarized by the title of one of his articles (1996a): *Factor analysis is not just a model in pure mathematics*. Mulaik agreed with Maraun that meaning in a linguistic convention is fixed and constituted by rules. But their agreement ends here. Mulaik departed from Maraun by asserting that the language game of common factor analysis is not just played in the realm of pure mathematics; it is also about things in the world. He emphasized that factor indeterminacy could be resolved by assigning an empirical referent for a common factor of the model. The rationale is as follows: even though attributes of objects, including mathematical attributes, exist independently of observers, the attributes do not always exist in our perception. Rather, our accumulated experience helps us to see things that we could not see before. The grammar of rules does not exist independently of human beings. Instead, rules and conventions are developed from our experience. Saying that a factor exists in a purely mathematical world, in which its intrinsic properties are defined by self–contained rules, is like saying that a triangle is a geometric figure because its criterion of identity is internal to geometry. But in applying geometry to surveying, a triangle is defined by three points, each on a different mountain peak, thus giving it a criterion of identity not exclusive to geometry.

Again, I tend to support Mulaik's position because confining explanations of mathematical objects within the mathematical world is problematic. There are many examples of mathematical theories that have been substantively revised in light of new evidence from our experience outside the mathematical realm. This point has been thoroughly discussed in the previous chapter and thus will not be repeated here. To paraphrase Mulaik, factor analysis is not a model in pure mathematics because there may be no distinct demarcation between pure and applied mathematics.

Realism and latent constructs

Realism of the unobservable

Baird and Maraun never mentioned anti–realism or implied any anti–realist orientation. At most their notion tends to support the demarcation between mathematics and interpretation and to frame factor indeterminacy in the mathematico–grammatical domain. To some extent it is like Carnap's (1956, 1971) notion of maintaining the dichotomy between analytic and synthetic knowledge, and also classifying mathematical questions as internal questions appealing to logic and convention. Arguing for this dichotomy does not necessarily lead to realism. Insisting on factor interpretation based upon an empirical referent inevitably opens the door to this question: What is this empirical referent? Is it situated in another linguistic convention, just like mathematical notations are sensible only in a mathematico–grammatical convention? Does the statement "spatial intelligence is a latent factor of drawing skills" simply re–express the functional equation "V1 = LVF1+E1" in another language? On one hand, Mulaik (1996b) traced meaning in language back to agreements within the intellectual community; on the other hand, he went beyond convention to embrace a realist position on the empirical referent of latent factors:

> But agreement of researchers on a particular solution is facilitated, I believe, by the constraints of past social agreements reinforced by invariant features of the environment as to what is objectively the way to describe what is in the world, given in the science and the knowledge acquired up to the present point. These agreements, I believe, are not purely a matter of social consensus on something totally arbitrary, that is, pure constructs, as the post–modernist deconstructionists would like to argue. Rather we agree because the world is the way it is, is perceived as independent of ourselves, and responds in invariant ways, not always to our liking. In the meantime, we individual humans respond and categorize the world perceptually and behaviorally in similar ways so that we arrive at agreement in our judgments. Without such agreement in our judgments—even more, without commitment to objectivity as a value—and without a world that responds in invariant ways, we could not and would not conduct ourselves according to rules. Our experience of an objective world, our commitment to our physics, our biology, our psychology thus constrains the kinds of interpretations that we give to our factors, so that we do not feel the freedom that the mathematics of factor indeterminacy suggests that we have when interpreting factors (p. 586).

The issue of realism and anti–realism is very important to factor analysis in the context of causal inferences, because to a realist in order to establish the cause and effect relationship between entities, those entities must be somehow perceived as real. In an episode of *Star Trek*, it can be entertaining to see how the photon fluctuation in a warp engine "causes" the starship to explode. However, the so–called cause and effect in science fiction is just a 3D animation effect generated by computers. There is no photon fluctuation, and neither the warp engine nor the starship is real. Thus, it would not be amusing to see an engineer in real life seriously talking about the causal relationship between photon fluctuation and warp engines; we would be more likely to decide that he needs psychotherapy! By the same token, if a psychologist talks about how depression causes poor job performance, but she treats the constructs "depression" and "performance" as fictitious, she is misusing language in a similar way. If "depression" and "performance" are not treated as real entities, then at most the psychologist could issue a statement like "the factor called X that summaries A to D behaviors and the one called Y that summaries E to F behaviors have a negative correlation." If correlation alone is adequate for theorizing, researchers could arbitrarily name factors X, Y, Z, A, B, C, rather than assigning names that are conceptually sensible and isomorphic to the empirical world (e.g. anxiety, depression, obsession, performance). When sensible names are assigned to factors, the hidden assumption is that there exists some degree of mapping between the theoretical and empirical worlds.

But how could the causal relationship between factors and observed items be validated? Arguments against CCP show that by mathematics alone, the causal relationship cannot be established. No matter how high the correlation coefficients are and how stable the factor structure appears to be, it still seems to be a leap of faith to claim the clustering as a causal phenomenon. Take planet clustering and motion as a metaphor. When astronomers observe that there are nine planets orbiting around the sun in a solar system, they can theorize that a hidden force causes the planets to behave in this manner. This causal claim is said to be data–driven rather than a leap of faith. Although we cannot see forces of orbits, multiple observations of planetary movements imply the existence of the gravitational forces. The clustering of observed items around an eigenvector is just as empirical as the clustering of planets around a solar system. Thurstone (1947), an early psychometrican who co–developed factor analysis with other researchers, also used the analogy of forces in physics to support the use of factors: "A simple example is the concept force. No one has ever seen a force. Only the movement of objects is seen. The faith of science is that some schematic representation is possible by which complexities of movement can be conceptually unified into order" (p. 51).

Operationalism and generalization

The mapping between the referents and the latent constructs is not a problem to researchers who subscribe to operationalism. There are different variants of operationalism. In the classical sense, which has some degree of association with logical positivism, a construct is nothing more than a set of operations, and thus operationalism is about the meaning of the referent. To be specific, based on the assumption that all meaning is empirical, the observed variables, which contain the empirical content, constitutes genuine cognitive significance of latent constructs. Although mathematical sentences, such as a linear equation of a factor model, is not empirically meaningful, logic and mathematics, to logical positivists, are construed by grammatical convention, and also meaning is constituted in correspondence between the logical structure of mathematical sentences and empirical facts in the world. The classical operationalism holds an anti–realist and a–causal position about the referents of the concepts, because a theoretical statement cannot be verified, but at most confirmed, by empirical observations, and there is always more than one theory that is said to be corresponding to the observation, and vice versa. Nonetheless, fairly speaking, some logical positivist was aware of this problem of multiplicity (Hempel, 1954).

Another form of operationalism is called methodological operationalism, in which theoretical constructs are used as a "handle" for conducting research on a phenomenon; constructs are not synonymous with operations. These operationalists are not necessarily anti–realist or anti–causal (Bickhard, 2001; Feest, 2005). Nonetheless, for the sake of mathematical convenience they have to put aside those ontological issues. In either one of the above schools, researchers refrain from claiming that the theoretical constructs represent real entities.

Borsboom, Mellenbergh, & van Heerden (2003) hold a realist position regarding latent factors. They compared and contrasted the operationalist and realist positions, and argued that the latter is more acceptable than the former. Operationalism is a form of anti–realism which maintains a sharp distinction between theory and observations, and treats theoretical constructs as nothing more than instruments for the sake of operational convenience. Borsboom et al.

assert that operationalism and the latent construct theory are fundamentally incompatible. If a latent construct is just for operational convenience, then there should be a distinct latent factor for every single test researchers construct. From the operationalist view, it is even impossible to formulate the requirement of unidimensionality. As a result, operationalists would have difficulties making sense of Item Response Theory (IRT), which is a special case of factor analysis and assumes one single trait in the measurement. Borsboom et al. argued that realism is typically associated with causality. If latent factors are real rather than operational, then latent factors are causally responsible for observed items. In a similar vein, Stanley (1987) argued that the operational approach to factor analysis is ad hoc and thus uninteresting.

There are some counter–arguments to Borsboom et al.'s view. Empirically speaking, very often constructs do not demonstrate unidimensionality even though the theory says so. Reliability in terms of internal consistency, which is often measured by Cronbach's alpha, is a necessary but not sufficient condition for unidimensionality. However, meta–analyses of reliability across studies, also known as reliability generalization studies, have indicated that reliability information can fluctuate from sample to sample (Thompson, 2003; Vacha–Hasse, 1998). No wonder Thompson and Vacha–Haase (2000) went even further to proclaim that "psychometrics is datametrics" (p. 174). In other words, reliability attaches to the data rather than the psychological test. Moreover, Kelley (1940) also warned that constructs resulting from factor analysis are not timeless, spaceless, populationless truths.

At first glance, factors seem better interpreted in the context of operationalism. However, fluctuation in the measurement model does not necessarily deny the realness of constructs. In the physical sciences, the measurement of tangible things also leads to inconsistent results. As indicated in Figure 5.1, the factor model takes measurement errors into consideration. In the meta–analyses mentioned above, although some inconsistency of reliability was found, those researchers were still able to make generalizations about reliability. If constructs were entirely operational, there would be no need to conduct meta–analyses at all, and studying generalization would be a waste of time. Every researcher could write his/her own survey items and invent his/her own construct in each individual study. The hidden assumption of generalization study is that there are certain invariant elements present in constructs in spite of measurement errors.

Nonetheless, this issue remains inconclusive because the preceding Borsboom et al.'s argument seems to be based upon the contentious Inference to the Best Explanation (IBE) developed by Harman (1965, 1968). The first step of IBE is to evaluate all available competing hypotheses. Next, IBE leads us to adopt the most coherent and complete explanatory account that can fit into our total explanatory picture of the world while no competing hypothesis would do as well. The argument for the realist view to latent constructs goes like this: between operationalism and realism, the latter is in a better position to facilitate causal explanation. In order to explain things in causal terms, constructs had better be real. However, this IBE does not establish a solid case that constructs are real; it simply asserts that between the two rivals, realism is a better choice than operationalism. But is it possible that somewhere there is a better theory than realism and operationalism that has not been discovered yet? To some researchers, forcing us to accept an explanation out of a "bad lot" is problematic. This is the so–called "bad lot argument" (Psillos, 1996; Van Fraassen, 1989).

Assumptions of quantification and additivity

Boresboom and Mellenbergh (2004) further defended realism by responding to the criticism raised by Michell (2000), who argued that the assumptions that underly latent factors are viable and the measured attribute must be additive in structure are never empirically tested. Michell argued that variables are quantifiable based upon the philosophy of the Pythagorean school, which maintains that the underlying deep structure of everything in the universe is numeric. Many early psychometricians (e.g. Spearman, Cattell) accepted as an article of faith the Pythagorean notion that psychological tests must measure something, even if what was measured was not known. In factor analysis, correlated items are combined to form a coherent factor in the sense that this group of item scores will be added together to generate a composite score. This practice is based on another untested assumption that the factor structure is additive.

Figure 5.2. An example of a Rasch model

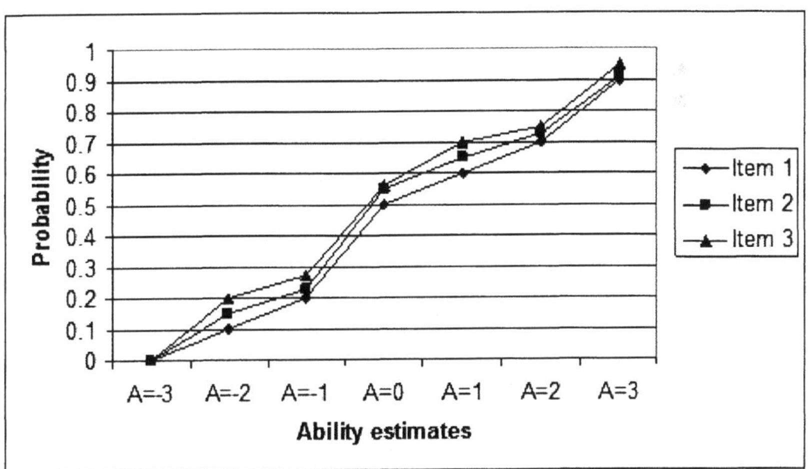

Michell is by no means anti–realist. Rather, his concern is with whether measuring variables on a continuous scale could reflect the deep (real) structure of the world. As a remedy, Michell (2004) suggested alternatives such as non–parametric methods. But are other alternatives equally guilty of having untested assumptions? How could one substantiate the claim that non–parametric methods, discrete scales, or qualitative data could represent the deep structure of the world or occupy a better ontological status?

In defense of realism, Boresboom and Mellenbergh asserted that in some cases a violation of additivity is consistent with a realist position, and indeed a realist position on attributes connects naturally to the latent factor framework. Take a Rasch model or one–parameter logistic model as an example (see Figure 5.2). All three Item Characteristic Curves (ICC) show a "clean" pattern; there is no question that these three items satisfy the additive condition and the assumption of unidimensionality.

But it is not like that all the time. Now consider a 3–parameter IRT model as shown in Figure 5.3. In this model examinees of higher ability (A = 3) have a lower probability (p = 0.1) of answering the item correctly, while it is more likely (P = 0.8) that examinees who are not sophisticated (A = –3) will respond correctly. It is possible that the item was constructed in a way that intelligent people tend to approach the problem in a complicated manner while less intelligent people just give a straight–forward answer. For example, if the question was "Does light always travel in a straight line?" examinees who are familiar with Einstein's physics would know that the direction of light can be distorted by gravitational force and thus answer "no" while novices would answer "yes" based on common sense.

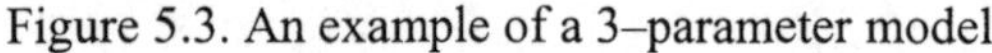
Figure 5.3. An example of a 3–parameter model

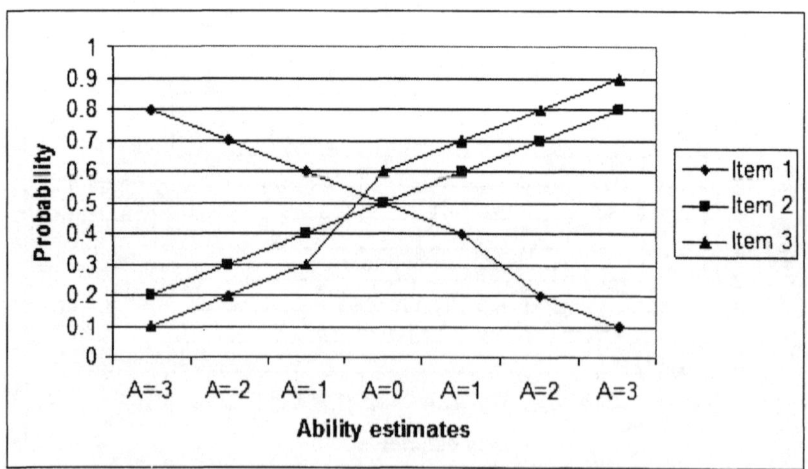

The preceding example was cited by Boresboom and Mellenbergh as an illustration of nonadditivity. I would like to expand this illustration by adding the following example: Examinees of high intelligence (A = 3) have a probability of .9 to give the correct answer for item 3, but the probability drops to .8 for item 2. In other words, for intelligent test takers item 2 is more difficult than item 3.

However, it is the reverse for less prepared examinees (A = –3). For them the probability of answering item 2 is .2 but that of item 3 is .1. Thus, for the less prepared test takers, item 3 seems to be harder than item 2. This illustrates the point that this latent construct model violates additivity. By accepting such a model, it becomes clear that a realist conception of quantifying attributes does not necessarily entail additivity. Boresboom and Mellenbergh asserted that for the realist, the fact that the exact mapping between the quantity and the construct cannot be proven is not disastrous, as Michell suggested, because additive representation is not the ultimate goal of psychometrics.

The constructivist approach to latent factors

Besides operationalism and realism, constructivism is arguably one of the most popular views to the ontological status of the referents of constructs shared by many social scientists. There are at least three forms of Constructivism: Scientific Constructivism, strong Constructivism, and very strong Constructivism. In scientific Constructivism, all scientific concepts used in the academic community are taken to be humanly constructed, but this view does not necessarily extend to concepts in our everyday life. However, this distinction seems to be blurred. For example, no doubt IQ is "constructed" by psychometricians with sophisticated theories and measurement instruments. But this concept is also treated as a part of our every day's life in a less sophisticated fashion. Hence, strong Constructivism removes this demarcation and bluntly claims that all concepts about facts we can ever possess are humanly constructed; thus, some aspects of reality owe their existence to social processes. Very strong Constructivism goes even further to say that because concepts about the world are socially constructed and there is no independent reality (Kukla, 2000).

It is understandable why the latent construct approach becomes a battle ground between realists and anti–realists, for the last version of constructivism, which denies an independent reality, tends to also deny the possibilities of making causal inferences out of the relationships among constructs. To be specific, if constructs are nothing more than mere fictions, they don't have any causal power to bring about physical events and the so–called cause and effect relations just happen in our mind. Nevertheless, researchers who subscribe to a scientific or strong constructivist position do not necessarily negate viability of causal inferences if their conviction regarding constructs is just that perception of reality has a social component.

By citing Goodman (1954/1983)'s "New riddle of induction," Hacking (1999) demonstrates the social dimension of constructs and how projection may go wrong (see Chapter 3). Goodman demonstrated that whenever we reach a conclusion based upon inductive reasoning, we could use the same rules of inference, but different criteria of classification, to draw an opposite conclusion. Hacking cited the example of "child abuse," a construct that has been taken for granted by many Americans, to demonstrate the new riddle. Hacking pointed out that actually the concept of "child abuse" in the current form did not exist in other cultures. Cruelty to children just emerged as a social issue during the Victorian period, but "child abuse" as a social science concept was formulated in America around 1960. In Hacking view, unlike natural kinds in natural science (e.g. gene, electrons) that are unresponsive to human conceptualization, constructs in social science are regarded as "interactive kind," which are subject to self–fulfilling prophecy.

At first glance, the preceding criticism is a serious challenge to the latent construct approach. However, it is important to distinguish the statement "cases of child abuse increase as the construct becomes popular" from the statement "child abuse is a social construction and thus is not 'real'." To be specific, when the construct "child abuse" was introduced, this concept might be misused and as a result many faked or exaggerated cases are reported. But can the "abuse" of child abuse logically lead to the conclusion that there is no such thing as child abuse? Hacking never embraces this position, and indeed he is moderately sympathetic to the phenomenon. Further, it would be an over–reaction to deny the value of a tool just because our presence or intervention affects the subject matter under study. Nevertheless, Hacking's example should be taken seriously by researchers, who adopt factor analysis and the latent construct approach, as a warning sign: Accepting a construct as an objective and invariant entity independent of human inquiry may be problematic; one should keep an open mind that a construct is subject to change under different circumstances. When the construct approach is conducted in an exploratory rather than confirmatory mode, new meanings of a construct, rather than an invariant structure, should be expected.

This chapter will not attempt to resolve the ontological issue of latent constructs once and for all. Rather, I will adapt the position of Laudan (1977) to tackle the issue of latent constructs. According to Laudan, "unsolved problems generally count as problems only when they are no longer unsolved" (p. 18). In other words, problems can be successfully identified only after they are solved. To be specific, we may not be sure whether an empirical effect is genuine; experimental results are difficult to reproduce; measurement instruments are unreliable. Also, before a problem is solved, it is unclear to which domain of science it belongs, and therefore unclear which theory should be employed to solve it. For example, should the observation that the moon seems larger near the horizon be answered by astronomical theories or by psychological models? Is the formation of crystals a problem for chemistry, biology, or geology? Are shooting stars a problem for astronomy or meteorology? In the 15th century the extra–terrestrial domain was considered immutable and thus meteors were assumed to be present in the lower atmosphere. Needless to say, any mathematical model representing shooting stars were purely fictional. Now we know the answer because we have solved this problem. However, can the same reasoning be applied to the latent construct approach? A century ago was it premature for a psychological researcher to assert that the entities in his/her model for explaining why the moon seems bigger near the horizon must be real? Indeed, ontologically unknown constructs should not be a hindrance to causal discovery. Contrary to Borsboom, I do not see that methodological operationalism and realism are mutually exclusive, or that operationalism is totally incompatible with the latent construct approach, or that without a firm ontological commitment to the constructs under study, talking about causal inferences is meaningless. On the other hand, I cannot see how constructivism can hinder us from making causal inferences even if some aspects of reality is tied to social processes or that constructs and humans have some kind of interaction. Why can't a researcher start from an exploratory mode with operational fictions, but eventually confirm or disconfirm that constructs as refer to real entities that carry causal efficacy? Further, why can't we go further to treat all inquiries as exploratory analyses and keep an open kind to revise the meanings of particular constructs?

Conclusion

Factor analysis alone cannot be a tool for causal discovery. It is undeniable that factor analysis has been under severe criticism in the arenas of philosophy of science, psychology, and statistics. Nonetheless, it is important to point out that most of these criticisms are applied to Exploratory Factor Analysis rather than confirmatory factor analysis. The function of the former is mainly to suggest a measurement model for further testing in the latter. But even this function has been questioned; Baird questioned whether EFA, as a merely information–transformation technique, can generate any hypothesis or model at all. By the same token, Maraun suggested that factor indeterminacy is insurmountable and any approach appealing to criteria external to mathematics is just subjective interpretation. Mulaik rejected both of the above claims by maintaining a tight integration between computation and interpretation. The demarcation of computation and interpretation is a variation of the dichotomy between logical and synthetic questions, which is a questionable epistemology. Counter examples of Reichenbach's common cause principle demonstrate that statistical relationships alone may not lead to meaningful conclusions; rather, empirical knowledge is required to determine the presence or absence of common cause or latent construct on a case–to–case basis.

Realism is central to the controversy pertaining to latent constructs. Both Boresboom et al. and Mulaik are firm in rejecting an operational approach to latent constructs. No matter how the reliability of latent constructs fluctuates from situation to situation, researchers tacitly assume some invariant structures so that it is possible to make generalizations and conduct meta–analyses across studies. Further, Boresboom and Mellenbergh made an insightful point that while the assumption of quantifying constructs is not proven, violations of additivity do not affect a realist view of latent constructs because Item Response Theory, which is an application of latent construct theory, does not entail additivity. Nonetheless, constructs derived from factor modeling should not be treated as universal and invariant concepts. As demonstrated by Hacking, certain constructs have a social component.

It is noteworthy that the Structural Equation Model is composed of the factor model and the path model, and in SEM this factor model is CFA. Nonetheless, EFA and CFA can work together in the sense that the former suggests a factor structure and the latter provides support for the proposed factor model. In addition, some applications of SEM/CFA are also exploratory in nature. For example, TETRAD, a SEM software application invented by Scheines, Glymour, & Spirtes (2005), can explore virtually all possible path combinations of a structural model and reporting the alleged best fit model for the data set. Further, according to Peirce (1934/1960), long term scientific inquiry is a self–correcting process; earlier theories will inevitably be revised or rejected by later theories. In this sense, all causal conclusions, no matter how confirmatory they are, must be exploratory in essence because these confirmed conclusions are subject to further investigations.

This chapter by no means exhausts all major philosophical controversies pertaining to factor analysis. Other important issues, such as whether extracting the proper number of factors is essential to factor analysis (Bollen, 2000; Hayduk & Glaser, 2000a, 200b; Herting, 2000; Markus, 2000; Mulaik & Millsap, 2000) and whether the vanishing tetrad approach is superior to conventional factor analysis in terms of removing impure indictors in a unidimensional factor model and distinguishing effect indicators from causal indicators (Bollen, 1990; Bollen, & Ting, 1993, 1998, 2000; Hipp, & Bollen, 2003; Hipp, Bauer, & Bollen, 2005), continue to be battle grounds among philosophers of science, statisticians and social scientists. However, covering these topics is beyond the scope of this introductory chapter.

Chapter 6 Causal inferences and Duhem–Quine thesis

Weaknesses of theorization and experimentation

The Structural Equation Model (SEM), which is a widely used statistical technique for causal inferences, is composed of the factor model and the path model. Philosophical issues of factor analysis have been discussed in the previous chapter and thus this chapter will shift the focus to the structural component of SEM. The efficacy of SEM and its variant TETRAD, will be discussed in the philosophical context of the Duhem–Quine thesis, simplicity, identifibility (testability), empirical adequacy (it means fitness, but it has nothing to do with gymnastics), and probabilistic causality. The path model, which is a linear approximation, is criticized as an over–simplification of the empirical world, which is said to be non–linear in nature. However, computational tractability, simplicity, and fitness together provide a strong justification for causal models. Although the untested assumptions in these causal models are challenged by critics, these models are good tools for causal analysis based upon partial knowledge. Given the consideration of realness, simplicity, and fitness, and the validity of probabilistic causation, this is the author's conviction that SEM is adequate to answer the Duhem–Quine question.

In everyday life, both scholars and non–scholars try to "theorize" things that happen around themselves. However, based upon empirical studies, psychologist Baron (2000) found that this theorization of causality is often flawed due to selection bias, prior belief, and the interaction of both. To be specific, people tend to pay attention to facts that confirm their prior belief regarding a particular issue.

Hoyle (1995) also asserted that use of theory is the most problematic approach to identify causal relationships, for usually there are competing theories that seem to be equally adequate in casual explanation. Hoyle considered research design the most powerful mean for generating casual inferences, because a good research design could rule out rival hypotheses. This notion has been widely adopted by social scientists and statisticians. Classical books on experimental design (e.g. Campbell & Stanley, 1963, Cook & Campbell, 1979, Kerlinger, 1986) emphasized that in experimental settings researchers could exercise a high degree of control and manipulation of various factors. If threats against internal validity and external validity are controlled, and error variances are suppressed, then it is possible to rule out rival explanations. It is generally agreed that in experimental settings strong causal inferences could be made, whereas in quasi–experiments causal inferences are weaker but still possible. However, in non–experiments correlation or association should be reported as descriptive findings only.

Although experimental design could remediate some flaws of theorization, it is by no mean bulletproof. French physicist and philosopher Duhem (1954) said that usually a complex array of variables, hypotheses, and auxiliary assumptions may be involved in a study. Even if a complex set of theories is rejected, the theory remains inconclusive. For associationists such as Karl Pearson, this is a typical argument that relationships may be spurious and thus causal inferences cannot be affirmed. Following the thread of the Duhem's notion, Quine (1951) went even further to say that if some ad hoc assumptions are altered or added, any disputed theories could be accepted. The combination of Duhem's and Quine's notions was termed as the "Duhem–Quine thesis." This thesis accurately points out some potential problems of experimentation. Even though the experimenter could take as many variables into account as possible, reduce as many error variances as possible, and maximize the experimental error, the interaction of all variables and remaining noise together could still make the research question unsettled. Further, many issues are not subject to experimental manipulation. For example, it is unethical for the experimenter to assign a sample to a smoking group and another to a non–smoking group to study whether cancer and smoking is causally related. Consequently, the notion of the experimental school confines some issues into the domain of association only (non–causality).

In recent years, mathematical approaches were proposed as tools to strengthen causal inferences. The Structural Equation Model, as well as TETRAD and the graph theory, which are extensions of SEM, are noticeable "causationist" schools. In the following sections, the characteristics of these schools of thought will be introduced and the philosophical issues related to these schools will be discussed.

Structural Equation Modeling

Structural equation model has gained popularity among social scientists since 1970s. According to Pearl (2000), the causal elements of SEM are not paid much attention by researchers. Economists view structural models as convenient representations of density functions, and social scientists see them as summaries of covariance matrices. For over a decade, both Pearl (2000) and Glymour & Cooper (1999) have devoted much effort to reinstate the causal interpretation of SEM.

In conventional experiments that involve many variables and relationships, researchers may perform several separate ANOVA and regression analyses. SEM is a different approach, in which variables are organized in a structural fashion. SEM is a synthesis of the latent factor model and the structural model.

After latent constructs (factors) are identified, the relationships among these constructs are arranged to form "chains" or "paths." The example illustrated in Figure 6.1 is given by Lomax (1992). Based upon literature review, a researcher hypothesizes that "home background" could be a predictor to "school achievement," and "school achievement" could predict "career success", he defines such vague concepts as home background, school achievement, and career success by the factor model. Afterwards, a chain (path) of cause and effect is drawn among constructs. Then he/she employs SEM techniques to examine the fitness between the data and the model. Please keep in mind that this example is simplified. A real–life SEM could be mch more complicated. Because of the complexity of SEM, there are numerous possible ways to fit the data with the model. The fitness indices become the evidence of the causal inference in SEM. This point will be further explained in a later section.

Figure 6.1. Example of a simple SEM

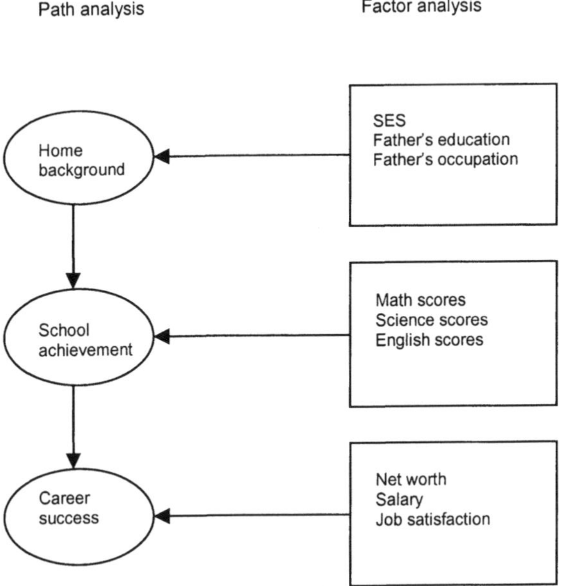

Linearity and simplicity

A structural model is a linear model. Critics are skeptical whether a linear model could represent and causally explain complex phenomena in the empirical world (e.g. Ling, 1982; Freedman, 1987, 1997). Ling called the causal inference by path models "a form of statistical fantasy" (p. 490), and Freedman called it "a faulty research paradigm" (p. 102). As a matter of fact, many times relationships in the real world do not fall into a linear pattern. In many datasets, the residuals between the linear fit and the data points are manifested in scatterplots. It seems natural that the line should go through all data points in a non–linear fashion. It is understandable why people believe that the linear model is an over–simplification of the world.

But even if the true causal structure is not linear, it does not mean that the causal relationship cannot be detected using linear modeling (Korb & Wallace, 1997). Further, Glymour, Scheines, Spirtes, and Kelly (1987) defended the sufficiency of linearity by using the fitness argument. According to Glymour et al., sciences have always proceeded by *approximation* and *idealization*. Linear approximation is not literally true, of course. Nevertheless, the principal justification for a linear model is that it explains the correlation data very well and no alternative linear model is readily available which provides a comparably good explanation of the correlations. In addition, linear models are conceptually simple, computationally tractable, and often empirically adequate.

It is important to point out that all three criteria must be presented together. Computational tractability is a manifestation of testability and repeatability. When data could be computed and the procedure can be replicated by the same algorithm, the model is said to be testable. Testability is a pre–requisite of empirical adequacy (fitness). If a model cannot be verified or falsified, no one could tell whether the data fits the model or not.

Simplicity alone is not a good criterion of judging the validity of the model. First, simplicity does not warrant whether the model is true. Simplicity is relevant to the pragmatic issue of research methodology, but is irrelevant to the epistemic aspect (van Fraassen, 1980). It is a common practice that when researchers face two equally adequate models in terms of explanatory power, they tend to choose the simpler model. However, perhaps the complicated one is closer to the truth. Thus, this theory choice is pragmatic rather than epistemic.

Second, simplicity is a relative concept. On some occasions the balance between fit and parsimony can be objectified by mathematics. For example, when comparing regression models with different sets of predictors, model comparison and variable selection procedures can be employed to determine whether the increase of R^2 can justify the increased complexity of the model. However, linear models in SEM are not necessarily simpler than non–linear models in regression analysis, and there is no objective way to tell whether one is simpler than another.

Further, even within the same research methodology, simplicity is still a relative concept. For example, in the regression context, how many variables should be retained to formulate a simple model is tied to the fitness criterion. In other words, researchers attempt to achieve the balance of fit and parsimony. The issue of simplicity and fitness will be further discussed in the section concerning identification. In short, simplicity alone might be open to attack, but combining simplicity, tractability, and fitness provide a strong justification of using linear models.

Identification and testability

As mentioned before, testability is one of the criteria of establishing a valid model. Identification is a special case of testability in SEM. Pearl (2000) asserted that in a structural equation such as Y = BX+E, the causal connection between X and Y must have no other value except B. He used a circuit board as a metaphor to SEM. In a circuit board, in which different components are joined by different paths, it shows not only how the circuit behaves under normal conditions, but also shows how the circuit would mis–behave under millions of abnormal conditions. While there are many ways for a signal to go through the circuit, only one correct way allows the signal to reach the destination so that the electronic device could perform the proper function. By the same token, a structural model formed by a web of complex relationships can have a million ways of model mis–specification. Assume that there is only one way that the model can be properly specified. If one unique solution is found out of many possible combinations, then a cause and effect relationship can be claimed. The uniqueness of the solution is tied to the issue of identification.

Figure 6.2. Insufficient data for falsification

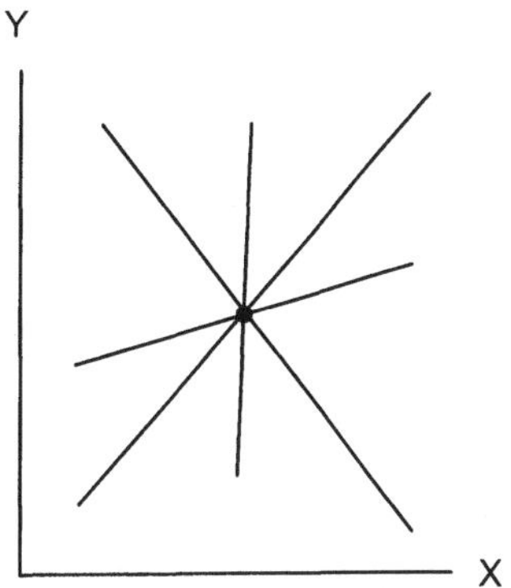

When there are more unknown parameters than the number of equations, this situation is called under–identification. For example, given the equation X+Y=2, this equation may yield infinite sets of solutions i.e. (X=1, Y=1), (X=3, Y=–1), (X=2, Y=0) . . . etc. For example, in Figure 6.2, the equation can be written as Y = a + bX. However, a line could fit the datum in any direction. In other words, X and Y could take any value. The influence of the Popperian principle of falsifibility can be found in this case. When the resulting equations fail to specify a unique solution, the model is said to be unfalsifiable, because it is capable of perfectly fitting any data. To be specific, if a model is "always right" and there is no way to disprove it, this model is useless. Thus, in SEM testability could be viewed as falsifibility.

If there are two equations such as X+Y=2 and 2X+Y=4, then the problem is more solvable. But the condition is still less than desirable. When there are two data points in the graph (see Figure 6.3), the statistician could draw a perfectly fitted line to connect two data points. Anyone could obtain two data points in any study and always come up with a "perfect solution." Thus, this model is also not falsifiable.

Figure 6.3. Perfectly fit data that cannot be falsified

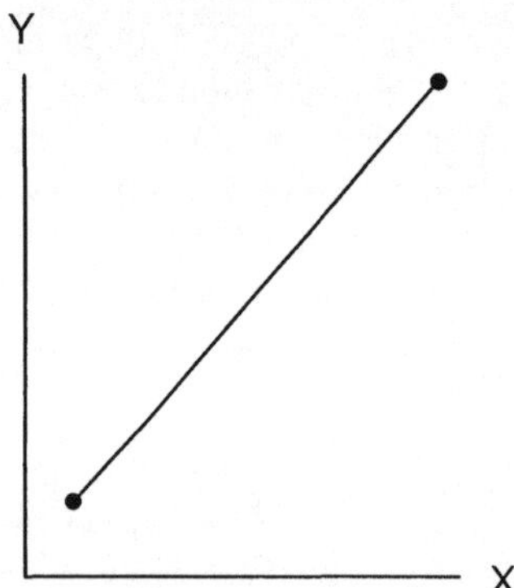

When there is just enough information to get a value for every parameter, the model is said to be just–identified. However, when there are more equations than unknown parameters, the model is considered over–identified. With over–identification, there is also no exact solution. This condition at first seems unfortunate, but it is actually a blessing in disguise. Although we may not obtain an exact solution, we may define a criterion and obtain the most adequate solution (Chou & Bentler, 1995). Following this thread, Pearl endorsed the use of over–identified models for data/model fit.

Petrovic (2000) further explained the importance of identification in causal interpretation by relating simplicity to fitness. If SEM would not have causal meaning, we should be able to compare observationally equivalent models solely on the basis of their parsimony rather than considering their respective choice of parameters. Why does the researcher burden himself/herself with an over–identified model when a simpler just–identified model could provide a satisfactory answer and save some CPU cycles? It is because an over–identified model could provide a better fit in terms of uniqueness.

At a quick glance, the identification approach looks similar to the one used by experimenters as mentioned in the beginning. The goal of careful experimental design and hypothesis testing is to rule out rival hypotheses. If SEM that seeks for data/model fit is nothing more than finding the best explanation out of rival models, then why is it considered an improvement over conventional methods? Nevertheless, there are major differences between the experimental school and the SEM school. In the experimental school, non–experimental and observational studies are not qualified to generate strong causal claims. However, Glymour et al. asserted that using SEM causal inferences are still possible with non–experimental data. In attempt to support this claim, Glymour et al. developed a program named TETRAD as a supplement for SEM software programs such as LISREL and EQS. Since TETRAD is co–developed by Spirtes, Glymour, and Scheines, this module is also known as SGS. Given the input as the covariance structure (joint distributions of variables), TETRAD is capable of generating paths among factors/variables. It is important to note that TETRAD does not output a unique path model and affirm the causal relationships. Instead, the output from TETRAD is a family of path models, which could be compatible with the covariance matrix. The automated path generation is an aid to, but not a replacement of, subsequent testing by human researchers.

Vanishing tetrads

The search algorithm in TETRAD, as its name implies, utilizes the Spearman's tetrad difference equations or vanishing tetrads (Hart & Spearman, 1913), and at least four indictors (measured variables) per factor is required. Tetrad refers to the difference between the product of a pair of covariances and the product of another pair among four random variables. For example, if there are four variables, namely, X1, X2, X3, and X4, there will be three tetrad difference equations:

$$D1 = \sigma_{12}\sigma_{34} - \sigma_{13}\sigma_{24}$$
$$D2 = \sigma_{13}\sigma_{24} - \sigma_{14}\sigma_{32}$$
$$D3 = \sigma_{14}\sigma_{42} - \sigma_{12}\sigma_{43}$$

If the tetrads are zero, they are called vanishing tetrads, which indicate that the four variables share a common latent factor. In other words, the researcher should obtain zero partial correlations when the model is *linear*. In TETRAD, significance tests are conducted on partial correlations to determine whether two variables are independent given fixed values for some set of other variables. This requirement is called conditional independence, which will be discussed in a later section.

Although the tetrad difference equation was the first approach in attempt to detect latent constructs, it was eventually over–shadowed by other techniques such as principal components (Hotelling, 1933), maximum likelihood (Lawley & Maxwell, 1971) and weighted least squares (Browne, 1984). Nonetheless, after the vanishing tetrad approach was revived by Glymour and his colleagues in recent years, many other researchers also endorsed it in various applications. For example, when Mulaik and Millasp (2000) defended use of four indicators per factor in their four–step approach for testing a SEM, they praised the tetrad approach for its merits of over–determining the latent variable. To be specific, one can always find a perfect fit between a uni–dimensional factor model with three positively correlated indicators. In this case no test of the single–factor model is possible with this set up. However, four positively correlated variables may not have a single common factor, and therefore, this over–identified common–factor model is testable or refutable.

Problem of sequential search

Actually, path searching is not something entirely new. Popular SEM software applications such as LISREL and EQS have their own automated path searching algorithms. Nevertheless, Ting (1998) found that the hit rates (the success rates of uncovering the right causal structure) of TETRAD's automatic search procedure reach 95% for large samples (n=2000) and 52% for small samples (n=200), which are higher than those offered by LISREL and EQS.

More importantly, Scheines et al. (1998) asserted that many path searching algorithms of existing SEM packages, such as LISREL and EQS, employ a form of stepwise search, which is an extension of a flawed strategy in stepwise regression. A stepwise regression is a statistical procedure, which starts with a large pool of potential predictors and then narrows down the list by certain variable selection methods. Glymour (2001) disapproved stepwise regression by saying:

> Regression does a funny thing: to evaluate the influence of one regressor on X, it conditions on all other regressors, but not on any proper subsets of other regressors. Stepwise regression procedures typically do investigate the dependence of a regressor and X conditional on various subsets of other regressors, but they do so completely ad hoc ways, with no demonstrable connection between the procedures and getting to the truth about causal structure. Regression and stepwise regression reflect intuitions from experimental design and elsewhere that absence of causation has something to do with conditional independence. They simply don't get the something right (p. 197).

While the above diagnosis of the weaknesses of stepwise regression is accurate, many readers may find it hard to follow, especially when the procedure of stepwise regression is not explained in detail. In the following Glymour's point will be elaborated. Simply put, the purpose of a regression model is to find out to what extent the outcome (dependent variable) can be predicted by the independent variables. The strength of this prediction is indicated by R^2, also known as variance explained or strength of determination. We expect that a regression model with strong predictive power is indicated by the one that has the high variance explained. However, it should be noted that if the researcher adds too many variables into the model, collinearity (inter–dependence among variables) may occur and the variance and parameter estimates are inflated.

When there are too many variables, we may acknowledge that the model is too complex to be useful and thus we need to select a subset of variables. One commonly employed remedy is stepwise regression, which is a sequential procedure for examining the impact of each variable on the model. In each step, any variable that cannot contribute much to the variance explained would be dropped. However, this methodology is valid *if and only if* all or most of the predictors are independent. Collinear regressors (regressors with a high degree of correlation) would return inaccurate results. Consider a model with an outcome variable, Y, and four non–orthogonal (correlated) regressors, X1–X4 (Figure 6.4). In this case, we cannot tell which individual variable contributes most of the variance explained. If X1 enters the model first, it seems to contribute the largest amount of variance explained. X2 seems to be less influential because its contribution to the variance explained has been overlapped by the first variable, and X3 also seems to be less significant because it is "overshowded" by X1 and X2. As Glymour pointed out, when a stepwise regression is used, the variable examined is conditional on all other variables, and thus the actual role of the variable in the model could never be unveiled in this fashion.

Figure 6.4. Venn diagram of correlated predictors.

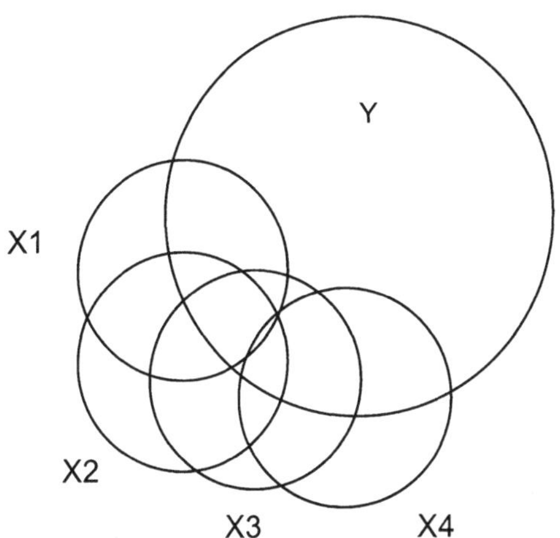

Indeed, the more correlated the regressors are, the more their ranked "importance" depends on the selection order (Bring, 1996). We can interpret the result of step regression as an indication of the importance of independent variables *if and only if* all predictors are orthogonal. In Figure 6.5 we have a "clean" model, in which the individual contribution to the variance explained by each variable is clearly identified. Thus, we can assert that X1 and X4 are more influential on the dependent variable than X2 and X3. However, in social sciences the ideal case is hardly close to the reality.

Figure 6.5. Venn diagram of orthogonal predictors.

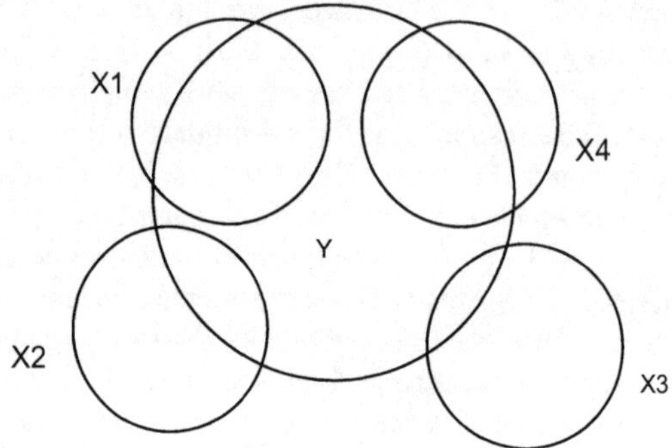

The problem of regression as a causal recovery tool does not end here. In addition, Clogg and Haritou (1997) pointed out that one usually cannot tell whether the causal assumptions with respect to the error term in regression can hold or not. In regression the value of the outcome variable (Y) is predicted given the value of the regressor (X). In every model there always exist certain errors, in which the data could not fit the model, or there are residuals between the actual value and the predicted value. Regression has several assumptions regarding the error term:

1. The expected error term has average value zero: E(e)= 0.
2. The variance of the error (or the conditional variance of Y given X) is constant.
3. The errors are independent or uncorrelated E(e1,e2)=0
4. There are no outliers.
5. The errors are normally distributed.

However, the so–called causal effect in regression, which is the beta weight, also known as the regression coefficients, is not identifiable if the assumption of zero correlation or zero covariance between the predictor and the error term is not true. This is just assumed in order to equate the beta weight with the causal effect. If we do not know that this covariance is zero, we cannot determine the true value of this covariance from the data. However, the preceding causal assumption cannot be checked with the data used for the regression analysis. Even worse is that when the number of predictors increases, the magnitude of the causal assumptions, which are derived from the number of paired covariance, substantively increases. In short, causal inferences in regression are driven more by non–verified assumptions than by data.

Hence, Glymour asserted that regression is not a valid tool for discovering the causal structure among variables and constructs. As a remedy, the search algorithms developed by the TETRAD team is based on conditional independence among variables, rather than conditioning a variable on all other variables. Conditional independence will be discussed in the next chapter pertaining to Causal Markov Condition.

Graphy theory

Local fitness testing

While Pearl (2000) rigorously defended SEM, he also developed the graph theory as an enhancement to SEM. The graph theory is composed of a set of new languages as opposed to conventional algebraic notations in statistics. Pearl asserted that algebraic notations fail to capture the causal structure among variables. When relationships are expressed in terms of functions and equations, the association could not be interpreted as causation without further justification. For example, Y = A + BX can be rewritten as X = (Y – A) / B. Thus, X could not be viewed as a cause of Y because the positions of X and Y could be swapped around the equation even if B is the only value that could solve the equation. In other words, the relationship between X and Y is not directional.

Using a circuit analogy, Pearl argued that a circuit diagram captures the very essence of causation because a circuit diagram could predict outcomes but equations cannot. In a circuit the layout of paths is directional instead of functional. By drawing causal diagrams in a graphical model, one could go beyond testing equations to testing possible directions of equivalent models. In brief, "X is a cause of Y" should be represented by the symbol "→" rather than "=" for the former indicates a direction.

Figure 6.6 is a simple graph that denotes the causal relationship among three variables. In this example, X1 is a direct cause of X2 whereas X2 is a direct cause of X3. There is no feedback or cyclic loop in which X3 causes X1, and thus these graphs are called Directed Acyclic Graphs (DAG). Users of EQS and AMOS (software packages for SEM) may think that it is very straightforward to construct a causal model by dragging and dropping circles or rectangles across the screen, and then connecting them with directional arrows. Actually many statisticians and philosophers have a hard time to follow the mathematical details of Pearl's graph theory. Hence, the subsequent discussion will concentrate on the conceptual and application aspects of Pearl's theory.

Figure 6.6. Basic DAG

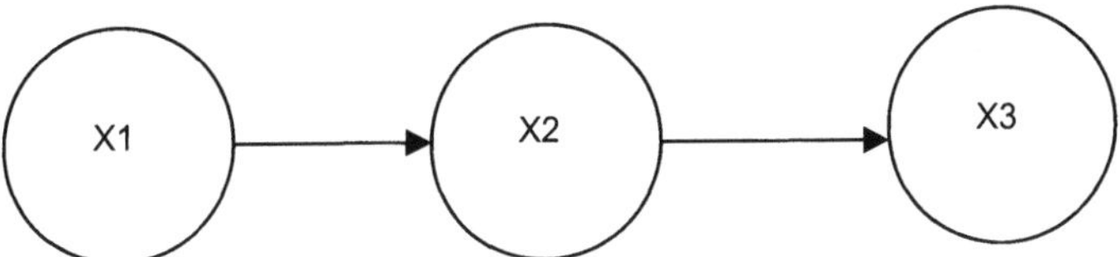

According to Pearl, data/model fitness and over–identification are necessary, but not sufficient conditions to infer cause and effect relationships. Pearl pointed out two potential problems of fitness tests:

1. If some parameters are not identifiable, the first phase of the test may fail to reach stable estimates for the parameters and the investigator must simply abandon the test.
2. If the model does not fit the data adequately, the researcher receives little information about which modeling assumptions are wrong.

In this case, the global fitness test is not helpful. As Duheim pointed out, when a complex set of variables and hypotheses goes wrong, a global answer at most could tell the researcher that something is wrong somewhere. To rectify this situation, Pearl suggested that local fitness testing is a better alternative. Local fitness testing examines the restrictions implied by the model one by one. It is considered more reliable than the global testing because it involves fewer degrees of freedom and is not affected by irrelevant measurement error. As discussed before, every measurement model carries certain errors. By using local fitness test the errors are localized.

Pearl's approach is directly opposed to Laudan's idea. In answering the Duheim challenge mentioned earlier, Laudan (1997) argued that when a complex set of theories is tested and generates an anomaly, the researcher should not try to localize blame or distribute credit to specific portions of the model. Rather, the rational strategy is to select a better set because the anomaly affects each element within the complex. Pearl's approach is considerably superior to Laudan's as a solution to the Duheim's problem. Laudan's idea resembles the global test thinking, which could hinder scientific research from accumulation of learning and progress. In contrast, Pearl's idea of local fitness testing can provide information for further model refinement. Unless the entire model is seriously mis–specified and global fitness testing correctly rejects the entire model, local fitness testing is no doubt a better choice.

Covariance equivalent models

In the graph theory, two models are considered equivalent if their reproduced covariance matrices are identical, regardless of the direction of the arrows. For example, X →Y is equivalent to X ← Y if the covariance structure between X and Y in the first model is the same as that of the second one. When there are many variables, different combinations of paths form numerous equivalent alternative models. Pearl relates the significance of equivalent models to the falsifiability criterion. In this way, the researcher does not test a single model but a whole class of observationally equivalent models. This class of equivalent models can be constructed and inspected graphically. If one unique solution comes up from many alternative models, a firm causal inference can be made.

The logic of Glymouir's TETRAD is very similar to Pearl's approach. TETRAD also output a pattern (class) of possible path models that are covariance equivalent. However, it may be the case that there are SEMs which are not covariance equivalent, but nonetheless fit the data almost equally well. This problem is addressed by outputting multiple patterns of possible SEMs.

Testing covariance equivalent and other possible fit models could also be viewed as an expansion of the counterfactual model. Counterfactual questions, as the name implies, are "what–if" questions. When X occurs and Y follows, the researcher could not jump to the conclusion that X causes Y. The relationship between X and Y could be "because of," "in spite of," or "regardless of." A responsible researcher would ask, "What would have happened to Y if X were not present?" In other words, the researcher does not base his/her judgment solely on the existing outcome, but also other potential outcomes. Thus, this model is also known as the potential outcome model.

Randomized or controlled experiments often have a counterfactual aspect (Brady, 2002). To be specific, the control group gives the information about how Y behaves when X is absent while the treatment group tells the experimenter about how Y reacts when X is present. However, the counterfactual approach taken by experiments is limited in two senses. First, causal inferences cannot be made to non–experimental data. Second, the experimenter can manipulate just a few scenarios.

Similarly, testing covariance equivalent and other fit models is also asking "what–if" questions. However, the researcher who employs the graphical model exhausts all possible scenarios by manipulating the model graphically (reversing arrows). For example, he/she may consider, "what would happens if we assume that Y causes X and Z causes Y, instead of assuming X causes Y, and Y causes Z?" Moreover, manipulating possible models enables the researcher to draw causal interpretations from non–experimental data. Some researchers mis–perceived SEM as a competitor to randomized experiments (Pearl, 1995). Indeed, besides exploring more "what–if" scenarios, SEM extends the counterfactual model, in that the actual outcome from a given function may serve as an input to subsequent potential outcome functions (Greenland, 2000).

Criticisms

Probabilistic vs. deterministic causality

Although the aforementioned causal models are philosophically sound and mathematically sophisticated, objections against these models are still visible in the academic arena. For example, while discussing causality in sociology, Abbott (1998) deliberately removed the mathematical models from his writing since he doubted the validity of probabilistic causation. In the same vein of prominent sociologist Durkheim, Abbott contended that causality means determination, which is necessary and sufficient.

Probabilistic causation and deterministic causation is an old topic in philosophy. Determinists asserted that scientific laws could only be founded on certainty and on an absolute determinism, not on a probability (Hacking, 1992). In scientific determinism, every outcome is a necessity. i.e., given the cause, the effect must occur. This idea originated from French mathematician Laplace. Based on the Newtonian physics, Laplace claimed that everything is determined by physical laws. If a powerful intellect (called Laplace's demon) fully comprehends the Newtonian law, and knows the position and momentum of every particle in the universe, no doubt he could predict every event in the history of the universe. Laplace's determinism was applied to the realm of extended, spatial, material substance. Later determinism was expanded to the realm of psychological and sociological events.

Philosophers have been puzzled by how one could implement causal relations in a non–deterministic context. Mulaik and James (1995), who are vocal endorsers of SEM, use the Item Response Theory (IRT) to argue for the probabilistic causal model. In IRT, item difficulty and subject ability (theta) jointly determine a specific probability distribution on the response variable. Varying ability and varying item difficulty varies the probability distribution of outcomes on the response variable. In IRT, estimation of subject theta is aided by the Bayesian approach, which updates the probability based upon new information (Mislevy, 1993). The probability that the examinee could answer a question correctly is contingent upon his/her ability. And his estimated ability is contingent upon his/her ongoing performance, especially in an adaptive test. In this scenario, it is more appropriate to interpret causation in a probabilistic fashion. By the same token, the probabilistic property of SEM should not be viewed as a sign of invalidity.

Pearl (2000) is well–aware of the issue of probabilistic causality. In the graphical model, Bayesian Networks (BN) are employed to encode causal relations. In contrast to the determinist view of Laplace, causal relationships defined in BN are assumed to be probabilistic. Pearl (2001) argues that conventional statistics has difficulties in expressing causal concepts because statistics deals with static conditions. However, causal analysis involves a web of interacting variables and changing conditions, and thus BN is more applicable to causal analysis. In the graphical framework, BN performs three roles:

1. to represent the causal assumptions about the environment;
2. to facilitate economical representation of joint probability functions;
3. to facilitate efficient inferences from observations.

Pearl argued that owing to the wide acceptance of quantum mechanics, natural laws are considered probabilistic and determinism is just a convenient approximation. Quantum mechanics may be very remote to ordinate people. Nonetheless, Salmon (1984) pointed out that probabilistic causality, rather than deterministic causality, is more aligned to our common sense in everyday life. For example, heavy smokers do not necessarily get lung cancer. It is only probable that a heavy smoker could become a cancer patient. In advocating probabilistic causality, Salmon did not deny the existence of sufficient causes. However, sufficient causes constitute a limiting case of probabilistic cases, which seems to be restrictive.

Untested and strong assumptions

The most vocal critic against SEM is Freedman. Freedman (1997) denounced Glymour's TETRAD program and criticized that "causation has to do with empirical reality, not with mathematical proofs based on axioms. The issue is not one of theorems, but of the connection between theorems and reality" (p. 76). In another paper that also refuted TETRAD, Freedman and Humphreys (1998) repeated the same notion, "There is no coherent ground—just based on the mathematics—for thinking that the graphs represent causation. . . . The mathematics in SGS will not be of much interest to philosophers seeking to clarify the meaning of causality" (p. 3).

Interestingly enough, Freedman's criticisms against Glymour and Pearl can also be framed in the Duhem question: "If assumptions A, B, C . . . hold, then H can be tested against the data. However, if A, B, C . . . remain in doubt, so must inferences about H" (p. 102). When facing an expected outcome, Duhem might say the theory remains inconclusive. In contrast, Freedman simply rejected the whole theory altogether. In Freedman's eyes, untested assumptions are just "maintained hypotheses." Freedman (2005) argued that the causal model suggested by both Glymour and Pearl carried many untested assumptions and the only empirical data are the covariance structure.

With regard to the validity of the assumptions for the path model, Freedman (1987) pointed out three possible threats:

1. Measurement error in the exogenous (independent) variables.
2. Nonlinear relationship between the endogenous (dependent) and exogenous variables.
3. Omitted variables.

Social scientists use latent factor models to address the first problem. However, Freedman said that this solution involves another set of assumptions. For example, it is assumed that there are repeated measurements linearly related to the latent factors. Pertaining to the second problem, Freedman said that when the variables are related in a non–linear fashion, the estimated coefficient would be biased. About the last problem, Freedman asserted that missing important variables could lead to a mis–specified model. He mocked that "this problem too is well known to workers in the field, and their solution is to expand the system by adding more variables. . . . Current social science theory cannot deliver that sort of specification with any degree of reliability, and current statistical theory needs this information to get started" (p. 109). Besides the preceding assumptions, Freedman (1997) also questioned other assumptions embedded in SEM and TETRAD such as faithfulness and causal Markov conditions, which will be illustrated in the next chapter. In brief, Freedman dismissed all popular reasons of accepting SEM assumptions:

> In the social sciences, however, statistical assumptions are rarely made explicit, let alone validated. Questions provoke reactions that cover the gamut from indignation to obscurantism. *We know all that. Nothing is perfect. Linearity has to be a good first approximation. The assumptions are reasonable. The assumptions do not matter. The assumptions are conservative. You cannot prove the assumptions are wrong. The bias will cancel. We can model the bias. We are only doing what everybody else does. Now we use more sophisticated techniques. What would you do? The decision–maker has to be better off with us than without us. We all have mental models; not using a model is still a model* (p. 103). (Italic appears in the original text.)

Use of latent factors and linear models has been discussed in previous sections. Freedman identified measurement error as one of the problems of the factor model. If error–free measurement is required in research, I am afraid that most research studies would be "mission impossible." This section will concentrate on the problem of missing variables. It is true that certain variables that are crucial causes to the outcome may be overlooked by the researcher. However, it is totally acceptable to miss some variables and then expand the system by adding more later. It is curious that Freedman denied adding more variables as a viable solution because model specification with a high degree of certainty is difficult. Demanding the researcher to identify all relevant causal variables with certainty is like expecting the researcher to be a Laplace's demon, who has the full knowledge of the whole world. We conduct research exactly because we don't know the cause and effect, not because we know everything. Our knowledge of the world is incomplete and it is perfectly fine to admit that any model or theory is fallible.

Nevertheless, even if the researcher possesses the intelligence of the Laplace's demon, is it necessary for him/her to include all relevant variables into the model? Like linearity, simplicity is also a reason that the researcher may omit certain "important" variables. All models are mis–specified in the sense that some variables are always excluded from the model. For example, a student asked me what variables cause school performance. I told him/her about my fifty–variable model: Study long hours, earn more money, marry a good wife/husband, buy a reliable car, watch less TV, browse more often on the Web, exercise more often, attend church more often, pray more often, go to fewer movies, play fewer video games, cut your hair more often, drink more milk and coffee . . . etc. Needless to say, this over–specified model is not useful at all. It is understood that Freedman was concerned with "important variables," not trivial variables. In this example, Freedman might worry that the most important variable "study long hours" could be left out while others such as "drink more milk and coffee" are retained. Nonetheless, methodologically speaking it is not a bad thing to leave out important variables, because the model will be simple enough to falsify or to be practical, such as suggesting some viabale course of actions.

One question implied by the Duhem thesis is: Could theories be refuted? Quine (1951) argued that by adding or adjusting ad hoc hypotheses, any disputed theory could be accepted. If the model fails to fit the data, the researcher may say, "Perhaps some important variables are missing." In this manner, the same theory could be tested over and over by adding more variables endlessly. On the other hand, Freedman used the same argument to refuse the validity of causal models: A model is invalid if some important variables are missing. Neither Quine nor Freedman could answer the Duhem question adequately. No model could fit the data perfectly. Again, this type of question could also be endless no matter how fit or unfit the model is. Therefore, advocates of causal models have explicitly spelled out the criterion of identification to set the parameters of testability.

In response to Freedman, Bentler (1987), one of the developers of EQS (a software program for SEM), defended the value of SEM in terms of simplicity and fitness test. Bentler stated that the central question of SEM is whether $\sigma=\sigma(\theta)$, where σ is a vector of population parameters and θ is a vector of smaller dimension than σ. For example, say there are 1000+ elements in σ and the researcher can find 100 parameters to characterize σ, the researcher will have obtained a tremendous simplification in representing the data. Further, goodness of fit of any model might be judged by the size of residuals (the difference between the predicted and the actual) or by fit indices. Bentler argued that to consider SEM as worthless, Freedman rejected a valuable idea and his action was discarding "the baby with the bathwater."

At first glance Freedman's strong demand for empirical support and skepticism of untested assumptions are reasonable. However, science does not progress based upon empiricism and a high degree of certainty. When Copernicus and Galileo developed the heliocentric model, there were not sufficient empirical data to support their claim. Before the introduction of the high–powered microscope, subatomic entities were considered untested assumptions. In the modern era, many sciences also proceed with untested assumptions and theoretical constructs. For example, the mental entities and processes proposed by cognitive psychologists are derived from a web of tested and untested assumptions. Asking for empirical substantiation and denouncing untested assumptions would inevitably reverse psychology to behaviorism. Inferences, by nature, are actions that take the researcher from one point to another. A typical example is that we usually draw an inference from a sample to a population, in which the size is infinite and the distribution is unknown. This is the type of uncertainty that researchers must live with unless the research goal is simply Pearsonian description, in which no inference is made.

In reply to Freedman's challenge, Spirtes and Scheines (1997) admitted that the TETRAD method is incomplete and there may be many other kinds of assumptions that should be investigated. Nevertheless, this is a systematic examination using partial knowledge. Scheines et al. (1998) further articulated the benefits of using assumptions in the context of causal model building. The bolder assumptions the researcher makes, the more knowledge he/she can learn about the causal structure:

> The result . . . do not free one from having to make assumptions; instead, they make rigorous and explicit what can and cannot be learned about the world if one is willing to assume that causal relations are approximately linear and additive, that there is no feedback, that error terms are i.i.d and uncorrelated, and that the Causal Independence and Faithfulness assumptions are satisfied, then quite a lot can be learned about the causal structure underlying the data. If one is only willing to make weaker assumptions, then less can be learned (p. 2).

Lastly, Freedman devoted tremendous effort to argue against causal models, but didn't spend a page to argue for a–causal models or suggest any better alternative. In the conclusion of Freedman's paper (1987), he said, "This kind of negative article may seem incomplete. Path analysts will ask, not unreasonably, 'Well, what would you do?' To this question, I have no general answer" (p. 125). Even though he did not give an answer, other researchers would take no answer as an answer. Based on Freedman's a–causal attitude, Abbott (1998) asserted that sociology should depart from causal accounting and spend more effort on descriptive work. Studying phenomena without knowing why is just like operating a "black–box." This attitude sets the clock backward. Take computing as a metaphor. It is not good enough for a computer programmer to correctly describe the signs of a system crash. A competent programmer should know what causes the system crash and is able to diagnose the problem.

Seeking for correctness

Although TETRAD can be used for modeling both SEM and Bayesian networks, the testing method of TETRAD is still classical or Fisherian, not Bayesian. TETRAD is subject to the risk of inflating Type I errors because multiple tests are used (Korb & Wallace, 1997). Also, its parameter estimator, which contains consistency as a property, implicitly assumes that consistency leads to correctness. Needless to say, Bayesians who do not accept the population parameter as an invariant constant find TETRAD problematic.

The concept of consistency originates from the Fisherian school: As the sample size increases, the difference between the estimated and the true parameters should be smaller and smaller, and should eventually converge to zero. If this criterion is fulfilled, this estimator is said to be consistent. The historical context of developing "consistency" is related to the quest for certainty (Howie, 2002; also see Chapter 1). Fisher, who disliked vagueness and subjectivity, was strongly opposed to Bayesian's subjective probability. For Fisher it was absurd to view properties of probability as varying from time to time, from place to place, and from person to person; probability should carry objective and invariant properties. Along with consistency, there are two other criteria of estimators that are said to establish the objective and invariant properties, namely, unbiasedness and efficiency. If the estimated parameter is the same as the true parameter, this estimation is considered unbiased. An efficient estimator is the one that has achieved the lowest possible variance among all other estimators, and thus it is the most precise one.

TETRAD introduced the concept of "pointwise consistency" as an extension of the Fisherian notion in the context of SEM. Specifically, search procedures in TETRAD are said to be "pointwise consistent" in the sense that they guaranteed to converge almost certainly to correct information about the true causal structure in the large sample limit, given that the structure and the sample data satisfy various commonly made assumptions, such as multi–normality and linearity (Scheines, Glymour, & Spirtes, 2005). This Fisherian orientation has been strongly questioned by critics who doubt the existence of invariant and objective parameters.

Conclusion

The Duhem question is central to this discussion: When multiple variables, hypotheses, auxiliary assumptions exist, how could a researcher reach a conclusion or infer a causal and effect interpretation? To answer the Duhem question, the mathematical approach, such as Structural equation models, TETRAD, and graphical models, attempts to exhaust numerous possible combinations of paths. Other components of these causal models are also rigorously defended. Linearity of path models is justified in the context of achieving simplicity and fitness. By employing Bayesian Networks, probabilistic causality is considered legitimate and even better than deterministic causality. Although there are certain untested assumptions in these causal models, theories are fallible and scientific inquiry essentially carries some degree of uncertainty, yet SEM is still a good tool to make causal inferences based upon incomplete knowledge.

Last but not least, although TETRAD is said to be a tool for both Causal Bayes Net and SEM, and also probabilistic causation can be justified by invoking BN, it is noteworthy that the BN approach in causal modeling is not entirely based on Bayesian statistics. Interestingly enough, many years ago Glymour (1980) had admitted that he is not a Bayesian, and indeed the testing procedures of TETRAD are tied to the frequency school of probability or the Fisherian hypothesis testing. While counterfactual reasoning drove R. A. Fisher to conceptualize probabilistic inferences in terms of comparing an observed statistics against a theoretical distribution in the long run (see Chapter 1), Bayesians assert that for non-repeatable events probability is undefined by relative frequency in the long run. While Fisherians aim to estimate a true population parameter, Bayesians regard the parameter as a variable rather than a constant. But philosophical commensurability between Fisherianism and Bayesianism has not been visible on the horizon yet (Berger, 2000, 2001).

Chapter 7 Causal Markov condition, faithfulness assumption, and virtual intervention

Conditioning and intervention

Causality is an intriguing but controversial topic in philosophy, statistics, and the social sciences. Since the introduction of Pearson's Product Moment Correlation Coefficient, many statisticians and social scientists have been conducting research based upon association (see Chapter 1). For a long time the question about whether quantitative methodologies could lead us to causal inferences has remained unsettled.

There are some sound reasons to justify why people are skeptical toward causal inferences yielded by statistical models. Yule (1926) pointed out that sometimes we could get nonsense–correlations between time–series. For instance, if you plot GNP, educational level, or anything against time, you may see some significant correlation. On the other hand, even though bad research studies exist, it does not mean that we should abandon the endeavors altogether. In recent years, Glymour and his CMU group (Glymour, 1982, 1983; Glymour, Scheines, Spirtes, & Kelly, 1987; Glymour, 1999; Glymour & Cooper, 1999) have been devoting efforts to the TETRAD project in an attempt to affirm causal inferences based upon correlational information and non–experimental data. Not surprisingly, many scholars have voiced either their support or objections to the TETRAD approach.

Interestingly enough, numbers per se could not determine whether causal information could be extracted from the data or the mathematical model. Basically, both proponents and opponents of using statistical approach in causality utilize the same numeric information. For instance, Structural Equation Modeling, the causal model endorsed by Glymour and Pearl (2000), is composed of a measurement model and a path model. In a measurement model, Pearson's Product Moment Correlation Coefficient, which is assocational in essence and a–causal in origin, is used for factor analysis. In addition, today the widely used hypothesis testing by statisticians and social scientists is a fusion of Fisher, Pearson, and Neyman's models. As mentioned in Chapter 1, Pearson accepted association only and de–emphasized causality. Regardless of whether you believe in causality or not, you may still conduct hypothesis testing, run Pearson's

Correlation Coefficient, and/or do factor analysis, unless you totally reject quantitative methods.

If numbers and mathematics alone could not settle the debate of causality, then where could we go to investigate the problem? I believe that the problem is concerned with the philosophical aspects, such as the unproved assumptions of statistical modeling. In this paper, two major assumptions of Glymour's TETRAD will be discussed. The arguments against these assumptions by Nancy Cartwright as well as those for these assumptions by James Woodward will be evaluated.

As mentioned in the beginning, when researchers compute the association of observational (non–experimental) data, sometime the relationships might seem to be nonsense. In order to gain more insights, careful statisticians might partition the data by grouping variables or other lurking variables. This kind of activity can be considered "conditioning." For example, in a research study regarding the relationship between the birth weight of babies and the age of mothers (an example dataset included in DataDesk, Data Description, Inc., 1999), the regression model using the full dataset indicates that as the age of mothers increases, the birth weight of babies increases. This relationship is counter–intuitive because usually as the mother gets older and older, the chance to give birth to a healthy baby is lower and lower.

However, when the dataset is partitioned by a grouping variable, race, the issue becomes more complicated. The positive relationship between birth weight and age is true among whites. For blacks, the relationship is negative, while for other ethnic groups the regression slope is almost flat, and therefore no significant relationship is implied. Please keep in mind that this study is non–experimental for the researcher did not manipulate age, race, and birth. Conditioning this kind of observational data always faces this problem: No broad generalization about relationships could be firmly made because further conditioning and partitioning may reverse the relationship discovered in the aggregate dataset.

According to Meek and Glymour (1994), computing probabilities by conditioning on an event is very different from computing probabilities upon an intervention to bring about that event. While talking about intervention, readers may get an impression that researchers are talking about conducting experiments, in which human interventions are imposed on various scenarios. Indeed, in Glymour's and Woodward's view, intervention does not necessarily happen at the data collection stage. At the data analysis stage, data manipulation and model building can also be viewed as a different kind of intervention.

Meek and Glymour compared the Fisherian tradition with their own work to show the continuity between both. Fisher's design of experiment could achieve two objectives: (1) To ensure that treatment assignment has no common causes and are independent if treatment has no effect on outcome; (2) to determine a definite joint probability distribution for treatment and outcome under the assumption of no effect (null hypothesis). On one hand, Fisher's design of experiment requires randomization of group assignment to rule out common causes.

On the other hand, Meek and Glymour asserted that causal claims entail claims about intervention or manipulation. If the research study is not experimental, then how could the logic of the Fisherian school be applied to causal inferences of non–experimental data? Spirtes, Glymour & Scheines (1993) proposed that two assumptions could be employed to bridge the gap between the causal structure and the non–experimental data: the Causal Markov Condition (CMC) and the Faithfulness assumption (FA). In their view, equipped with these two assumptions, researchers could draw causal inferences as if intervention or manipulation had been made to the data.

Causal Markov Condition

In a causal model, joint probability distribution over the variables must satisfy CMC (Druzdzel & Glymour, 1995). In CMC, each variable is probabilistically independent from its non–descendants, conditional on its parents. In Figure 7.1, suppose that X1 and X2 are probabilistically independent from each other, and they both contribute to the effect of X3. X4 is independent from X1 and X2, conditional on X3. If X1 and X2 were not probabilistically independent, the model would be problematic. For example, in a regression model when independent variables are highly correlated, the problem of multicollinearity exists and the model is not interpretable. The Causal Markov Condition is the assumption of the path model, in which relationships among variables are structured. The path model is one of the components of the Structural Equation Model adopted by causationists.

Figure 7.1. Example of the Causal Markov Condition

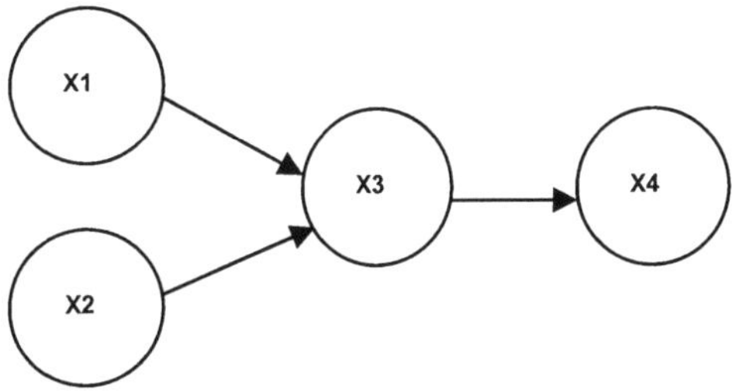

Shipley (2000) used an example in ecology to illustrate CMC: In studying transition of vegetation, ecologists realize that a location occupied by a species S1 in time t will be replaced by species S2 at time t+1. This is considered a *Markovian process* in the sense that changes in the vegetation at t+1 depends on most of the state of the vegetation at t, but not the distant past, such as t–1, t–2, and t–3. Simply put, in causal modeling once the researcher knows the direct cause of an event (X3→X4 in Figure 7.1), then knowledge of indirect causes

(X1, X2) do not provide additional information. The previous chapter mentioned that Glymour was critical of sequential search procedures because in a stepwise process each variable is selected or deselected by conditioning one variable on all others. On the contrary, the search algorithm based on CMC treat relationships among variables as conditionally independence from the indirect causes.

The Causal Markov Condition also implies the common cause principle proposed by Reichenbach (1956) and advocated by Glymour and his colleagues (Glymour, 1982; Glymour, Scheines, Spirtes, & Kelly, 1987). According to the common cause principle, if a system of variables satisfies the Markov Condition, and they have a high degree of association, then there might exist a latent construct (factor) causing them (see Chapter 5). The common cause principle is the underlying assumption of the factor model, which is also a building block of the Structural Equation Model.

Faithfulness assumption

According to the faithfulness assumption, statistical constraints arise from structure, not coincidence. As the name implies, FA supposes that probabilistic dependencies will faithfully reveal causal connections. In other words, all independence and conditional independence relations among observed variables are consequences of the CMC applied to the true causal structure. For example, a research study (as cited in Glymour, 1987) indicates that providing financial aid to released prisoners did not reduce recidivism. An alternate explanation is that free money discourages employment, and unemployment has a positive effect on recidivism while financial aid tends to lower recidivism. As a result, these two effects cancel out each other (Figure 7.2). However, the faithfulness assumption rules out this explanation.

Figure 7.2. Example of the Faithfulness assumption.

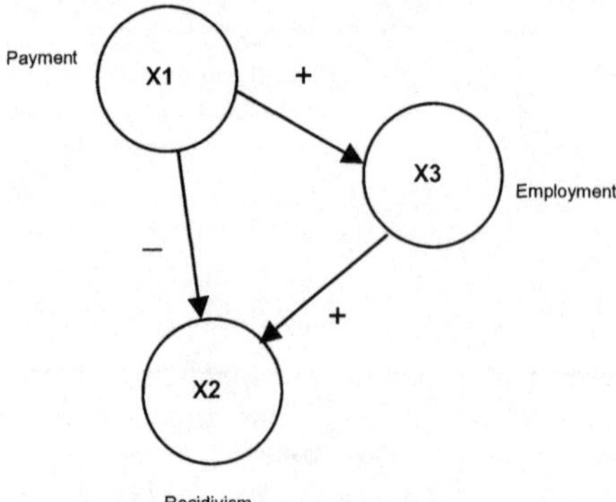

Meek and Glymour (1994) proposed that when probabilities satisfy CMC and FA and when the intervention is ideal in the sense of manipulation, casual inferences are legitimate. This notion is termed the "manipulation theorem." To be specific, given an external intervention on a variable A in a causal model, the researcher can derive the posterior probability distribution over the entire model by simply modifying the conditional probability distribution of A. If this intervention is strong enough to set A to a specific value, the researcher can view the intervention as the only cause of A. Nothing else in the model needs to be modified, as the causal structure of the system remains unchanged.

Cartwright's arguments against causation

Empiricist view: No causes in, no causes out

Many philosophers are opposed to the CMC, FA, and manipulation or intervention in the modeling level. Due to space constraints, this paper will concentrate on Nancy Cartwight only. Cartwright (1999) emphasized the point of "no causes in, no causes out" (p. 39). To be specific, there is no way to get casual information from equations and associations. New causal knowledge must be built only from old, empirical causal knowledge. In other words, the empiricist's rule embraced by Cartwright is that the relevant data are the data that will fix the truth or falsity of the hypothesis, given the other known facts. Glymour et al. included all possible combinations of variables and paths in the model and then irrelevant ones were eliminated. Cartwright questioned that if relevant variables and genuine causes are not included at the beginning, then this elimination approach is useless. For these reasons, Cartwright strongly criticized Glymour et al.'s theory:

> Because Glymour, Scheines, Kelly, and Spirtes employ the hypothetico–deductive method, they must proceed in the opposite order. Their basic strategy for judging among models is two–staged: first list all the relevant relations that hold in data, then scan the structures to see which accounts for the greatest number of these relations in the simplest way. That means that they need to find some specific set of relations that will be relevant for every model. But, from the empiricist point of view, no such thing exists (p. 78).

In questioning the applicability of CMC, Cartwright (1999) used a classical example to argue that researchers may take the risk of confusing a co–symptom with a cause: In R.A. Fisher's opinion, smoking does not cause lung cancer. Rather, smoking and lung cancer are caused by a common cause: a special gene that increases the tendency to smoke and to get cancer. Not surprisingly, Cartwright asserted that to investigate a hypothesis like this, one must conduct a randomized experiment instead of counting on CMC and mathematical intervention of non–experimental data.

Actually, Glymour and his TETRAD group do not rely on equations alone. Rather, they still use empirical data though the data are non–experimental. It seems that in Cartwright's view, non–experimental data are not "empirical" enough. First, it is a well–known fact that most data in astronomy and geology are not experimental, yet many conclusions in these disciplines are qualified to be causal inferences. Second, according to the abductive logic, new knowledge does not necessarily arise from old, empirical knowledge (see Chapter 3).

A simple definition of empirical data is data that are collected through sensory input and could be verified by sensory channels or logical means. When observational data of various variables are measured and computed, are their statistical properties empirical? Assuming that the data values of these variables indicate a high degree of internal consistency and a single dimension, and thus these variables satisfy the common cause principle and are collapsed into a single factor, can we regard properties such as "internal consistency" (in psychometric sense, not in logical sense) and "unidimensionaity" empirical? My answer is "yes" because they are absolutely verifiable.

Further, assume that I took an IQ test and achieved a score of 200; is the psychometric attribute "high intelligence" empirical? According to strict empiricists, the answer is "no" because the score is not obtained by repeated experiments. Gaining a high score in one single test could be due to pure luck. Right before the test is administered to me, I might take Ginkgo Biloba or read a book carrying IQ test items that are similar to the test. To estimate my IQ score in a scientific manner, I have to retake the same test several times and to demonstrate a high degree of stability of test score over time. However, in many experimental studies subjects are tested or measured just once. In theory, the subjects' memory about the test should be wiped out so that no carry over effect is present when subjects are retested. Needless to say, it is impossible and unethical to erase people's memory. Indeed, reliability of many experimental scores is established by mathematical modeling. To be specific, by thought experiment the true score model assumes that if the same person takes the same test over and over, error scores would scatter around the true score, and the observed score is the composite of the true score and the error score. Hence, mathematical models are applied to minimize the error score (Yu, 2001).

Last but not least, it is doubtful whether objecting that a model may leave out some genuine causes or relevant variables and so rejecting the method could help scientific progress at all. First, who could affirm that all relevant variables are included in the model except the omnipotent God? Second, is it really necessarily to include all relevant variables? In defense of his standpoint, Glymour (1999b) wrote,

> Cartwright is perhaps correct that the whole truth about anything is very complex; but, quite properly, science is seldom interested in the whole truth, or aided by insistence upon it. In my view, an inquiry that correctly found the causes of most of the variations in a social phenomenon and neglected small causes would be a triumph (p. 59).

Probabilistic causation and Simpson's paradox

In addition, while Glymour et al. based their causal modeling on probability, Cartwright (1999) believed that causal laws cannot be reduced to probabilistic laws and thus CMC is questionable. According to Cartwright, "probabilities may be a guide to causes, but they are like a symptom of a disease: there is no general formula to get from symptom to disease" (p. 243). Nevertheless, she did not reject CMC altogether. Rather she pointed out that there is not a universal condition that can be imposed on all causal structures. By citing the Simpson's Paradox (1951), in which the conclusion drawn from the aggregate data is contradicted by the conclusion drawn from the contingency table based upon the same data, Cartwight (1983, 1999b) asserted that universal causal inferences are misleading. The so–called causal relationship is always confined to a particular population. For instance, in England once a 20–year follow–up study was conducted to examine the survival rate and death rate of smokers and non–smokers. The result implied a significant positive effect of smoking because only 24% of smokers died compared to 31% of non–smokers. However, when the data were broken down by age group in a contingency table, it was found that there were more older people in the non–smoker group (Appleton & French, 1996). Based on the Simpson's Paradox, Dupre and Cartwright (1988) suggested that there are only probabilistic capacities, but no probabilistic causal laws at all. In Cartwright's view, causal explanation depends on the stability of capacities. In contrast to probabilistic causation that is relative to grouping variables, capacities remain the same when removed from the context in which they are measured.

Inconsistent results happen all the time. If we reject probabilistic causation because there is inconsistency, many research projects would become impossible. As a matter of fact, the discovery of Simpson's paradox does not discourage researchers from drawing generalizations. Instead, different techniques have been employed by statisticians and social scientists to counteract the potential threat of Simpson's Paradox. For example, by simulation, Hsu (1989) found that when the sample size is small, randomization tends to make groups become non–equivalent and increase the possibility of Simpson's Paradox. Thus, after randomization with a small sample size, researchers are encouraged to check the group characteristics on different dimensions (e.g. race, sex, age . . . etc.), and re–assignment of group membership is recommended if non–equivalent groups exist. Further, to avoid the Simpson's Paradox, Olkin (2000) recommended that researchers employ meta–analysis rather than pooling. In pooling, data sets are first combined and then groups are compared. As a result, the conclusion drawn from the combined data set could be misleading, while insights about the research question are hidden in partitioned data. On the contrary, in meta–analysis (Glass, 1976; Glass & Smith, 1981; Hunter & Schmidt, 1990; Yu, 2005a) groups in different data sets are compared first in terms of effect size, and then the comparisons are combined to infer a generalization. In other words, the information of partitioned datasets is given consideration first.

However, while inconsistency of causal inferences can be, to some degree, defended by employing meta–analysis, researchers should also be aware of certain shortcomings of this methodology:

1. *Assumption of standardized effects*: In some branches of meta–analysis, computation of effect size is based upon a pooled variance or an adjusted variance. In response to this practice, Berk and Freedman (2003) are skeptical to the merit of meta–analysis. In their view, the claimed merit of meta–analysis is illusory. First, many meta–analyses use studies from both randomized experiments and observational studies. In the former, it is usually the case that subjects are not drawn at random from populations with a common variance. In observational studies there is no randomization at all. Thus, it is gratuitous to assume that standardized effects are constant across studies.

2. *Social dependence*: Further, Berk and Freedman questioned the assumed independence of studies for meta–analysis. Researchers are trained in similar ways, read the same papers, talk to each other, write proposals for the same funding agencies, and publish the findings to the same pool of peer–review journals. Earlier studies lead to later studies in the sense that each generation of doctoral students trains the next. They questioned whether this social dependence compromises statistical independence.

3. *Publication bias*: Another common problem of meta–analysis is publication bias, also know as the file–drawer problem (Rosenthal, 1979): Publication bias leads to the censoring of studies with non–significant results. As a remedy, Keng and Beretvas (2005) developed methodology to quantify the effect that publication bias can have on correlation estimation.

4. *Logic of coutroom*: Root (2003) challenged the merits of meta–analysis at the philosophical level. According to Root, standard hypothesis testing is based upon the logic of physical sciences, in which the researcher must gamble with the unknown future, in the sense that the prediction derived from the hypothesis may not be in alignment to the proposed theory. However, meta–analysis is implicitly tied to the logic of courtroom, in which collected evidence is used to explain past events. In a retrospective methodology such as meta–analysis, the synthesizer has the luxury of choosing what past studies to be included. Using gambling as an analogy, Root pointed out that computing probabilities based on known facts is like betting money in a game after the result is known.

Counter–example of Faithfulness assumption

Cartwright (1999a) was skeptical toward the universality of FA. In FA, it is not acceptable to have two equally powerful causal effects cancel out each other. Nonetheless, Cartwright gave one counter–example: Consider the case of fiber optics. Low–loss optical fibers can carry information at gigabits per second over a long distance. But pulse broadening effects inherent to fiber optics can also smear data as they travel along the cable. In this case, the same original source emits two opposite effects that tend to cancel out each other. In order to make fiber optics useful, network engineers must apply complicated engineering schemes to enhance the first effect and suppress the latter simultaneously. Thus, Cartwright (2001) argued that the researcher must gather the background information about the causal structure under study instead of blindly following FA under all circumstances. Any conclusions the researcher draws about causal inferences based upon FA can only be as secure as our models of that structure and its operation. That's why Cartwright insisted on "no models in, no causes out" (1999, p. 17).

Actually these so–called "counter–examples" can be found everywhere. Take another networking scheme as an example: Consider Ethernet and Category 5 cabling. Ethernet follows a bus topology, and thus any one in the network could send out any data packet at any time. As a result, data packets may collide with each other. Again, engineers must apply complicated methods to make Ethernet useable. Medicine is another example. A few years ago I was very sick for a long time in spite of visiting clinics over and over. Later I was told that my illness was prolonged because while the medicine that I took cured a certain kind of disease, it also weakened my body and made me vulnerable to other diseases.

Nevertheless, when we examine these cases carefully, we could find that there were no violations of FA. In the networking examples, the positive and negative effects must be exactly equal in intensity so that when networking cables are installed, nothing would happen. But it is not true. In the first case, the signals are indeed sent into the fiber optics but they disintegrate as they travel a longer distance. In the second case, the Ethernet network is still functioning except that data collisions happen all the time. In the example of taking medicine, "feeling sick," like "economic problem" and "social ill," is too ambiguous to be an effect. Indeed feeling sick due to one symptom is different from feeling sick due to another. In other words, the positive and negative effects do not cancel out each other. If the government increases spending to increase the employment rate, the inflation rate may increase, too. But it is incorrect to say that the two effects of government spending cancel out each other because "economic problems" still exist.

Further, without the faithfulness assumption, any model could always be defensible by the argument of "canceling–out." When the welfare program administered to released prisoners is not successful in reducing recidivism, it is said that both the encouraging effect and the discouraging are at work. The same approach can be used to explain any failure or ineffectiveness. If a doctor prescribes the wrong medicine to me and thus my illness is never cured, he could also argue that his medicine works but the drug has a side effect to make me feel bad. A good treatment should be a robust one. By applying FA, researchers are forced to give a verifiable and clear–cut causal conclusion instead of explaining away failure.

Woodward's arguments for causal inferences

Interventions

Although James Woodward and Clark Glymour are not in the same research camp and indeed Glymour (in press) was mildly critical of certain Woodward's ideas, they share much common ground in the perspective of manipulation and intervention. As most people notice, Glymour's idea of intervention is not the same as the conventional sense. In conventional experiments, human intervention is imposed on different settings, and then how subjects react to the intervention is recorded. In Glymour's approach, intervention is imposed on numbers, and how numbers react to the intervention is evaluated. But whether it is a true "intervention" is still debatable.

Woodward (2000, 2001, 2003) argued that a process or event could qualify as an intervention even if it does not involve human action. In other words, a purely "natural" process involving no animate beings at all can qualify as an intervention if causal information is embedded. This kind of research is often described by scientists as a "natural experiment." Moreover, even when manipulations are carried out by human beings, it is the causal features of those manipulations that matter for recognizing and characterizing causal relationships. For example, an intervention on variable X with respect to a second variable Y is a causal process that changes X in an appropriately exogenous way, so that if a change in Y occurs, it occurs only by virtue of the change in X, and not as a result of some other set of causal factors.

In experiments human intervention actually happens in the real world. In the mathematical realm, intervention or manipulation happens in a counterfactual fashion, or in the possible worlds. The intervention yields answers to questions like "what would happen to Y if X1 were added to the model and the coefficient of X2 were down–weighted?" In this case, whether or not the interventions that set the value of Xs and Y are carried out by human beings and whether or not they have in fact taken place is irrelevant (Hausman & Woodward, 1999).

Following this idea, intervention in the sense of TETRAD is legitimate. Human intervention in experiments does not create causal information or make the data ready for causal inferences. Causal properties have already been embedded in the subject matter and experimental control is just a way to reveal the causal information. If the data are non–experimental, causal characteristics are still within the data. Mathematical intervention, by the same token, is to make the causal relationship more obvious, if there is any. In TETRAD, causal structure is represented in a system of equations. When the researcher changes the variables and/or the coefficients of the equations, he/she is changing the mechanism(s) or relationship(s) represented by it. Woodward (1999) stated that we can view this as a matter of intervening on the dependent variable in the equation so that the value of that variable is now fixed by the intervention rather than by the variables that previously determined its value.

According to Woodward (2003), manipulating equations is just like conducting thought experiments in a theoretical sense. Conventional wisdom suggests that one may conclude causal relationships that are exploitable for the purposes of control in practical, experimental, and "applied" science contexts. However, it seems counter–intuitive to think of causal relationships in "pure" or theoretical sciences in this way. In Chapter 4, I have argued against a sharp distinction between pure and applied mathematics, and it is my conviction that the same type of argument can be extended to the demarcation between pure and applied sciences in the context of manipulation and causal inferences. Woodward (2003) was also opposed to this deeply rooted common sense in the scientific community by asking:

> Does this mean that there are two quite distinct notions of causation, one appropriate for practical contexts and the other for theoretical context? What happens when, because of technological advances, it becomes possible to carry out an experimental manipulation to test a causal claim in what was previously a nonexperimental area of science or to apply what was previously purely theoretical causal knowledge to manipulate nature in new ways? Do causal claims that previously part of theoretical science undergo a fundamental change in meaning in such cases? (p. 37)

Woodward asserted that the meaning or role of causal claims should be the same in both situations. But to be fair to the skeptics, very often the problem of causal claims in non–experimental studies is not concerned with thought experiments or theoretical studies. Rather, it pertains to quasi–experiments or observational studies, in which experimental manipulation of variables to test cause–and–effect relationships (e.g. alter the amount of drug given to the patients) is absent.

Experimental manipulation is tied to internal validity, which refers specifically to whether an experimental treatment or condition makes a difference or not and whether there is sufficient evidence to support the causal claim in a coherent fashion. Although causal claims or treatment effectiveness concluded from experimental studies have been well accepted by the scientific community for many decades, recently its certainty is under attack by some medical researchers. A former director (personal communication, June 30, 2005) of a large US health insurance network pointed out the unpleasant fact that in recent years many pharmaceutical companies were forced to recall or to make disclaimers on certain drugs like Celebrex, Vioxx, Zyprexa, and Baycol that had been initially approved by FDA. In spite of the safety assurance backed up by rigorous tests in laboratory settings, harmful side effects of those drugs to humans were unexpectedly found after the drugs were released to the market. The director contended that clinical testing yields high internal validity but low external validity, which refers to the generalizibility of the treatment outcomes to a larger population. As a remedy, now health information systems or health informatics are developed to analyze data with methodologies that allow virtual manipulation at the modeling level to investigate how medical treatments work in a dynamic system like the "real" world. SEM is an example of this. It does not mean that from now on medical researchers will throw away experiments and will totally rely on non–experimental studies for making inferences to treatment effectiveness. Rather both experimental and observational approaches will work together for obtaining a thorough understanding of the phenomenon. Nonetheless, the moral of this story is that superiority of experimental studies in terms of causal claims may no longer be regarded as unchallenged dogmas.

Invariance

The idea of invariance introduced by Woodward is also relevant to Glymour's idea. It is important to note that in Woodward's framework, the concepts of invariance and interventions are closely related. For example, if Y=a+bX+e is a correct description of the causal relationship between X and Y, by intervening the value of X, the value of Y should change correspondingly within a reasonable range of data values. To be specific, in Woodward's view (2001) a causal generalization need not be universal. Rather, it could be just invariant, which means it is stable or robust in the sense that it would continue to hold under a relevant class of changes. This claim concerning causality is less ambitious than Cartwright's capacities, which aims to achieve context–free causation. Woodward (1998) asserted that many claims in social sciences are made within a limited range of circumstances. For example, interventions that change the money supply may change the price level in some range of circumstances, but not in others. Woodward (1999) and Hausman and Woodward (1999) gave a humorous example: If I water my plant with 1–3 liters of water, my plant would grow. If I water the same plant with 1,000 liters of water and the plant dies, it does not negate the statement "water causes plants to grow."

This simple argument provides a sound rationale for using linear modeling in TETRAD (Glymour, 1987). One popular argument against linear models is that it is too simplified to capture the complexity of the real world. In many situations, relationships between variables are non–linear. The relationship between stress and performance is a classical example. Psychologists found that for most people, as the stress level increases, the performance level increases correspondingly. Nonetheless, the regression slope is reversed when too much pressure is imposed. Following Woodward's argument, if a professor assigned five term papers, six examinations, and ten presentations to her students, and as a result the whole class failed, is it right for her to say, "It seems that pressure does not improve performance in all situations. Now this causal law breaks down!" The main point here is that the validity of a causal model requires invariance within a reasonable range of data values. Cases such as giving 1,000 liters of water to plants and six exams to a class must be dismissed.

Conclusion

In summary, in order to make causal interpretation of non–experimental data, the researcher must have some type of manipulation, rather than conditioning, of variables. The Causal Markov Condition and its sister, the common cause principle, provide the assumptions to structure relationships among variables in the path model and to load different variables into common latent constructs in the factor model. In addition, the Faithfulness assumption rules out those models in which statistical independence relations follow as a result of special coincidences among the parameter values. Putting all these together, TETRAD uses algorithms to examine all possible paths among variables to search for a plausible causal explanation. During this process intervention is imposed on the data and hence causal claims are justified.

Cartwright argued for "no causes in, no causes out," which means without background knowledge based upon empirical data, relevant variables and genuine causes may be omitted from the model. In this case, path searching and model building by sophisticated algorithms may be useless. The counter–arguments are that empirical data should not be narrowly defined in a restrictive sense, and the aim of the scientific investigation is not to examine all relevant variables. Cartwright objected to probabilistic causations and CMC by citing the Simpson's Paradox. However, statistical methodology is going toward broader generalizations in spite of the threat of the Simpson's paradox. Furthermore, Cartwright gave a counter–example to the faithfulness assumption and warned that FA should not be adopted without careful investigation of the background information. Nevertheless, rejecting FA may take the risk that any failure can be justified by adopting the notion that two equally powerful forces cancel out each other.

Woodward stated that even with non–experimental data, interventions are still possible because interventions are not necessarily carried out by humans at the stage of data collection. In data analysis, data values and equation parameters can be manipulated in a counterfactual manner. Moreover, the idea of invariance proposed by Woodward could be used to justify the linearity assumption of TETRAD.

Both Cartwright and Woodward made many other points rejecting or supporting TETRAD that could not be covered by this short chapter. Additionally, besides Cartwright and Woodward, many other scholars from various disciplines, such as sociology, computer science, and mathematics, have participated in this type of discussion. This phenomenon shows that causality has become an inter–disciplinary subject matter. Even among philosophers discussion of this issue goes beyond pure philosophy. For example, although the primary role of Cartwright and Woodward is that of philosopher, Cartwright is versed in economics and Woodward has a mathematical background. Fruitful results are expected when input from such a wide variety of perspectives is integrated.

Chapter 8 Statistical God of the gaps?

Divine providence and Fisher's counter–argument

The Bernoulli distribution is the simplest discrete distribution, which is constructed by only two possible outcomes. For example, if you toss a coin, the outcome will be either a "head" or a "tail." In reproduction, the outcome is either a boy or a girl. Usually the dichotomous results are denoted as "1" or '0." In theory, the probability of obtaining "1" or "0" should be .5, but in reality it is not always the case. Bernoulli observed that in human reproduction the sex ratio of males and females was about 18:17.

In 1710 Dr. John Arbuthnot, the physician of the Queen of England, argued that the sex ratio at birth was a manifestation of Divine Providence. He pointed out that equal numbers of both genders at birth would be counter–productive to society. For example, during his time all soldiers were men and therefore men suffer a greater death rate than women. Fortunately, in actuality there are always more males than females and as a result some miraculous equilibrium is reached. When William Derham commenced the third series of Boyle Lectures in 1711, he illustrated the amazing structure of the world by repeating the same argument as Arbuthnot's: Male surplus is very useful for the supplies of war, the seas and other expenses of the men above the women. In 1756 de Moivre, a pioneer in probability theory and trigonometry, also asserted that the phenomenon discovered by John Arbuthnot is indeed an effect of intelligence and design (as cited in Hacking, 1975; Sober, 2002).

But two centuries later R. A. Fisher (1930) refuted the above argument of design by introducing the concept of "parental investment." Based on the assumption that fixed resources (R) are equally distributed to each sex (R/2), the parent should have more sons when sons are less expensive to produce and maintain. By the same token, if sons and daughters were equally costly, the parent should have been produced an even mix. But actually sons die sooner on average than daughters and thus sons will require a smaller investment. As a result, parents have more sons than daughters and therefore the male bias at birth can be explained in a naturalistic approach. As mentioned in Chapter 1, one of Fisher's major research areas was evolution. Fisher's counter–argument against Arbuthnot's notion of Divine Providence laid the foundation for both evolutionary biology and game theory, which were fused to be a new discipline named Evolutionary Game Theory in the 1960s. Thus, Fisher was credited as the pioneer of Evolutionary Game Theory (Alexander, 2003).

Hence, Fisher's counter–argument can be reframed in the context of evolution as follows: The puzzling phenomenon that the sex ratio is approximately equal when many "extra" males never mate occurs in many mammals. The human population in London is just one of numerous examples. Those males that do not reproduce offspring seem to be redundant. But Fisher realized that if we measure individual fitness in terms of the expected number of descendants, then individual fitness depends on the distribution of both genders in the population. A larger number of females in the population would enhance male's individual fitness. Conversely, a greater number of males would lead to a higher female's individual fitness. According to Fisher, this evolutionary dynamics lead to the equilibrium of sex ratio. Not surprisingly, to most statisticians, biologists, and game theorists, Fisher's theory is more convincing than Arbuthnot's.

Misuse of statistics by Arbuthnot, Derham, and de Moivre are typical examples of invoking "God of the gaps" because in those cases a theological argument was hastily applied as the ultimate causal explanation to a surprising phenomenon while essential details were omitted. On the other hand, even if particular mathematical details are carefully constructed, we may still be invoking the "mathematical or statistical God of gaps argument" when mathematical properties are treated as the *sole* source of explanatory power. To illustrate this kind of research risk, the case study of evolutionary game theory is used as an example in the following discussion. It is important to note that this chapter is by no means to equate Evolutionary Game Theory with the statistical God of the gaps argument, because Evolutionary Game theorists are well aware of other non–mathematical approaches as valid causal explanations to cultural phenomena.

Modern evolutionary game theory

Based upon evolutionary game theory, philosopher of science Brian Skyrms (1996, 2000a, 2003) developed simulation–based models to explain cultural phenomena, such as distributive justice and the formation of social networks. The starting point adopted by Skyrms is Fisher's statistical solution to the sex–ratio problem. Like Fisher, Skyrms employed a mathematical model of evolution to explain human behavior. By using Monte Carlo simulations, Skyrms demonstrated how certain behaviors and population structures (e.g., the concept of fairness, social networks) could eventually emerge after many generations regardless of what the initial conditions are. It gives a plausible account of how a stable system could be invaded under different combinations of topology in the population and under various strategies adopted by players.

There are two distinct characteristics in the Skyrmsian approach. First, it takes no account of relevant genetic bases for behavioral dispositions as suggested by evolutionary biologists (Tennant, 1999). Second, in contrast to evolutionary psychology, which emphasizes specific psychological factors of human behavior, the Skyrmsian approach is evolutionary generalist; it is a *mathematical abstraction* instead of an empirical modeling; it entirely omits the psychological mechanisms and evolutionary histories from which humans emerge (D'Arms, Batterman & Gorny, 1998). The above two features are interrelated in terms of their emphasis on global structure instead of individual attributes as well as on mathematical abstraction instead of empirical detail. To compensate for the lack of detail in explaining human behavior, Skyrms established the merits of his approach by using the criteria of mathematical properties such as representativeness, robustness, and flexibility.

Particularist and generalist accounts

Evolutionary psychology is a fairly new discipline, emerging over the past few decades. It is important to point out that although evolutionary psychology is considered a particularist account of human behavior, it is not interested in studying different behaviors in different situations. Rather, its focus is on human nature in the context of how selection pressure shapes a universal cognitive mechanism. The ancestor of evolutionary psychology is sociobiology, which also aims to explain human behavior through human nature. Most sociobiologists are genetic determinists, though some are more subtly so than others (Ruse & Wilson 1985). However, most evolutionary psychologists do not focus on genetic explanations at the exclusion of other explanations. In other words, evolutionary psychology is not genetically deterministic. Further, sociobiological accounts often fail in generalizing from crucial details of particular ecologies and ontogenies of the species whose behaviors they seek to explain. As a remedy, evolutionary psychology has moved toward a particularist approach to the evolutionary explanation of human behaviors by giving the details of psychological mechanisms (de Waal, 2002; Edwards, 2003).

Evolutionary Game Theory does not emphasize any universal human cognitive process or human nature. To be explicit, the Skyrmsian mathematical model regards cognitive details as unimportant. Resentment of particularists, such as D'Arms (1996), toward generalists is understandable because it seems that evolutionary game theory falls back to the age of sociobiology. Without some kind of fine–grain story of the biological or psychological mechanism that brings about the behavior in question, the generalist's account could be mis–used as a form of "mathematical or statistical God of the gaps" because invoking a highly abstract model could explain too many things. In Christian apologetics, when intelligent design is invoked as the ultimate answer to any phenomenon which has not been explained by science, this approach is mocked as "God of the gaps." By the same token, when the evolutionary dynamic is used while the details of evolution are unexplained, it may also be some sort of "mathematical or statistical God of the gaps." As a counter–argument, Alexander (2000) maintained that the particular and the generalist accounts are compatible. What the generalist explanation provides is an explanation for why such behavior was selected in the first place, whereas the particular approach shows how certain specific mechanisms serve to produce certain behaviors.

Robustness and stability

Skyrms defended his position by introducing certain mathematical properties, including representativeness, robustness, and flexibility, to explain why psychological state, cultural context, social condition, and other details are irrelevant. Among the three properties, the notion of robustness is the most important one. According to Skyrms (2000b), an equilibrium is said to be stable and a model is regarded as robust if the dynamics carry every possible initial state in the interior state space to that equilibrium. If stability and robustness are achieved, a mathematical model can have explanatory value even when we are completely uncertain about the detail of the initial state in the system. Nonetheless, Skyrms admitted that even a structurally stable model might, after all, be badly mis–specified.

Strictly speaking, "stability" and "robustness" are two different concepts. A model demonstrated to be stable is not necessarily also robust. In measurement and statistics, stability is synonymous with temporal reliability and reproducibility (Yu, 2005b). If the same initial conditions are given, it is expected that all simulations would yield the same or similar results no matter how many simulations are run. In this case no procedure for altering initial conditions is involved. Skyrms is entirely right that a stable model could be totally mis–specified. When I use a curved ruler to measure my height a hundred times and all results consistently show that I am six feet tall, no doubt the measurement model is stable, but it does not carry any explanatory value to my physical condition.

In statistics, the term "robustness" can be interpreted literally. Consider this analogy: If a person is robust (strong), he will be immune to hazardous conditions such as extremely cold or extremely hot weather. If a statistical test is robust, the validity of the test result will not be affected by poorly structured data. In other words, it is resistant against violations of parametric assumptions. Robustness has a more technical definition: If the actual Type I error rate of a test is close to the proclaimed Type I error rate, say 0.05, the test is considered robust. In the context of Monte Carlo simulation, a robust model must be defined by a criterion of convergence or a specific cut–off value for the error rate. The explanatory value of robustness study in statistics has been a controversial topic because both the initial conditions and the cut–off criterion are said to be artificial and arbitrary. Also, more seriously, robustness is a long run concept. This is not very impressive when certain values converge after running a large number of simulations. Some patterns would eventually emerge from a random, structured, or mixed process in the long run. Borrowing John Maynard Keynes's phrase "in the long run we are all dead," I would question the robustness criterion by saying "in the long run many things can converge." Further, when a robust model is imposed on specific data, there is a big logical gap between the general model and the particular data. It is legitimate to question how one could know that a robust model could be applied to the issue in question. In short, a stable model could be consistently wrong, and a robust model might have no connection to reality. Thus, it is not surprising that Barrett et al. (1999) challenged Skyrms by arguing that we need to ask whether our ancestors really solved problems in the same manner as playing games (e.g. the prisoners' dilemma). They contended that mathematical models are one thing, but empirical reality is another. Much more empirical work is needed to show how the Skyrmsian model and reality are connected.

Difficulties in accounting for changes

Although it is doubtful that the generalist account of evolutionary game theory could supersede the particularist account of evolutionary psychology, this does not imply that the Skyrmsian approach is flawed. On the contrary, mathematical modeling in Evolutionary Game Theory is indispensable because it can account for the dynamic aspect of a model. To be explicit, it could effectively explain how a system could be destabilized and how an equilibrium could eventually be restored.

Nonetheless, the particularist account introduced by evolutionary psychology is not trouble–free. While evolutionary psychologists are proud of giving detail in their explanation, very often the detail can only explain a phenomenon in a specific setting; it fails to explain why changes in those norms and conventions occur later. For example, from the perspective of evolutionary psychology, men are pre–programmed to have as many women as possible in order to maximize the probability of procreation (Wright, 1994). However, if this aspect of so–called "human nature" had been hard–wired into every man's cognitive structure, it is very difficult to imagine how these static traits could be transformed, as they clearly would have to have been in many men. As a matter of fact, today the mainstream norm is fidelity insteasd of polygamy. In addition, Thornhill and Palmer (2000) argue that rape may have been favored by natural selection because it furthers male reproduction. In opposition to learning theory, which proposes that rape is a kind of unnatural and learned behavior through socialization, these evolutionary psychologists assert that rape is natural and genetically driven. Regardless of how much psychological detail the theory illustrates, this theory is not applicable across all situations. Rape may be acceptable in a small number of societies, but in most cultures rape is considered both immoral and illegal. No convincing answer to why this is the case is offered by evolutionary psychologists.

As mentioned before, sociobiology is a precursor of evolutionary psychology, and not surprisingly, they face similar criticisms. During the 1970s, because of the perception that behaviors seem to be unalterable in his framework, E. O. Wilson was accused of being a right–wing extremist who hijacked science to cover up racism and sex discrimination (Rossano, 2003). Even if we put aside the agenda of political correctness, by the same token, evolutionary psychology also has difficulties in accounting for behavioral changes of a population. To be fair to evolutionary psychologists, they are not so naïve as to say that hard–wired psychological mechanisms exclude any cultural evolution and social learning. As mentioned previously, most evolutionary psychologists are not biological determinists. The issue is that the complexity of psychological mechanisms is a strong factor in evolutionary psychology; the more complex the mind is to start with, the more complex culture and society can become (Gander, 2003). The more complex culture and society can become, the more resistance to change the society can face. In a modeling perspective, a high level of complexity creates tremendous difficulties in formulating a model of change. In this sense, evolutionary game theory seems to be a better analytical tool for the dynamic aspect of cultural evolution than evolutionary psychology and sacrifice of certain detail is inevitable.

Actually, not only are the particular and the generalist approaches not mutually exclusive, but they also could be complementary to each other in the sense that the particularist account can specify input variables for a simulation–based methodology while the mathematical approach can evaluate the long run stability and the robustness of a specified model. For example, the tendency of reciprocity among players is essential to the Skyrmsian game scenarios. In response to the Skyrmsian conception of morality, evolutionary psychologist Dennis Krebes (2000) elaborated on the behavioral pattern of reciprocity by incorporating insight from psychology. To be specific, Krebes argued that Evolutionary Game Theory could explain morality because we are biologically disposed to maximize others' tendency to practice the "Golden Rule" in their interactions with us. In other words, we preach this principle to create the impression that we practice it and expect the same to be done to us by others. Moreover, Krebes argued that humans inherit dispositions to invoke certain cooperative strategies that define moral development in Kohlberg's theory.

In examining the robustness claim of the Skyrmsian model, Ernst (2001) also suggested that for Skyrms's project to be carried through, the evolutionary models must be informed by the empirical work of evolutionary biologists, anthropologists, and primatologists. As mentioned in an earlier section, a stable and robust model may be a mis–specified model after all. A particular account can definitely be helpful in specifying a proper model. However, particularists such as psychologists, biologists, sociologists and anthropologists may provide too many diverse details to formulate a coherent global picture of cultural evolution. Also, a high level of complexity is detrimental to a model of change. The beauty of mathematics/statistics is in its ability to simplify the detail, suppress the noise, and smooth the residuals. When a positive feedback loop is formed between evolutionary psychology and evolutionary game theory, the chasm between modeling and reality might eventually be bridged.

Theory of force and statistical interpretation

According to Walsh, Lewens, and Ariew (2002), there are two major approaches to viewing the nature of evolutionary theory, namely, *the theory of force* and the *statistical interpretation*. The following two scenarios were used to illustrate the differences between these two approaches. In the first scenario, a feather is dropped from a height of one meter. In the second, ten coins are randomly drawn from an urn containing 1000 coins: 500 with heads up, 500 tails up. In both cases we might make a prediction about the outcomes. We might predict that the feather will fall within a certain scope. In the coin–drawing case, we predict a distribution of heads and tails resulted from drawing. However, there is a significant difference between the two predictions. In the former, the trajectory of the falling feather is generated by the forces known by our physical laws. In the latter, the expected outcome does not result from attending to the forces acting on the coins. Instead, certain probability laws are at work, and the population structure must be taken into consideration. In other words, in the former case, particular details such as the force of gravity, the wind speed, the distance between the dropping point and the ground, and other conditions pertaining to physical laws should be taken into account to explain the outcome. In the latter the issue is purely mathematical and thus it is legitimate to apply mathematical criteria to evaluate the prediction. Furthermore, Walsh et al. asserted that the error types in these two approaches are totally different. In the case of falling feather, errors in prediction result from ignorance of detail, e.g., a scientist might not measure the wind speed correctly. However, in the coin–drawing scenario, the nature of the error is statistical, such as random fluctuations. There are two phenomena to be explained in evolution: The individual properties and the population structure, which are approached by some researchers from a theory of force and statistical explanation.

Conclusion

The above analogy could be well applied to the distinction between evolutionary psychology and Skyrmsian mathematical modeling. The particularist account offered by evolutionary psychologists is a theory of force, in which specific causal agents, such as psychological drives, are said to bring out behavioral consequences. On the other hand, the Skyrmsian simulation–based approach is obviously a mathematically–based model, in which robustness can add weight to the explanatory power of a prediction. It is important to point out that the essence and purpose of these two types of theories are fundamentally different, and thus applying the criteria of one to dismiss another, or vice versa, is unfair and counterproductive.

In statistics most phenomena could be answered by blanket concepts like the following: "The score of group A is high in the first test and low in the second one because of random fluctuations." "The score is high in the fist test and low in the second one because of regression to the mean." "Sometime the score is high and sometime it is low. This variation forms a normal curve. Many things in the world happen according to the bell curve effect." "The sample distribution is skew. But according to the Central Limit Theorem, the sampling distribution will be normal if replications are done." Needless to say, this kind of "universal" answer does not give any detail. Readers still have no clue why the test score is high in one test but low in another or why the sample distribution is skew. That is exactly the "statistical God of the gaps" argument! What they need to know are the mental state of the test takers, the content of the items, the background information of the population, and other relevant details. For a similar reason, philosopher of science Glymour (1998) is critical of the explanatory power of the bell curve argument in the social sciences because the so–called bell curve effect has no causal power. In short, although the goal of statistics is to study the aggregate pattern of the subject matter with reference to some distributions, we also need to illustrate the *qualitative* detail of the agents that cause changes in variables.

References

Abbott, A. (1998). The causal devolution. *Sociological Methods & Research, 27,* 148–180.

Aldrich, J. (1995). Correlations genuine and spurious in Pearson and Yule. *Statistical Science, 10,* 364–376.

Aldrich, J. (1997). R. A. Fisher and the making of maximum likelihood 1912–1922. *Statistical Science, 12,* 162–176.

Alexander, J. M. (2000). Evolutionary explanations of distributive justice. *Philosophy of Science, 67,* 490–516.

Alexander, J. M. (2003). Evolutionary game theory. *Stanford Encyclopedia of Philosophy.* Retrieved November 13, 2005, from http://plato.stanford.edu/entries/game–evolutionary

Almeder, R. (1980). *The philosophy of Charles S. Peirce: A critical introduction.* New Jersey: Rowman & Littlefield.

Anderson, D. R. (1987). *Creativity and the philosophy of C. S. Peirce.* Boston: Martinus Nijoff Publishers.

Anderson, J. R. (1990). *The adaptive character of thought.* Hillsdale, NJ: Erlbaum.

Appleton, D. R. & French, J. M. (1996). Ignoring a covariate: An example of Simpson's paradox. *American Statistician, 50,* 340–341.

Arntzenius, F. (1992). The common cause principle. *Proceedings of the Biennial meeting of the Philosophy of science association, Vol. 2: Symposia and Invited Papers,* 227–237.

Arntzenius, F. (2005). Reichenbach's common cause principle. *Stanford Encyclopedia of Philosophy.* Retrieved October 14, 2005, from: http://plato.stanford.edu/entries/physics–Rpcc/

Ayer, A. J. (1934). Demonstration of the impossibility of metaphysics. *Mind (New Series), 43,* 335–345.

Ayer, A. J. (1936). The principle of verifiability. *Mind (New Series), 45,* 199–203.

Ayer, A. J. (1946). *Language, truth, and logic (2nd ed).* London: V. Gollancz.

Bacon, F. (1620, 1960). *The new organon, and related writings.* New York: Liberal Arts Press.

Bailey, D. H., & Borwein, J. M. (2001). Experimental mathematics: Recent developments and future outlook. In B. Engquist, & W. Schmid, (Eds.), *Mathematics unlimited: 2001 and beyond* (pp. 51–65). New York: Springer.

Baird, D. (1983). The Fisher/Pearson chi–squared controversy: A turning point for inductive inference. *British Journal for the Philosophy of Science, 34,* 105–118.

Baird, D. (1987). Exploratory factor analysis, instruments and the logic of discovery. *Journal for Philosophy of Science, 38,* 319–337.

Baron, J. (2000). *Thinking and deciding (3rd ed.).* Cambridge: Cambridge University Press.

Bartholomew, D. (2002). Old and new approaches to latent variable modeling In G. A. Marcoulides & I. Moustaki. (Eds.), *Latent variable and latent structure models* (pp. 1–9). Mahwah, NJ: Lawrence Erlbaum.

Behrens, J. T. (1997). Principles and procedures of exploratory data analysis. *Psychological Methods, 2,* 131–160.

Behrens, J. T., & Yu, C. H. (2003). Exploratory data analysis. In J. A. Schinka & W. F. Velicer, (Eds.), *Handbook of psychology Volume 2: Research methods in Psychology* (pp. 33–64). New Jersey: John Wiley & Sons, Inc.

Bennett, J. H. (1983). (Ed.). *Natural selection, heredity, and eugenics.* Oxford: Clarendon Press.

Bentler, P. (1987). Structural modeling and the scientific method: Comments on Freedman's critique. *Journal of Educational Statistics, 12,* 151–157.

Berg, B. L. (2001). *Qualitative research methods for the social sciences.* Boston, MA: Allyn & Bacon.

Berger, J. (2000). Bayesian analysis: A look at today and thoughts of tomorrow. *Journal of American Statistical Association, 95,* 1269–1276.

Berger, J. (2001, August*). Could Fisher, Jeffreys, and Neyman have agreed on testing?* Paper presented at the Joint Statistical Meeting , Atlanta, GA.

Berk, R.A. & Freedman, D. (2003). Statistical assumptions as empirical commitments. In T. G. Blomberg & S. Cohen (Eds.), *Law, Punishment, and Social Control: Essays in Honor of Sheldon Messinger (2nd ed)* (pp. 235–254). New York: Aldine.

Bernardo, J. M., & Smith, A. F. M. (1994). *Bayesian theory.* Chichester, NY: John Wiley & Sons.

Bickhard, M. H. (2001). The tragedy of operationalism. *Theory and Psychology, 11,* 35–44.

Blalock, H. M. (1964*). Causal inferences in nonexperimental research.* Chapel Hill: University of North Carolina Press.

Bogdan, R., & Taylor, S. (1975*). Introduction to qualitative research: A phenomenological approach to the social sciences.* New York: John Wiley & Sons.

Bollen, K. (2000). Modeling strategies: In search of the Holy Grail. *Structural Equation Modeling, 7,* 74–81.

Bollen, K.A. (1990). Outlier screening and a distribution: Free Test for Vanishing Tetrads. *Sociological Methods and Research, 19,* 80–92.

Bollen, K.A. and Ting, K. (1993). Confirmatory tetrad analysis. *Sociological Methodology, 23,* 147–75.

Bollen, K.A. and Ting, K. (1998). Bootstrapping a test statistic for vanishing tetrads. *Sociological Methods and Research 27,* 77–102.

Bollen, K.A. and Ting, K. (2000). A tetrad test for causal indicators. *Psychological Methods, 5,* 3–22

Bond, T. G., & Fox, C. M. (2001). *Applying the Rasch model: Fundamental measurement in the human sciences.* New Jersey: Lawrence Erlbaum Associates.

Borsboom, D., Mellenbergh, G. J. (2004). Why psychometrics is not pathological: A comment on Michell. *Theory and Psychology, 14,* 105–120.

Borsboom, D., Mellenbergh, G. J., & Van Heerden, J. (2003). The theoretical status of latent variables. *Psychological Review, 110,* 203–219.

Bowler, P. J. (1989). *Evolution: The history of an idea.* Los Angeles, CA: University of California Press.

Box, G. E. P. (1953). Non–normality and tests on variances. *Biometrika, 40,* 318–335.

Bozeman, T. D. (1977). *Protestants in an age of science: The Baconian ideal and antebellum American religious thought.* Chapel Hill, NC: University of North Carolina Press.

Brady, H. (2002). *Models of causal inference: Going beyond the Neyman-Rubin-Holland Theory.* Retrieved November 19, 2005, from http://polmeth.wustl.edu/retrieve.php?id=87

Bredo, E., & Feinberg, W. (1982). The positivist approach to social and educational research. In E. Bredo & W. Feinberg (Eds.), *Knowledge and values in social and educational research* (pp. 13–27). Philadelphia: Temple University Press.

Brenner–Golomb, N. (1993). R. A. Fisher's philosophical approach to inductive inference. In Keren G. & Lewis, C. (Eds.), *A handbook for data analysis in the behavioral sciences* (pp. 283–307). Hillsdale, NJ: LEA.

Bring, J. (1996). A geometric approach to compare variables in a regression model. *American Statistician, 50,* 57–62.

Bronowski, J. (1965/1972). *Science and human values.* New York: Harper and Row.

Brown, R. (1963). *Explanation in social science—A constructive analysis of "explanations"and their outcome in the social sciences: Sociology, anthropology, economics, history, demography, political science, psychology.* Chicago, IL: Aldine Publishing Company.

Browne, M. W. (1984). Asymptotic distribution free methods in analysis of covariance structures. *British Journal of Mathematical and Statistical Psychology, 37,* 62–83.

Buchler, J. (1940). The accidents of Peirce's system. *Journal of Philosophy, 37,* 264–269.

Burrell, D. B. (1968). Knowing as a passionate and personal quest: C. S. Peirce. In M. Novak (Ed.), *American Philosophy and Future* (pp. 107–137). New York: Charles Scribner's Sons.

Callaway, H. G. (1999*). Intelligence, Community, and Cartesian Doubt.* Retrieved October 13, 2005, from http://www.door.net/arisbe/menu/library/aboutcsp/callaway/intell.htm

Campbell, D. & Stanley, J. (1963). *Experimental and quasi–experimental designs for research.* Chicago, IL: Rand–McNally.

Campbell, D. T. (1995). The postpositivist, nonfoundational, hermeneutic epistemology exemplified in the works of Donald W. Fiske. In P. E. Schrout & S. T. Fiske (Eds.*), Personality research, methods, and theory: A festschrift* *honoring Donald W. Fiske* (pp. 13–27). Hillsdale, NJ: Lawrence Erlbaum Associates.

Carnap, R. (1937). *The logical syntax of language.* London: Routledge & Kegan Paul Ltd.

Carnap, R. (1952). *The cognition of inductive methods.* Chicago, IL: University of Chicago Press.

Carnap, R. (1956*). Meaning and necessity: A study in semantics and modal.* Chicago, IL: University of Chicago Press.

Carnap, R. (1959). The elimination of metaphysics through logical analysis of language. In A. J. Ayer (Ed.), *Logical positivism* (pp. 60–81). New York: Free Press.

Carnap, R. (1971). Foundations of logic and mathematics. In O. Neurath, R. Carnap, & C. Morris, (Eds.), *Foundations of the unity of science, toward an international encyclopedia of unified science* (pp. 139–212). Chicago: University of Chicago Press.

Cartwright, N. (1983). *How the laws of physics lie.* Oxford: Oxford University Press.

Cartwright, N. (1989). *Nature's capacities and their measurement.* Oxford: Oxford University Press.

Cartwright, N. (1999a). Causal diversity and the Markov Condition. *Synthese, 12,* 3–27.

Cartwright, N. (1999b). *The dappled world.* Cambridge: Cambridge University Press.

Cartwright, N. (2001).What is wrong with Bayes Nets? *Monist, 84,* 242–276.

Chaitin, G. J. (1998). *The limits of mathematics: A course on information theory and the limits of formal reasoning*. Singapore: Springer–Verlag.

Chou, C. H., & Bentler, P. M. (1995). Estimates and tests in structural equation modeling. In R. H. Hoyle (Eds.), *Structural equation modeling: Concepts, issues, and applications* (pp. 37–55). Thousand Oaks, CA: Sage Publications.

Christensen, L. B. (1988). *Experimental methodology.* Boston: Allyn and Bacon.

Clark, A. M. (1998). The qualitative–quantitative debate: Moving from positivism and confrontation to post–positivism and reconciliation. *Journal of Advanced Nursing, 27,* 1242–1249.

Cliff, N. (1996). *Ordinal methods for behavioral data analysis.* Mahwah, NJ: Erlbaum.

Clogg, C., and Haritou, A. (1997). The regression method of causal inference and a dilemma confronting this method. In Vaughn R. McKim, and Stephen P. Turner (Eds.), *Causality in Crisis: Statistical Methods and the Search for Causal Knowledge in the Social Sciences* (pp. 83–112). Norte Dame, IN: University of Norte Dame Press.

Coffa, J. A. (1991). *The semantic tradition from Kant to Carnap.* New York: Cambridge University Press.

Cohen, J. (1990). Things I have learned (so far). *American Psychologist, 45,* 1304–1312.

Cook, P. (1999). *Introduction to exploring data: Normal distribution.* Retrieved November 13, 2005, from http://exploringdata.cqu.edu.au/normdist.htm

Cook, T. D. (1985). Post–positivist critical multiplism. In R. L. Shotland & M. M. Mark (Eds.), *Social science and social policy* (pp. 21–62). Beverly Hills, CA: Sage.

Cook, T. D. (1991). Clarifying the warrant for generalized causal inferences in quasi–experimentation. In M. W. McLaughlin & D. Phillips (Eds.), *Evaluation and education at quarter century* (pp. 115–144). Chicago: NSSE.

Cook, T. D. (1993). A quasi–sampling theory of the generalization of causal relationships. In L. Sechrest & A. G. Scott (Eds.), *Understanding causes and generalizing about them* (pp. 39–83). San Francisco, CA: Jossey–Bass.

Cook, T. D., & Campbell, D. T. (1979). *Quasi–experimentation: Design and analysis issues for field settings.* Boston, MA: Houghton Mifflin Company.

Cook, T. D., & Shadish, W. R. (1994). Social experiments: Some developments over the past fifteen years. *Annual Review of Psychology, 45,* 545–580.

Copleston, F. (1946/1985). *A history of philosophy (Book One).* New York: Image.

Cox, D. R. (1958). Some problems connected with statistical inference. *Annals of Mathematical Statistics, 29,* 357–372.

Creath, R. (1990a). Carnap, Quine, and the rejection of intuition. In R. B. Barrett & R. F. Gibson (Eds.), *Perspectives on Quine* (pp. 55–66). Cambridge, MA: Basil Blackwell.

Creath, R. (Ed.). (1990b). *Dear Carnap, Dean Van: the Quine–Carnap correspondence and related work.* Berkeley, CA: University of California Press.

Creath, R. (1991). Every dogma has its day. *Erkenntnis, 35,* 347–389.

Cronbach, L. J. (1982). *Designing evaluations of educational and social programs.* San Francisco, CA: Jossey–Bass.

Cronbach, L. J. (1989). Construct validation after thirty years. In R. L. Linn (Ed.), *Intelligence: Measurement, theory, and public policy* (pp. 141–171). Urbana, IL: University of Illinois Press.

Cronbach, L. J., & Meehl, P. E. (1955). Construct validity in psychological tests. *Psychological Bulletin, 52,* 281–302.

D'Arms, J. (1996). Sex, fairness, and the theory of games. *Journal of Philosophy, 93,* 615–627.

D'Arms, J., Batterman, R. & Gorny, K. (1998). Game theoretic explanations and the evolution of justice. *Philosophy of Science, 65,* 76–102.

Data Description, Inc. (1999). DataDesk [Computer software and manual] Retrieved October 15, 2005, from http://www.datadesk.com

de Regt, H. (1994). *Representing the world by scientific theories: The case for scientific realism.* Tilburg, The Netherlands: Tilburg University Press,

de Waal, F. (2002). Evolutionary psychology: The wheat and the chaff. *Current Directions in Psychological Sciences, 11,* 187–194.

DesCartes, R. (1641/1964). *Philosophy essays: Discourse on method, meditations; Rules for the direction of the mind.* Indianapolis: Bobbs–Merrill.

DeVito, S. (1997). A gruesome problem for the curve–fitting solution. *British Journal for the Philosophy of Science, 48,* 391–396.

Devitt, M. (1991). *Realism and truth (2nd ed.).* Cambridge, MA: B. Blackwell.

Diaconis, P., and Efron, B. (1983). Computer–intensive methods in statistics. *Scientific American, May,* 116–130.

Dootson, S. (1995). An in–depth study of triangulation. *Journal of Advanced Nursing, 22,* 183–187.

Drozdek, A., & Keagy, T. (1994). A case for realism in mathematics. *Monist, 77,* 329–344.

Druzdzel, M, & Glymour, C. (1995, March–April). *Having the right tool: Causal graphs in teaching research design.* Paper presented at the University of Pittsburgh Teaching Excellence Conference, Pittsburgh, PA.

Duhem, P. M. M. (1954). *The aim and structure of physical theory.* Princeton, NJ: Princeton University Press.

Dupres, J., & Cartwright, N. (1988). Probability and causality: Why Hume and indeterminism don't mix. *Nous, 22,* 521–536.

Edgington, E. S.(1995). *Randomization tests.* New York: M. Dekker.

Edwards, J. (2003). Evolutionary psychology and politics. *Economy and Society, 32,* 280–298.

Efron, B., & Tibshirani, R. J. (1993). *An introduction to the bootstrap.* New York: Chapman & Hall.

Eliason, S. R. (1993). *Maximum likelihood estimation: Logic and practice.* Newbury Park, CA: Sage.

Embretson, S. E., & Reise, S. (2000). *Item response theory for psychologists.* Mahwah, NJ: Lawrence Erlbaum Associates.

Erlandson, D. A., Harris, E. L., Skipper, B. L., & Allen, S. D. (1993). *Doing naturalistic inquiry: A guide to methods.* Newbury Park, CA: Sage Publications.

Ernst, Z. (2001). Explaining the social contract. *British Journal of Philosophy of Science, 52,* 1–24.

Everitt, B. S. (1999). *Chance rule: An informal guide to probability, risk, and statistics.* New York: Springer.

Feest, U. (2005). Operationism in psychology: What the debate is about, what the debate should be about. *Journal of History of the Behavioral Sciences, 41,* 131–149.

Feibleman, J. (1945). Peirce's use of Kant. *The Journal of Philosophy, 42,* 365–377.

Feldman, M. (1998, February 28). Re: Rethinking quantitative social research. Message posted to news://sci.stat.consult

Fielding, N., & Fielding, J. (1986). *Linking data.* Beverly Hills, CA: Sage Publications.

Fisher, R. A. (1930). Inverse probability. *Proceedings of the Cambridge Philosophical Society, 26,* 528–535.

Fisher, R. A. (1935). The logic of inductive inference. *Journal of the Royal Statistical Society, 98,* 39–82.

Fisher, R. A. (1936). Has Mendel's work been rediscovered? *Annals of Science, 1,* 115–117.

Fisher, R. A. (1949). *The theory of inbreeding.* Edinburg: Oliver and Boyd.

Fisher, R. A. (1955). Statistical methods and scientific induction. *Journal of the Royal Statistical Society B, 17,* 69–78.

Fisher, R. A. (1956). *Statistical methods and scientific inference.* Edinburgh: Oliver and Boyd.

Fisher, R. A. (1958). *The genetical theory of natural selection.* New York: Dover Publications.

Fisher, R. A. (1990). *Statistical inference and analysis: selected correspondence* (edited by J.H. Bennett). New York: Oxford University Press, 1990.

Fisher–Box, J. (1978). *R. A. Fisher: The life of a scientist.* New York: John Wiley.

Forster, M. (1999). Model selection in science: The problem of language variance. *British Journal for the Philosophy of Science, 50,* 83–102.

Forster, M., & Sober, E. (1994). How to tell when simpler, more unified, or less ad hoc theories will provide more accurate predictions. *British Journal for the Philosophy of Science, 45,* 1–35.

Forster, P. D. (1993). Peirce on the progress and the authority of science. *Transaction of the Charles S. Peirce Society, 29,* 421–452.

Freedman, D. & Humphreys, P. (1998) *Are there algorithms that discover causal structure? Technical Report 514.* Berkeley, CA: University of California, Berkeley.

Freedman, D. (1987). As others see us: A case study in path analysis. *Journal of Educational Studies, 12,* 101–128.

Freedman, D. (1995). Discussion of causal diagrams for empirical research by J. Pearl. *Biometrika, 82,* 692–693.

Freedman, D. (1997). From Association to Causation via Regression. *Advances in Applied Mathematics, 18,* 59–110.

Freedman, D. (2005). *Statistical models for causation.* Retrieved November 19, 2005, from http://www.stat.berkeley.edu/~census/651.pdf

Frege, G. (1884/1960). *The foundations of arithmetic (2nd ed.).* New York: Harper.

Friedman, M. (1991). The re–evaluation of logical positivism. *The Journal of Philosophy, 88,* 505–519.

Friedman, M. (2002). Kant, Kuhn, and the rationality of science. *Philosophy of Science, 69,* 171–190.

Gander, E. (2003). *On our minds: How evolutionary psychology is reshaping the nature–versus–nurture debate.* Baltimore, MD: John Hopkins University Press.

Geary, R. C. (1947). Testing for normality. *Biometrika, 34,* 209–241.

Gerbing, D., & Hamiliton, J. (1996). Viability of Exploratory Factor Analysis as a precursor to confirmatory factor analysis. *Structural Equation Modeling, 3,* 62–72.

Gigerenzer, G. & Edwards, A. (2003). Simple tools for understanding risks: from innumeracy to insight. *BioMedical Journal, 327,* 741–744.

Gigerenzer, G., Swijtink, Z., Porter, T., Daston, L., Beatty, J., Kruger, L. (1989). *The empire of chance: How probability changed science and everyday life.* Cambridge: Cambridge University Press.

Gillham, N. W. (2001). *A life of Sir Francis Galton: From African exploration to the birth of eugenics.* Oxford: Oxford University Press.

Glaser, B. G., & Strauss, A. L. (1967). *Discovery of grounded theory: Strategies for qualitative research.* Chicago, IL: Aldine Pub. Co.

Glass, G. V. (1976). Primary, secondary, and meta–analysis of research. *Educational Researcher, 5,* 3–8.

Glass, G. V., McGraw, B., & Smith, M. L. (1981). *Meta–analysis in social research.* Beverly Hills, CA: Sage Publications.

Glesne, C., & Peshkin, A. (1992). *Becoming qualitative researchers: An introduction.* New York : Longman.

Gliner, J. A., & Morgan, G. A. (2000). *Research methods in applied settings: An integrated approach to design and analysis.* Mahwah, NJ: Lawrence Erlbaum Associates.

Glymour, C. (1980). *Theory and evidence.* Princeton: Princeton University Press.

Glymour, C. (1982). Casual inference and causal explanation. In R. McLaughlin (Ed.), *What? Where? When? Why? Essays on induction, space, and time, explanation* (pp. 179–191). Boston, MA: D. Reidel Publishing Company.

Glymour, C. (1986). Comments: Statistics and metaphysics. *Journal of the American Statistical Association, 81,* 964–966.

Glymour, C. (1998). What went wrong? Reflections on science by observations and the Bell Curve. *Philosophy of Science, 65,* 1–32.

Glymour, C. (1999a). A mind is a terrible thing to waste. *Philosophy of Science, 66,* 455–471.

Glymour, C. (1999b). Rabbit hunting. *Synthese, 121,* 55–78.

Glymour, C. (2001). *Mind's arrows: Bayes and Graphical causal models in psychology.* Cambridge, MA: MIT Press.

Glymour, C. (2005 May). *Bayes Nets and the automation of discovery.* Paper presented at the Second Annual Austin–Berkeley Formal Epistemology Workshop, Austin, TX.

Glymour, C. (in press). Review of James Woodward "Making things happen: A theory of causal explanation." *British Journal for Philosophy of Science.*

Glymour, C. & Cooper, G. F. (Eds.) (1999). *Computation, causation, and discovery.* Cambridge, MA: MIT Press.

Glymour, C., Scheines, R., Spirtes, P, & Kelly, K. (1987). *Discovering causal structure: Artificial intelligence, philosophy of science, and statistical modeling.* Orlando, FL: Academic Press.

Gödel, K. (1944). Russell's mathematical logic. In P. A. Schilpp, (Ed.), *The philosophy of Bertrand Russell* (pp. 125–153). Chicago: Northwestern University.

Gödel, K. (1947/1986). *Collected works*. New York: Oxford University Press.

Gonzalez, W. J. (1991). Intuitionistic mathematics and Wittgenstein. *History and Philosophy of Logic, 12,* 167–183.

Goodman, N. (1954/1983). *Facts, fictions, and forecast.* Indianapolis: Hackett.

Gopnik, A. & Schulz, L. (2004). Mechanisms of theory formation in young children. Trends in *Cognitive Sciences, 8,* 371–377.

Gould, S. J. (1988). The ontogeny of Sewall Wright and the phylogeny of evolution, *Isis, 79,* 273–281.

Greene, B. (2004). *The fabric of the cosmos: Space, time, and the texture of reality*. New York: Vintage Books.

Greenland, S. (2000). Causal analysis in the health sciences. *Journal of the American Statistical Association, 95,* 286–289.

Guba, G., & Lincoln, E. (1994). Competing paradigms in qualitative research. In N. K. Denzin, & Y. S. Lincoln (Eds.), *Handbook of qualitative research* (pp. 105–117). Thousand Oaks, CA: Sage Publications.

Haack, S. (1993). Peirce and logicism: Notes towards an exposition. *Transaction of the Charles S. Peirce Society, 29,* 33–67.

Hacking, I. (1975). *The emergence of probability: A philosophical study of early ideas about probability, induction and statistical inference.* NewYork : Cambridge University Press.

Hacking, I. (1983). *Representing and intervening: Introductory topics in the philosophy of natural science.* New York: Cambridge University Press.

Hacking, I. (1990). In praise of the diversity of probabilities. *Statistical Science, 5,* 450–454.

Hacking, I. (1992). *The taming of chance.* Cambridge, UK: Cambridge University Press.

Hacking, I. (1999). *The social construction of what?* Cambridge, MA: Harvard University Press.

Harman, G. (1965). The inference to the best explanation. *Philosophical Review, 74,* 1, 88–95.

Harman, G. (1968) Enumerative induction as inference to the best explanation. *Journal of Philosophy, 65,* 529–533.

Hart, B., & Spearman, C. (1913). General ability, its existence and nature. *British Journal of Psychology, 5,* 51–84.

Hausman, C. R. (1993). *Charles S. Peirce's evolutionary philosophy.* Cambridge: Cambridge University Press.

Hausman, D., & Woodward, J. (1999). Independence, invariance, and the Causal Markov Condition. *British Journal of Philosophy of Science, 50,* 521–583.

Hayduk, L. A., & Glaser, D. (2000). Jiving the four–step, waltzing around factor analysis, and other serious fun. *Structural Equation Modeling, 7,* 1–35.

Hayduk, L., & Glaser, D. (2000). Doing the four–step, right–2–3, wrong–2–3: A brief reply to Mulaik and Millsap; Bollen; Bentler; and Herting and Costner. *Structural Equation Modeling, 7,* 111–123.

Hempel, C. G. (1954). A logical appraisal of operationalism. *Scientific Monthly, 79,* 215–220.

Hempel, C. G. (1965) *Aspects of scientific explanation and other essays in the philosophy of science.* New York: Free Press.

Hempel, C. G. (1966). *Philosophy of natural science.* Englewood Cliffs, NJ: Prentice–Hall.

Hersh, R. (1997). *What is mathematics, really?* Oxford: Oxford University Press.

Herting, J. (2000). Another perspective on 'the proper number of factors' and the appropriate number of steps. *Structural Equation Modeling, 7,* 92–112.

Hill, W. (1996). Sewall Wright's "System of Mating." *Genetics, 143,* 1499–1506.

Hipp, J. and Bollen, K. A. (2003). "Model fit in structural equation models with censored, ordinal, and dichotomous variables: testing vanishing tetrads. *Sociological Methodology, 33,* 267–305.

Hipp, J., Bauer, D.J., & Bollen, K. A. (2005). Conducting tetrad tests of model fit and contrasts of tetrad–nested models: A new SAS macro. *Structural Equation Modeling, 12,* 76–93.

Hoffmann, M. (1997). *Is there a logic of abduction?* Paper presented at the 6th congress of the International Association for Semiotic Studies, Guadalajara, Mexico.

Hoffrage, U., Gigerenzer, G., Krauss, S., & Martignon, L. (2002). Representation facilities reasoning: What natural frequencies are and what they are not. *Cognition, 2002,* 343–352.

Hotelling, H. (1933). Analysis of a complex of statistical variables into principal components. *Journal of Educational Psychology, 24,* 4170441, 498–520.

Howe, K. R (1988). Against the quantitative–qualitative incompatibility thesis (or dogmas die hard). *Educational Researcher, 17,* 10–16.

Howie, D. (2002). Interpreting probability: Controversies and developments in the early twentieth century. Cambridge, UK: Cambridge University Press.

Howson, C., & Urbach, P. (1993). *Scientific reasoning: The Bayesian approach.* Chicago, IL: Open Court.

Hoyle, R. H. (Ed.) (1995). *Structural equation modeling: Concepts, issues, and applications.* Thousand Oaks, CA: Sage Publications.

Hoyle, R. H. (1995). The structural equation modeling approach: Basic concepts and fundamental issues. In R. H. Hoyle (Ed.), *Structural equation modeling: Concepts, issues, and applications* (pp. 1–15). Thousand Oaks: Sage Publications.

Hsu, L. M. (1989). Random sampling, randomization, and equivalence of contrasted groups in psychotherapy outcome research. *Journal of Consulting and Clinical Psychology, 57,* 131–137.

Hubbard, R., & Bayarri, M. J. (2003). Confusion over measures of evidence (p's) versus errors (alpha's) in classical statistical testing. *American Statistician, 57,* 171–178.

Hume, D. (1777/1912). *An enquiry concerning human understanding, and selections from a treatise of human nature.* Chicago: Open Court Pub. Co.

Hunter, J. E., & Schmidt, F. L. (1990). *Methods of meta–analysis: Correcting error and bias in research findings.* Newbury Park, CA: Sage Publications.

Huysamen, G. K. (1997). Parallels between qualitative research and sequentially performed quantitative research. *South African Journal of Psychology, 27,* 1–9.

Inman, H. F. (1994). Karl Pearson and R. A. Fisher on statistical tests: A 1935 exchange from Nature. *The American Statistician, 48,* 2–11.

Isaacson, D. (2000). Carnap, Quine, and logical truth. In D. Follesdal (Ed.). *Philosophy of Quine: General, reviews, and analytic/synthetic* (pp. 360–391). NewYork: Garland Publishing.

Jacquez, J. A., & Jacquez, G. M. (2002). Fisher's randomization test and Darwin's data—A footnote to the history of statistics. *Mathematical Biosciences, 180,* 23–28.

Jaffe, A., & Quinn, F. (1993). "Theoretical mathematics": Toward a cultural synthesis of mathematics and theoretical physics. *American Mathematics Society, 28,* 1–13.

Jaynes, E. T. (1995). *Probability theory: The logic of science.* Retrieved October 13, 1995, from http://omega.math.albany.edu:8008/JaynesBook.html

Jick, T. (1983). Mixing qualitative and quantitative methods: Triangulation in action. In Van Mannen (Ed.), *Qualitative methodology* (pp. 135–148). Beverly Hills, CA: Sage Publications.

Johnson, B. & Onwuegbuzie, A. (2004). Mixed methods research: A research paradigm whose time has come. *Educational Researcher, 33,* 14–26.

Joreskog, K. G. (1969). A general approach to confirmatory maximum likelihood factor analysis. *Psychometrika, 34,* 183–202.

Joreskog, K. G. (1970). A general method for analysis of covariance structures. *Biometrika, 57,* 239–251.

Joreskog, K. G. (1971). Statistical analysis of sets of congeneric tests. *Psychometrika, 36,* 109–132.

Joreskog, K. G. (1974). Analyzing psychological data by structural analysis of covariance matrices. In R.C. Atkinson, D.H. Krantz, R.D. Luce and P. Suppes (Eds.), *Contemporary developments in mathematical psychology* (Vol II, pp. 1–56). San Francisco: W.H. Freeman.

Joreskog, K. G. (1980). Structural analysis of covariance and correlation matrices. *Psychometrika, 43,* 443–477.

Joreskog, K. G. and Sorbom, D. (1979). *Advances in factor analysis and structural equation models.* Cambridge, MA: ABT Books.

Josephson, J. R. & Josephson, S. G. (1994). (Eds.) *Abductive inference: Computation, philosophy, technology.* Cambridge, UK: Cambridge University Press.

Kant, I. (1781/1969*). Critique of pure reason.* New York: Dutton.

Kelley, D. (1998*). The art of reasoning (3rd ed.).* New York: W. W. Norton & Co.

Kelley, T. L. (1940). Comment on Wilson and Worcester's Note on Factor Analysis. *Psychometrika, 5,* 117–120.

Keng, L, & Beretvas, N. (2005 April). *The effect of publication bias on correlation estimation.* Paper presented at the Annual Meeting of the American Educational Research Association, Montreal, Canada.

Keppel, G., & Zedeck, S. (1989). *Data analysis for research design: Analysis of Variance and Multiple Regression/Correlation approaches.* New York: W. H. Freeman.

Kerlinger, F. N. (1986). *Foundations of behavioral research (3rd ed.).* Forth Worth, TX: Holt, Rinehart and Winston.

Kieseppa, I. A. (2001). Statistical model selection criteria and the philosophical problem of underdetermination. *British Journal for the Philosophy of Science, 52,* 761–794.

Kline, R.B. (1998). *Principles and practice of structured equation modeling.* New York: The Guilford Press.

Koopmans, T. C., & Reiersol O. (1950). The identification of structural characteristics. *Annals of Mathematical Statistics, 21,* 165–181.

Korb, K. B., & Wallace, C. S. (1997). In search of the philosopher's stone: Remarks on Humphreys and Freedman's critique of causal discovery. *British Journal for the Philosophy of Science, 48,* 543–553.

Krebs, D. (2000). Evolutionary games and morality. *Journal of Consciousness Studies, 7,* 313–321.

Kuhn, T. S. (1962). *The structure of scientific revolutions.* Chicago: University of Chicago Press.

Kuhn, T. S. (1985). *The Copernican revolution.* Massachusetts, MA: Harvard University Press.

Kukla, A. (2000). *Social constructivism and the philosophy of science.* New York: Routledge.

Lakoff, G., & Nunez, R. E. (2000). *Where mathematics comes from: How the embodied mind brings mathematics into being.* New York: Basic Books.

Langenbach, M., Vaughn, C., & Aagaard, L. (1994). *An introduction to educational research.* Boston, MA: Allyn and Bacon.

Laudan, L. (1977). *Progress and its problems: Toward a theory of scientific growth.* Berkeley, CA : University of California Press.

Laudan, L. (1996). *Beyond positivism and relativism: Theory, method, and evidence.* Boulder, CO: Westview Press.

Lawley, D. N., & Maxwell, A. E. (1971). *Factor analysis as a statistical method.* London: Butterworth.

Leech, N. L., & Onwuegbuzie, A. J. (2004 April). *A typology of mixed research designs.* Paper presented at the Annual Meeting of the American Educational Research Association, Montreal, Canada.

Lehmann, E. L. (1993). The Fisher, Neyman–Pearson theories of testing hypotheses: One theory or two? *Journal of the American Statistical Association, 88,* 1242–1249.

Leplin, J. (1997). *A novel defense of scientific realism.* Oxford: Oxford University Press.

Letourneau, N., Allen, M. (1999). Post–positivistic critical multiplism: A beginning dialogue. *Journal of Advanced Nursing, 30,* 623–630.

Lieffer, K. M. (1999). An introductory prime on the appropriate use of exploratory and confirmatory factor analysis. *Research in the Schools, 6,* 75–92.

Linacre, (2000). Pierce, C.S. Almost the Peirce Model? *Rasch Measurement Transactions, 14,* 756–757.

Lindstrom, P. (2000). Quasi–realism in mathematics. *Monist, 83,* 122–149.

Ling, R. (1982). Review of "Correlation and causation" by David Kenny. *Journal of American Statistical Association, 77,* 481–491.

Lipton, P. (1991). *Inference to the best explanation.* New York: Routledge.

Lomax, R. G. (1992). *Statistical concepts: A second course for education and the behavioral sciences.* White Plains, NY: Longman.

Lord, F. (1980). *Applications of item response theory to practical testing problems.* Hillsdale, NJ: Lawrence Erlbaum Associates.

Ludbrook, J. & Dudley, H. (1998). Why permutation tests are superior to t and F tests in biomedical research. *American Statistician, 52,* 127–132.

Luker, B., Luker, B., Jr., Cobb, S. L., & Brown, R. (1998). Postmodernism, institutionalism, and statistics: Considerations for an institutionalist statistical method. *Journal of Economic Issues, 32,* 449–457.

MacCallum, R. C. (1995). Model specification: Procedures, strategies, and related issues. In R. H. Hoyle (Ed.), *Structural equation modeling: Concepts, issues, and applications* (pp. 16–36). Thousand Oaks, CA: Sage Publications.

Mach, E. (1941). *The sciences of mechanics.* La sale, IL: Open Court.

Magnello, M. E. (1996a). Karl Pearson's Gresham Lectures: W. F. R. Weldon, speciation and the origins of Pearsonian statistics. *British Journal for the History of Science, 29,* 43–64.

Magnello, M. E. (1996b). Karl Pearson's mathematization of inheritance: from ancestral heredity to Mendelian genetics (1895–1909). *Annals of Science, 55,* 33–94.

Mallows, C. L., & Tukey, J. W. (1982). An overview of techniques of data analysis, emphasizing its exploratory aspects. In J. T. de Oliveira & B. Epstein (Eds.), *Some recent advances in statistics* (pp. 111–172). London: Academic Press.

Maraun, M. (1996). Metaphor taken as truth: Indeterminacy in the factor analysis model. *Multivariate Behavioral Research, 31,* 517–538.

Markus, K. (2000). Conceptual shell games in the four–step debate. *Structural Equation Modeling, 7,* 163–173.

Markus, K. (2004). Varieties of causal modeling: How optimal research design varies by explanatory strategy. In K. van Montfort, J. Oud, & A. Satorra (Eds.), *Recent developments on structural equation models* (pp. 175–196). Boston, MA: Kluwer Academic Publishers.

McLaughlin, E. (1991). Oppositional poverty: The quantitative/qualitative divide and other dichotomies. *Sociological Review, 39,* 292–308.

Meehl, P. E. (1986). What social scientists don't understand. In D. W. Fiske & R. A. Schweder (Eds.), *Metatheory in social science: Pluralisms and subjectivities* (p. 325). Chicago: University of Chicago Press.

Meek, C., & Glymour, C. (1994). Conditioning and intervening. *British Journal of Philosophy, 45,* 1001–1021.

Merriam, S. B. (1998). *Qualitative research and case study: Applications in education.* San Francisco, CA: Jossey–Bass.

Michell, J. (1997). Quantitative science and the definition of measurement in psychology. *British Journal of Psychology, 88,* 355–386.

Michell, J. (2000). Normal science, pathological science and psychometrics. *Theory and Psychology, 10,* 639–667.

Michell, J. (2004). Item response models, pathological science and the shape of error: reply to Borsboom and Mellenbergh. *Theory and Psychology, 14,* 121–129.

Miles, M., & Huberman, A. (1984). *Qualitative data analysis.* Beverly Hills, CA: Sage Publications.

Minnameier, G. (2004). Peirce's suit of truth: Why inference to the best explanation and abduction ought not to be confused. *Erkenntnis, 60,* 75–105.

Mislevy, R. (1993). Some formulas for use with Bayesian ability estimates. Educational *& Psychological Measurement, 53,* 315–329.

Mislevy, R. (1994). Evidence in educational assessment. *Psychometrika, 59,* 439–483.

Moran, P. A. P., & Smith, C. A. B. (1966). *Commentary on R. A. Fishers paper on the correlation between relatives on the supposition of Mendelian inheritance.* London: Galton Laboratory, University College London.

Morrison, M. (2002). Modelling populations: Pearson and Fisher on Mendelism and Biometry. *British Journal of Philosophy of Science, 53,* 39–68.

Mulaik, S. (1991). Factor analysis, information–transforming instruments, and objectively: A reply and discussion. *British Journal for Philosophy of Science, 42,* 87–100.

Mulaik, S. (1993). Objectivity and multivariate statistics. *Multivariate Behavioral Research, 28,* 171–203.

Mulaik, S. (1996b). On Maraun's deconstructing of factor indeterminacy with constructed factors. *Multivariate Behavioral Research, 31,* 579–592.

Mulaik, S. A., & James, L. R. (1995). Objectivity and reasoning in science and structural equation modeling. In R. H. Hoyle (Eds.), *Structural equation modeling: Concepts, issues, and applications* (pp. 118–127). Thousand Oaks: Sage Publications.

Mulaik, S., & Millsap, R. (2000). Doing the Four–Step Right. *Structural Equation Modeling, 7,* 36–73.

Mulaik, Stanley. (1987). A brief history of the philosophical foundation of exploratory factor analysis. *Multivariate Behavioral Research, 22,* 267–305.

Mulaik, Stanley. (1996a). Factor analysis is not just a model in pure mathematics. *Multivariate Behavioral Research, 31,* 655–661.

Nation, J. R. (1997). *Research methods.* Upper Saddle River, NJ: Prentice Hall.

Neyman, J. & Pearson, E. S. (1928). On the use and interpretation of certain test criteria for purposes of statistical inference. Part I and II. *Biometrika, 20,* 174–240, 263–294.

Neyman, J. & Pearson, E. S. (1933a). The testing of statistical hypotheses in relation to probabilities a priori. *Proceedings of Cambridge Philosophical Society, 20,* 492–510.

Neyman, J. & Pearson, E. S. (1933b). On the problem of the most efficient tests of statistical hypotheses. *Philosophical Transactions of Royal Society; Series A, 231,* 289–337.

Neyman, J., & Pearson, E. S. (1933). On the problem of the most efficient tests of statistical hypotheses. *Philosophical Transactions of the Royal Society of London, Series A, 231,* 289–337.

Norton, B. J. (1975). Biology and philosophy: The methodological foundations of biometry. *Journal of History of Biology, 8,* 85–93.

Norton, B. J. (1983). Fisher's entrance into evolutionary science: The role of eugenics. In M. Grene (Ed.), *Dimensions of Darwinism: Themes and counterthemes in 20th century evolutionary theory* (pp. 19–30), Cambridge: Cambridge University Press.

Norton, B. J., & Pearson, E. S. (1976). A note on the background to, and refereeing of, R. A. Fisher's 1918 paper "On the correlation between relatives on the supposition of Mendelian inheritance." *Notes and Records of the Royal Society of London, 31,* 151–162.

O'Neill, L. (1993). Peirce and the nature of evidence. *Transaction of the Charles S. Peirce Society, 29,* 211–223.

Olkin, I. (2000, November). *Reconcilable differences: Gleaning insight from independent scientific studies.* ASU Phi Beta Kappa Lecturer Program, Tempe, Arizona.

Olson, C. L. (1976). On choosing a test statistic in multivariate analysis of variance. *Psychological Bulletin, 83,* 579–586.

Onwuegbuzie, A. J., & Leech, N. L. (2005, February). *Linking research questions to mixed methods data analysis procedures.* Paper presented at the annual meeting of the Southwest Educational Research Association, New Orleans, LA.

Ottens, J. & Shank, G. (1995). The role of abductive logic in understanding and using advanced empathy. *Counselor Education & Supervision, 34,* 199–213.

Parkhurst, D. (1985). Interpreting failure to reject a null hypothesis. *Bulletin of the Ecological Society of America, 66,* 301–302.

Parkhurst, D. (1990). Statistical hypothesis tests and statistical power in pure and applied science. In G. M. von Furstenberg (Ed.), *Acting under uncertainty: Multidisciplinary conceptions* (pp. 181–201). Boston, MA: Kluwer Academic Publishers.

Patomaki, H., & Wight, C. (2000). After postpositivism? The promises of critical realism. *International Studies Quarterly, 44,* 213–239.

Pawitan, Y. (2000). *Likelihood: Consensus and controversies.* Paper presented at the Conference of Applied Statistics in Ireland.

Pawitan, Y. (2001). *In all likelihood: Statistical modeling and inference using likelihood.* New York: Oxford University Press.

Pearl, J. (1995). Rejoinder to discussions of causal diagrams for empirical research. *Biometrika, 82,* 702–710.

Pearl, J. (2000). *Causality: Models, reasoning, and inference.* Cambridge, UK: Cambridge University Press.

Pearl, J. (2001). Causal inference in the health science: A conceptual introduction. *Health Services and Outcomes Research Methodology, 2,* 189–220.

Pearson, E. S. (1938). *Karl Pearson: An appreciation of some aspects of his life and work.* Cambridge: The University Press.

Pearson, E. S. (1955). Statistical concepts in their relation to reality. *Journal of the Royal Statistical Society, Series B, 17,* 204–207.

Pearson, K. & Filon, L. N. G. (1898) Mathematical contributions to the theory of evolution IV. On the probable errors of frequency constants and on the influence of random selection on variation and correlation. *Philosophical Transactions of the Royal Society A, 191,* 229–311.

Pearson, K. (1892/1937). *The grammar of science.* London: J. M. Dnt & Sons.

Pearson, K. (1894). Contributions to the mathematical theory of evolution. *Philosophical Transactions of the Royal Society A, 185,* 71–110.

Pearson, K. (1895). Contributions to the mathematical theory of evolution. II. Skew variation in homogeneous material. *Philosophical Transactions of the Royal Society A, 186,* 343–414.

Pearson, K. (1896) Mathematical contributions to the theory of evolution. III. Regression, heredity and panmixia. *Philosophical Transactions of the Royal Society A, 187,* 253–318.

Pearson, K. (1900) On the criterion that a given system of deviations from the probable in the case of correlated system of variables is such that it can be reasonably supposed to have arisen from random sampling. *Philosophical Magazine, 50,* 157–175.

Pedhazur, E. J. (1982). *Multiple regression in behavioral research: Explanation and predication (2nd ed.).* Forth Worth, TX: Harcourt Brace College Publishers.

Peirce, C. (1934/1960). *Collected papers of Charles Sanders Peirce.* Cambridge: Harvard University Press.

Peirce, C. S. (1868). Some consequences of four incapacities. *Journal of Speculative Philosophy, 2,* 140–157.

Peirce, C. S. (1877). The fixation of belief. *Popular Science Monthly, 12,* 1–15.

Peirce, C. S. (1878). Deduction, induction, and hypothesis. *Popular Science Monthly, 13,* 470–482.

Peirce, C. S. (1934/1960). *Collected papers of Charles Sanders Peirce.* Cambridge: Harvard University Press.

Peirce, C. S. (1954). Notes on positivism. In P. P. Wiener (Ed.), *Charles S. Peirce selected writing: Values in a universe of chance* (pp. 137–141). New York: Dover Publications.

Peirce, C. S. (1986). *Writings of Charles S. Peirce: A chronological edition (Volume 3: 1872–1878).* Bloomington: Indiana University Press.

Penrose, R. (1989). *The emperor's new mind: Concerning computers, minds, and the laws of physics.* Oxford: Oxford University Press.

Peterson, I. (July 27, 1991). Pick a sample. *Science News, 140,* 56–58.

Petrovic, M. (2000). *Probabilistic and structural causality.* Retrieved August 13, 2001, from http://www.soc.washington.edu/courses/soc582/misha3.html

Phillips D. (1987). *Philosophy, science and social Inquiry.* New York: Pergamon Press.

Phillips D. (1990a). Postpositivistic science: Myths and realities. In E. G. Guba (Ed.), *The paradigm dialogue* (pp. 31–45). Newbury Park, CA: Sage.

Phillips D. (1990b). Subjectivity and objectivity: An objective inquiry. In E. W. Eisner & A. Peshkin (Eds.), *Qualitative inquiry in education: The continuing debate* (pp. 19–37). New York: Teachers College Press.

Phillips D. C. (1992). *The social scientist's bestiary: A guide to fabled threats to, and defences of, naturalistic social science.* New York: Pergamon Press.

Phillips, D. C. (2000). *The expanded social scientist's bestiary.* New York: Rowman & Littlefield.

Phillips, D. C., & Burbules, N. (2000). *Postpositivism and educational research.* New York: Rowan & Littlefield.

Phillips, J. (1988). Diggers of deeper holes. *Nursing Science Quarterly, 1,* 149–151.

Piegorsch, W. W. (1990). Fisher's contributions to genetics and heredity, with special emphasis on the Gregor Mendel controversy. *Biometrics, 46,* 915–924.

Popper, K. R. (1959). *Logic of scientific discovery.* London: Hutchinson.

Popper, K. R. (1963). *Conjectures and refutations: The growth of scientific knowledge.* London: Routledge & K. Paul.

Popper, K. R. (1968). *Logic of scientific discovery.* New York: Harper & Row.

Popper, K. R. (1974). Replies to my critics. In P. A. Schilpp (Ed.), *The philosophy of Karl Popper* (pp. 963–1197). La Salle, IL.: Open Court.

Porter, T. (2004). *Karl Pearson: The scientific life in a statistical age.* Princeton, NJ: Princeton University Press.

Press, S. J., & Tanur, J. M. (2001). *The subjectivity of scientists and the Bayesian approach.* New York: John Wiley & Sons.

Province, W. (1971). *The origins of theoretical population genetics.* Chicago, IL: The University of Chicago Press.

Psillos, S. (1996). On Van Fraassen's critique of abductive reasoning. *Philosophical Quarterly, 46,* 31–47.

Psillos, S. (1999). *Scientific realism: How science tracks truth.* New York: Routledge.

Putname, H. (1995). Mathematical necessity reconsidered. In P. Leonardi & M. Santambrogio, (Eds.), *On Quine: New Essays* (pp. 267–282). Cambridge: Cambridge University Press.

Pyle, A. (Ed.). (1999). *Key Philosophers in Conversation: The Cogito interviews.* New York: Routledge.

Quine, W. V. (1951). Two dogmas of empiricism. *Philosophical Review, 60,* 20–43.

Quine, W. V. (1957). The scope and language of science. *British Journal for the Philosophical Science, 8,* 1–17.

Quine, W. V. (1966/1976). *The ways of paradox, and other essays.* Cambridge, MA: Harvard University Press.

Quine, W. V. (1982). *Methods of logic.* Cambridge, Mass.: Harvard University Press.

Quine, W. V. (1990/1992) *Pursuit of Truth (2nd ed.).* Cambridge, MA: Harvard University Press.

Rao, C. R. (1992). R. A. Fisher: The founder of modern statistics. *Statistical Science, 7,* 34–48.

Raykov, T., & Marcoulides, G. A. (2001). Can there be infinitely many models equivalent to a given covariance structure model? *Structural Equation Modeling, 8,* 142–149.

Reichardt, C. S., & Cook, T. D. (1979). Beyond qualitative versus quantitative methods. In T. D. Cook & C. S. Reichardt (Eds.), *Qualitative and quantitative methods in evaluation research* (pp. 7–32). Beverly Hills, CA: Sage Publications.

Reichenbach, H. (1938). *Experience and prediction: An analysis of the foundations and the structure of knowledge.* Chicago, IL: University of Chicago Press.

Reichenbach, H. (1956). *The direction of time.* Berkeley, CA: University of Los Angeles Press.

Reid, C. (1982). *Neyman—from life.* New York: Springer–Verlag.

Rennie, D. L. (1999). A matter of hermeneutics and the sociology of knowledge. In M. Kopala & L. A. Suzuki (Eds.), *Using qualitative methods in psychology* (pp. 3–14). Thousand Oaks, CA: Sage Publications.

Rescher, N. (1978). *Peirce's philosophy of science: Critical studies in his theory of induction and scientific method.* Notre dame: University of Notre Dame Press.

Roberts, P. C. (1989, December 11). America's self–loathing even has Japan convinced. *Business Week*, 22.

Root, D. (2003). Bacon, Boole, the EPA, and scientific standards. *Risk Analysis, 23,* 663–668.

Rosenthal, R. (1979). The "file–drawer problem" and tolerance for null results. *Psychological Bulletin, 86,* 638–641.

Rosenthal, S. B. (1993). Peirce's ultimate logical interpretant and dynamical object: A pragmatic perspective. *Transactions of the Charles S. Peirce Society, 29,* 195–210.

Rosnow, R., & Rosenthal, R. (1989). Statistical procedures and the justification of knowledge in psychological science. *American Psychologist, 44,* 1276–1284.

Rossano, M. (2003). *Evolutionary psychology*. New York: John Wiley & Sons.

Ruben, D. (1998). The philosophy of social sciences. In A. C. Grayling (Ed.), *Philosophy 2* (pp. 420–469). Oxford: Oxford University Press.

Ruse, M., & Wilson, E. O. (1985). The evolution of ethics. *New Scientist, 17,* 50–52.

Russell, B. & Whitehead, A. N. (1910). *Principia Mathematica.* Cambridge: Cambridge University Press.

Russell, B. (1913). On the notion of cause. *Proceeding of Aristotelian Society (New Series), 56,* 26–27.

Russell, B. (1919). *Introduction to mathematical philosophy.* London: Allen & Unwin.

Russell, B. (1945/72). *A history of Western philosophy.* New York: Touchstone.

Russell, B. (1959). Logical atomism. In A. J. Ayer (Ed.), *Logical positivism* (pp. 31–52). New York: Free Press.

Salmon, W. (1967). *The foundations of scientific inference.* Pittsburgh: University of Pittsburgh Press.

Salmon, W. (1984). *Scientific explanation and the causal structure of the world.* Princeton, NJ: Princeton University Press.

Salvucci, S., Walter, E., Conley, V, Fink, S, & Saba, M. (1997). *Measurement error studies at the National Center for Education Statistics.* Washington D. C.: U. S. Department of Education.

Samuelson, P. (1967). Economic forecast and science. In P. A. Samuelson, J. R. Coleman & F. Skidmore (Eds.), *Reading in Economics* (pp. 124–129). New York: McGraw–Hill.

Sanders, J. T. (1993). *Dimensions of scientific thought.* Nashville, TN: Camnichael & Carmichael.

Scheines, R., & Glymour, C., & Spirtes, P. (2005). The TETRAD project: Causal models and statistical data [Computer software and manual]. Retrieved October 13, 2005, from http://www.phil.cmu.edu/projects/tetrad/

Scheines, R., Spirtes, P., Glymour, C., Meek, C., & Richardson, T. (1998). The TETRAD project: Constraint based aids to causal model specification. *Multivariate Behavioral Research, 33,* 65–117.

Schlick, M. (1925/1974). *General theory of knowledge.* New York: Springer–Verlag.

Schlick, M. (1959). Positivism and realism. In A. J. Ayer (Ed.), *Logical positivism* (pp. 82–107). New York: Free Press.

Schuldenfrei, R. (1972). Quine in perspective. *Journal of Philosophy, 69,* 5–16.

Searle, J. (1998). *Mind, language, and society: Philosophy in the real world.* New York: Basic Books.

Shank, G. (1991, October). *Abduction: Teaching to the ground state of cognition.* Paper presented at the Bergamo Conference on Curriculum Theory and Classroom Practice, Dayton, OH.

Shipley, B. (2000). *Cause and correlation in biology: A user's guide to path analysis, structural equations and causal inference*. Cambridge: Cambridge University Press.

Simpson, E. H. (1951). The interpretation of interaction in contingency tables. *Journal of the Royal Statistical Society, Ser. B., 13,* 238–241.

Skyrms, B. (1975). *Choice and chance: An introduction to inductive logic (2nd ed.)*. Chicago, IL: University of Illinois Press.

Skyrms, B. (1996). *Evolution of the social contract*. Cambridge: Cambridge University Press.

Skyrms, B. (2000a). Game theory, rationality and evolution of the social contract. *Journal of Consciousness Studies, 7,* 269–284.

Skyrms, B. (2000b). Stability and explanatory significance of some simple evolutionary models. *Philosophy of Science, 67,* 94–113.

Skyrms, B. (2003). *Stag hunt and the evolution of social structure*. Cambridge: Cambridge University Press.

Sober, E. (2002). *Sex ratio theory, ancient and modern: An 18th century debate about intelligent design and the development of models in evolutionary theory*. Retrieved November 13, 2005, from http://philosophy.wisc.edu/sober/papers.htm

Spirtes, P., and Scheines, R. (1997). Reply to Freedman. In S. Turner and V. McKim (Eds.), *Causality in Crisis: Statistical Methods and the Search for Causal Knowledge in the Social Sciences.* (pp. 163–176). University of Notre Dame Press.

Spirtes, P., Glymour, C. & Scheines, R. (1993). *Causation, Prediction and Search.* Springer Verlag.

Staat, W. (1993). On abduction, deduction, induction and the categories. *Transactions of the Charles S. Peirce Society, 29,* 225–237.

Stigler, S. M. (1986). *The history of statistics: The measurement of uncertainty before 1900.* Cambridge, MA: The Belknap Press of Harvard University Press.

Stockford, S., Thompson, M., Lo, W. J., Chen, Y. H., Green, S., & Yu, C. H. (2001, October). *Confronting the statistical assumptions: New alternatives for comparing groups.* Paper presented at the Annual Meeting of Arizona Educational Researcher Organization, Tempe, AZ.

Suber, P. (1997). *Paradoxes of material implications*. Retrived October 28, 2005 from http://www.earlham.edu/~peters/courses/log/mat–imp.htm

Sullivan, P. F. (1991). On falsification interpretation of Peirce. *Transactions of the Charles S. Peirce Society, 27,* 197–219.

Tennant, N. (1999). Sex and the evolution of fair–dealing. *Philosophy of Science, 66,* 391–414.

Thagard, P., & Shelley, C. (1997). Abductive reasoning: Logic, visual thinking, and coherence. In M. Chiara (Eds), *Logic and scientific methods* (pp. 413–427). Dordrecht: Kluwer.

Thompson, B. (1992). A partial test distribution for cosines among factors across samples. In B. Thompson (Ed.), *Advances in Social Sciences Methodology* (Vol 2, pp. 81–97). Greenwich, CT: JAI Press.

Thompson, B. (2004). *Exploratory and confirmatory factor analysis: Understanding concepts and applications.* Washington, D. C.: American Psychological Association.

Thompson, B. (Ed). (2003). *Score reliability: Contemporary thinking on reliability issues.* Thousand Oaks, CA: Sage Publication.

Thompson, B., & Vacha–Haase, T. (2000). Psychometrics is datametrics: The test is not reliable. *Educational and Psychological Measurement, 60,* 174–195.

Thompson, D. W. (1959). *On growth and form.* Cambridge: Cambridge University Press.

Thompson, M. S., Green, S. B., Stockford, S. M., Chen, Y., & Lo, W. (2002, April). *The .05 level: The probability that the independent–samples t test should be applied?* Paper presented at the Annual Meeting of the American Education Researcher Association, New Orleans, LA.

Thornhill, R., & Palmer, C. (2000). *A natural history of rape: Biological bases of sexual coercion.* Cambridge, MA: MIT Press.

Thurstone, L. L. (1947). *Multiple–factor analysis: a development and expansion of the vectors of mind.* Chicago: The University of Chicago press.

Tieszen, R. (1992). Kurt Gödel and phenomenology. *Philosophy of Science, 59,* 176–194.

Tieszen, R. (1995). Mathematical realism and Gödel's incompleteness theorem. In P. Cortois (Ed.), *The many problems of realism* (pp. 217–246). Tilburg, Netherlands: Tiburg University Press.

Ting, K. (1998). The TETRAD approach to model respecification. *Multivariate Behavioral Research, 33,* 157–164.

Toothaker, L. E. (1993). *Multiple comparison procedures.* Newbury Park, CA: Sage Publications.

Trundle, R. (1994). *Ancient Greek philosophy: Its development and relevance to our time.* Brookfield: Avebury.

Tukey, J. W. (1977). *Exploratory data analysis.* Reading, MA: Addison–Wesley Publishing Company.

Tukey, J. W. (1980). We need both exploratory and confirmatory. *American Statistician, 34,* 23–25.

Tukey, J. W. (1986). *The collected works of John W. Tukey (Volume IV): Philosophy and principles of data analysis 1965–1986.* Monterey, CA: Wadsworth & Brooks/Cole.

Turney, P. (1999). The curving fitting problem: A solution. *British Journal for the Philosophy of Science, 41,* 509–530.

Tursman, R. (1987). *Peirce's theory of scientific discovery: A system of logic conceived as semiotic.* Indianapolis, Indiana: Indiana University Press.

Upton, G. (1992). Fisher's exact test. *Journal of the Royal Statistical Society. Series A (Statistics in Society), 155,* 395–402.

Vacha–Hasse, T. (1998). Reliability generalization: Exploring variance in measurement error affecting score reliability across studies. *Educational and Psychological Measurement, 58,* 6–20.

Van Fraassen, B. (1980). *The scientific image.* Oxford: Clarendon Press.

Van Fraassen, B. (1989). *Laws and symmetry.* Oxford: Oxford University Press.

Vincent, D. F. (1953). The origin and development of factor analysis. *Applied statistics, 2,* 107–117.

von Mises, R. (1928/1957). *Probability, statistics, and truth.* London: The Macmillan Company.

von Mises, R. (1964). *Mathematical theory of probability and statistics.* New York: Academic Press.

Walsh, D. M. (2003). Fit and diversity: Explaining adaptive evolution. *Philosophy of Science, 70,* 280–301.

Walsh, D. M., Lewens, T., & Ariew, A. (2002). The trials of life: Natural selection and random drift. *Philosophy of Science, 69,* 452–473.

Walsh, D., Lewens, T., & and Ariew, A. (2002). The trials of life: Natural selection and random drift. *Philosopher of Science, 69,* 452–473.

Wang, H. (1986). *Beyond analytic philosophy: Doing justice to what we know.* Cambridge, MA: MIT Press.

Ward, T., Vertue, F., & Haig, B. D. (1999). Abductive method and clinical assessment. *Behavior Change, 16,* 49–63.

Warner, M. (2001). Objectivity and emancipation in learning disabilities: Holism from the perspective of critical realism. *Journal of learning disabilities, 26,* 311–325.

Watkins, J. (1985). *Science and skepticism.* Princeton, NJ: Princeton University Press.

Webb, E. J., Campbell, D. T., Schwartz, R. D., Schrest, L., & Grove, J. B. (1981). *Nonreactive measures in the social sciences.* Boston, MA: Houghton Mifflin.

Weber, M. (1904/1976). *The protestant ethic and the spirit of capitalism.* New York: Charles Scribner's Son.

Weinberg, S. (1992). *Dreams of a final theory.* New York: Pantheon Books.

Weiss, P. (1940). The essence of Peirce's system. *Journal of Philosophy, 37,* 253–264.

Werkmeister, W. H. (1937a). Seven theses of logical positivism critically examined I. *The Philosophical Review, 46,* 276–297.

Werkmeister, W. H. (1937b). Seven theses of logical positivism critically examined II. *The Philosophical Review, 46,* 357–376.

Whitehead, A. N., & Russell, B. (1910/1950). *Principia mathematica (2nd ed.).* Cambridge, UK: Cambridge University Press.

Wiener, P. P. (1969). A Soviet philosopher's view of Peirce's pragmatism. In S. Morgenbesser, P. Suppes & M. White (Eds.), *Philosophy, Science, and Method* (pp. 595–601). New York: St. Martin's Press.

Williams, R. H., Zumbo, B. D., Ross, D., & Zimmerman, D. W. (2003). On the intellectual versatility of Karl Pearson. *Human Nature Review, 3,* 296–301.

Woodward, J. (1998). Causal independence and faithfulness. *Multivariate Behavioral Research, 33,* 129–148.

Woodward, J. (1999). Causal interpretation in systems of equations. *Synthese, 121,* 199–247.

Woodward, J. (2000). Explanation and invariance in the special sciences. *British Journal of Philosophy of Science, 51,* 197–254.

Woodward, J. (2001). Causation and manipulability. *Stanford Encyclopedia of Philosophy.* Retrieved October 13, 2005, from http://plato.stanford.edu/entries/causation–mani/

Woodward, J. (2003). *Making things happen.* Oxford: Oxford University Press.

Wright, B. D. (1999). Fundamental measurement for psychology. In S. E. Embretson & S. L. Hershberger (Eds.), *The new rules of measurement: What every educator and psychologist should know* (pp. 65–104). Hillsdale, New Jersey: Lawrence Erlbaum Associates.

Wright, B. D., & Masters, G. N. (1982). *Rating scale analysis.* Chicago, IL: MESA.

Wright, B. D., & Stone, M. H. (1979). *Best test design.* Chicago, IL: MESA.

Wright, R. (1994). *The moral animal: The new science of evolutionary psychology.* New York: Pantheon Books.

Yu, C. H. (2001). *An introduction to computing and interpreting Cronbach Coefficient Alpha in SAS.* Proceedings of 26th SAS User Group International Conference. Retrieved October 13, 2005, from www.asu.edu/sas/sugi26/stats/p246–26.pdf

Yu, C. H. (2002). *An overview of remedial tools for violations of parametric test assumptions in the SAS system.* Proceedings of 2002 Western Users of SAS Software Conference, 172–178.

Yu, C. H. (2003). Resampling methods: concepts, applications, and justification. *Practical Assessment, Research & Evaluation,* 8(19). Retrieved November 7, 2005, from http://PAREonline.net/getvn.asp?v=8&n=19

Yu, C. H. (2005a). *Meta–analysis and effect size.* Retrieved October 29, 2005, from http://www.creative–wisdom.com/teaching/WBI/es.shtml

Yu, C. H. (2005b). Test–retest reliability. In *Encyclopedia of Social Measurement* (Vol. 3, pp. 777–784). San Diego, CA: Academic Press.

Yu, C. H., Anthony, S., & Behrens, J. T. (1995, April). *Identification of misconceptions in learning central limit theorem and evaluation of computer–based instruction as a remedial tool.* Paper presented at the Annual Meeting of American Educational Researcher Association, San Francisco, CA (ERIC Document Reproduction Service No. ED 395 989).

Yu, C. H., Lo, W. J., & Stockford, S. (2001, August). *Using multimedia to visualize the concepts of degree of freedom, perfect–fitting, and over–fitting.* Paper presented at the Joint Statistical Meetings, Atlanta, GA.

Yule, G. U. (1926). Why do we sometimes get nonsense–correlations between time–series? A study in sampling and the nature of time–series. *Journal of Royal Statistical Society, 89,* 1–69.

Index

L

M

N

O

P

Q

R

S

T

U

V

W

About the author

Chong Ho Yu is currently the Director of Testing, Measurement, Assessment, and Research in the Digital Media Instructional Technology group at Arizona State University (ASU), USA. He holds a doctorate in Educational Psychology with a concentration in Measurement, Statistics, and Methodological Studies from ASU. He is also a doctoral candidate in Philosophy, specializing in philosophy of science, at the same institution. His research interests are diverse, including philosophy of quantitative methods, relationships between science and Christianity, alternate quantitative procedures, such as resampling, data visualization, and Exploratory Data Analysis, applications of instructional technology, applications of psychometrics, and aesthetics of photography; he had published articles and book chapters on preceding topics. His website is accessible at http://www.creative–wisdom.com